"With her empirical critique of the neo-liberal dogmas that dominate employment policies today, Catherine Casey has re-asserted the importance of social values not only for education but for work itself."

– *James Wickham, Trinity College Dublin*

"It is a brave soul who invites us to see a pernicious side to the idea of a 'knowledge-based economy'; so central has that idea become to both exponents of the neo-liberal hegemony and those who seek to humanize it. Catherine Casey is one such brave soul. She here documents in a highly scholarly way both the factual limitations to the idea and its less than benign implications for education, work and citizenship. Future enthusiasts for the knowledge-based economy will need to come to terms with her challenge."

– *Colin Crouch, Professor of Governance and Public Management,*
University of Warwick Business School, UK

Economy, Work and Education

Routledge Advances in Management and Business Studies

For a full list of titles in this series, please visit www.routledge.com

20 Work and Unseen Chronic Illness
Silent voices
Margaret Vickers

23 The Foundations of Management Knowledge
Edited by Paul Jeffcutt

25 Managing Technological Development
Hakan Hakansson and Alexandra Waluszewski

27 Business, Government and Sustainable Development
Gerard Keijzers

32 Technological Communities and Networks
International, National and Regional Perspectives
Dimitris G. Assimakopoulos

37 Critical Representations of Work and Organization in Popular Culture
Carl Rhodes and Robert Westwood

45 Challenges and Controversies in Management Research
Edited by Catherine Cassell and Bill Lee

46 Economy, Work and Education
Critical Connections
Catherine Casey

Economy, Work and Education

Critical Connections

Catherine Casey

Routledge
Taylor & Francis Group
NEW YORK AND LONDON

First published 2012
by Routledge
605 Third Avenue, New York, NY 10017

Simultaneously published in the UK
by Routledge
4 Park Square, Milton Park, Abingdon, Oxon OX14 4RN

Routledge is an imprint of the Taylor & Francis Group, an informa business

Library of Congress Cataloging-in-Publication Data
Casey, Catherine, J.
Economy, work and education : critical connections / by Catherine Casey.
p. cm. -- (Routledge advances in management and business studies ; 46)
Includes bibliographical references and index.
1. Information technology--Economic aspects. 2. Information society--Economic aspects. 3. Education--Economic aspects. 4. Labor market.
5. Economic development--Social aspects. I. Title.
HC79.I55C366 2011
330--dc22
2011005038

ISBN: 978-0-415-88671-0 (hbk)
ISBN: 978-0-203-80653-1 (ebk)

Typeset in Sabon
by Taylor & Francis Books

For Philip Wexler

Contents

Acknowledgements

I gratefully acknowledge the support for this project which I received from research grants at the University of Auckland, the University of Leicester, and the award of a James Cook Fellowship by the Royal Society of New Zealand. The research and writing of this book were also made possible by my term as a Visiting Scholar at the School of Political and Social Sciences at the European University Institute in Florence. I am very grateful for that visit and participation in the wonderful scholarly environment of that special place.

I thank with much appreciation friends and colleagues including Angelos Agalianos, Francesco Garibaldo, Michael Kuhn and James Wickham for their stimulating conversations over the matters explored in this book. More personally, I especially thank Nicola Gavey, Brett and Margaret Warburton, Judy Robson, Gill and John Denny, Ilene Wexler, and Pierre Grech Marguerat. I warmly thank Antje Fiedler for her research assistance and Margaret Tibbles for her careful reading of the draft manuscript. And I thank Philip Wexler to whom this book is dedicated with love and friendship.

Introduction

In recent decades a political economic discourse promoting liberal, highly competitive and principally knowledge-based economies has won a vast influence and launched institutional reform across much of the developed world. Business-led demands for ever-modernizing efficiencies, advanced technological applications, production growth and competitive advantage in a globalizing economy have stimulated intense emphasis on continual innovation in product and process, flexibility of production organization and demand for liberalization of market regulation. These transformation pressures, as economists view these events, generate increased complexity, risk and uncertainty. They attract much debate in social and economic arenas. Amid the diversity of views, there is agreement that the implications of these socio-economic dynamics for national economies, welfare states, civic communities and persons are immense. An academic interest in institutional varieties of capitalism finds useful, informative divergence among national responses. But, it must be said, a convergence toward adoption of neo-liberal governance models to facilitate dynamic competitiveness and expansive marketization is readily evident, certainly across the European welfare state countries. The neo-liberalization of capitalism has yielded a wildly uneven distribution of the advantages and costs that have ensued.

The governance regime of liberalized markets and rationalization of other social institutions to facilitate market economic dispersion shows little sign of alteration at the present time, even as the 2008 financial crisis brought the near collapse of global liberal capitalism. These patterns raise many serious concerns especially as institutional pathways may set future policy dependencies and limit or delay other options. Most immediately affected by these continuing transformation pressures are the spheres of work and of education.

Economic and political demands promote a "learning society" to accompany the knowledge-based economy. The key to successful competitiveness and expansion of the knowledge-based economy, it is widely believed, lies in accelerated educational expansion and skills development. Education, which has been undergoing a massive expansion occurring at a varying pace through the twentieth century, is now charged directly with servicing a privileged economic agenda of normalizing across the population the attainment of higher-level skills for application in labour market participation. This wide-spread policy development, which is especially salient in higher education, accords particular values to the qualities of human life – of learning and working – that have long been the bearers of more diverse and plural qualities in cultural life.

A generation ago, many thought that expanding the provision of education, especially higher education, to a much wider populace would lead to substantively more than economic expansion. It would lead to a vitalized and sophisticated democracy, a culture of participation and power distribution and rich human cultural development among many more people in society. Yet it now appears that education's social, cultural and personal good, like that of work, is being powerfully subordinated to the interests of economy. Learning for employment skills acquisition has come to assume a role beyond its due portion in a culturally rich human life. It appears now elevated as the primary composite task of the good citizen, the learner-worker of the learning economy/society. In this respect, as in others, economic policy has come to exert an inordinately influential role in social and cultural life.

The sphere of work has, for much longer than education, been subject to forces of economic rationalization. For many people, work is regarded virtually exclusively as an economic activity substantively devoid of other rationalities except as decorative remnants. Education, however, persists in being much more difficult to subjugate and control. Nonetheless, there is now intensifying and systematic pressure upon education to yield to economic rationalization and governance. Higher education appears in the vanguard of that programme of transformation. The increasing dominance of economic rationalities in shaping education, as well as work, raises serious questions not only for education, but also for the ways in which democratic societies may act to govern economic institutions and market activity in society.

In response to these concerns, many social critics are searching anew for viable prospects for a renewal of education's cultural dimensions and role in personal and social life. That search at the present time seems as fearsomely daunting as it is urgent. Nonetheless, in continuing the groundwork task of criticism necessary to that search, accompanying questions gain renewed force. Just as the university's corporate assimilation must be challenged, are there vital dimensions of work that are – or ought to be – irreducible to the economically rational? What are the prospects for a revitalization of these dimensions even as work appears to be an exhaustively rationalized sphere? Has the particular neo-liberal economic turn, which many put forward as the "new economy" of twenty-first century capitalism, triumphed over cultural spheres that were formally insubordinate to the imperatives of markets and business interests in the shaping and ends of human life? What are the prospects for collective, social, action in shaping these ultimate matters? These questions concerning the conditions and prospects for work and education critically connected to economy orient the searching discussions in this book.

The book takes up a twofold principal task. The first is to critically inquire into the current neo-liberal restoration of the privileging of elite interests in economic action, to trace its outcomes and effects, and to probe its salient contradictions in relation to education and work. A profoundly influential iteration of the neo-liberal turn has been the promotion of a knowledge-based economy which has been imagined as both the irrefutable successor to Keynesian managed capitalism and as normatively attractive to people in society. That discursive construct and its effects are the first main focus of attention. The second task is to offer some reflections in response to the problems and dilemmas the economic incursion now presents to socially interested citizens. This exploration considers sources of cultural innovations that may offer renewed scope for a revitalized social regulation of economy and a more imaginative horizon for both work and education. The route to this renovation is the intractably fraught yet necessary discrimination of the cultural tasks of education, and of work, from the rationalities of economy, technique and productivism. Its project is a regeneration and re-imagination of collective, public discourse on education, work and economy. It is the social refusal to render solely unto economy what cannot belong there.

A SOCIOLOGICAL APPROACH

The intricate complexities of the social and economic currents of recent decades may readily lead us to conclude that these forces are more than ever escaping our grasp, both in terms of our efforts to scientifically analyze them and in their political governance. Sociological analysis has been greatly affected by a protracted disciplinary crisis that has led to searching reflections and new thinking on sociology's role and contribution to contemporary social understandings. In the Anglophone world, much sociological work has turned to cultural analysis and philosophical excursions in an apparent retreat from social and economic analysis, even as economic practices were very much to the fore in classical sociological traditions. In the meantime, economists and corporate business leaders and their particular forms of analysis and demand have risen to gain greater social and cultural influence in the spaces of a virtually de-politicized public square.

The academic debates on contemporary social currents are very often dispersed across disciplines which are too frequently bound to those disciplinary norms and internecine squabbles. Disciplinary inabilities to pursue comprehensive social analysis have led to methodological and interpretive inadequacies that further hinder shared endeavours. Sophisticated, yet limited, mathematical models too often serve as default compensation for the lack of broader communicative and multi-dimensional inquiry. An obsession with quantification now blights the social sciences. C. Wright Mills' (1959) once-famous call of the "sociological imagination" founders in a productivism of micro and non-cumulative studies of idiosyncratically isolated or fleetingly fashionable phenomena, and a positivism of general linear analysis. These academic and research behaviours are perhaps now to be expected in the current climate in research and educational institutions in which heightened production pressures evident in the business world more intensely affect research and scholarly practices. Those pressures now actively hinder our scholarly and scientific efforts to develop advanced knowledge and understanding, and to contribute studied reflections to the much wider social tasks of criticism, imagination, proposition and intervention.

Observers have noted signs of a weakening of other cultural institutions, not only those of the academy, that help protect society from the market, and from the bureaucratic state. The role of mid-twentieth century democratic institutions that were hard-won in the years after World War II in the regulation of economic practices has manifestly weakened. Civil society institutions have rich potential for revitalization. But at present, in conditions of heightened private economic interest, weakened society and fragmented critical social science, developments in some sectors of social life – importantly business, technological and market practices – escape social institutional regulation in the interests of the many. Their imperatives, consequently, exert a distorted and powerful influence over many other sectors and dimensions of social life. The restored power in recent decades of elite economic and political interests in shaping the social and cultural climate in much of the Western world attests to this tendency. The confidence of social analysts that critical concerns about the consequences, especially those of increased inequalities, hierarchies, conflict and injustice, will be effectively addressed has faltered. Social analysts find themselves, just like the rest of the public, too often as policy-takers grumbling among themselves on the sidelines of an economically dominated social sphere.

Yet, nonetheless, the sociological project has a classical history and a classical task that remain no less valid today. There is no question that it is an immense challenge to seek to analyze current political and economic forces in social and cultural spheres today. Recognition of immeasurable social complexity is perhaps key among our sociological learnings after the postmodern crisis. The classical sociological vantage point, with its characteristic concern for society (which is not to be confused with the nation or state), is the formal vantage point of this study. That vantage point is further informed by a mid-twentieth century tradition of critical social theory that poses interrogation of social practices and exposure of ideological interests in forms of social organization. The fundamental argument for society that has permeated modern sociology recognizes a realm of human needs and aspirations that cannot be satisfied in the sphere of community, or in the practices of economy. The classical argument for society, evocatively expressed by Max Weber in the early twentieth century, favours recognition of a relationship of liberal autonomy in which tolerance between institutions guarantees freedom of spheres of activities from capitalist rationalities in the organization of human affairs, and enables those institutions to act in dynamic concertation to affect the regulation of economy and society.

A further word on the context of the current study is important. This study is not particularly concerned with the nation-state, although this category remains important in the governance of political entities and in the lives of so many of its citizens. The nation-state remains common in sociological, political and economic studies, especially those of a comparative nature, but a good sociological case can be made for consciously relegating methodological nationalism to other investigative purposes. Classical sociological interest lies in societies and these may not coincide with politically defined nation-states. Societies may be found in cities and regions that exist within national boundaries, but substantially cross them as well. Societies characterized by similar economic and industrial structures and institutions are empirically recognizable even as many aspects of culture, including linguistic, may vary considerably. This is especially the case with the category "European model welfare state society", a concept I adopt following the European scholars Crouch (1999), Esping-Andersen (2002) and Keating *et al.* (2003). Such a notion of the "European model welfare state society" can usefully be employed in full recognition of national and regional varieties within that generalized model. Other nation-states with some features in common with Europe and often consistently figuring highly on many OECD measures – such as Japan, Korea, Singapore – are not directly included in the discussions that follow. However, other countries – Australia, New Zealand, and, to some extent, Canada – feature welfare state economic and political models readily recognizable as those of the European social model. They are therefore implicated in the general category conception of the European model welfare state. However, the European Union, principally because of its excellent and prominent policy-making institutions and its highly visible pronouncement of its pursuit of the knowledge-based economy, serves as the collective benchmark and discursive focus in the discussions below.

EDUCATION AND WORK

Many specialist scholars have written excellent works in the fields of education and work. Many sociologists too have explored the complex developments of economy, technology, culture and society in recent decades. I attempt in this project to draw some of these discussions together, to contribute to a closer scholarly dialogue between interested thinkers who too often must labour and converse apart. That cross-disciplinary endeavour carries its inevitable pitfalls but it also offers the vantage point afforded from traversing the old boundaries and retrieving core concerns shared by many scholars and researchers. Among those shared concerns are the accelerated expansion of liberal marketized relations and an abrogation of social responsibilities. Under the neo-liberal regime, work and education are connected more closely than ever. Economic rationalities propose their systemic integration and harmonization. Much has been written about the problems of the neo-liberal economic and political turn of recent decades. Many hope that in the wake of the 2008 financial crisis that tide has ebbed and a more sober awareness of the need for social and political responsibility of governments and social institutions in governing economic activity may now be emerging. But one must be cautious in optimism while prodigious in hope. There is pressing evidence that the consequences of economic and political liberalization have exerted an institutionalization of certain cultural changes and affected popular assumptions in broad support of or compliance with a liberalized culture and diminished social sphere. A remarkable acceptance of the dominance of big business interests, of shareholders' and employers' priorities, of managerial power, and weakened collective action, appears in much socio-political life in Western countries.

The search for reasonably optimistic avenues for socially and culturally interested development in work, education and economy under current conditions is an enduring one. This study is a critical interrogation of contemporary neo-liberal economy and its unprecedented, ungoverned reach into so many spheres of life, especially education and work. The vantage point is a concern for persons who work, who seek education and learning and social participation, and whose life aspirations irrepressibly surpass those of economic activity.

OVERVIEW OF THE BOOK

Chapter 1 outlines the broad contours of the economic and social conditions now shaping the worlds of work and education. The scope of the discussions throughout lies in the decades close to the turn of the twenty-first century. The chapter reflects on sociological discussion of what many have regarded as the technological revolution, the sweep of neo-classical economics and the weakening of many socio-cultural institutions. It addresses the rise of a conception of knowledge that exclusively privileges technological and scientific forms of reason and competence. It considers forms of expert governance that have appeared in correspondence with these developments. Chapter 2 critically discusses historical factors in the collapse of the Keynesian model of managed capitalism and the turn of neo-liberalism. It explores the pursuit of innovation and the political and economic assumptions of accelerated competitiveness and liberalization as crucial and principal factors in the advanced economies.

Chapter 3 examines economic and political forces that shape the dominant patterns of work and production. Production is conceptualized to include diverse tangible and intangible goods and services in contemporary advanced economies. Discussion develops a meta-level analysis of general trends and patterns in production relations that are observable across industry sectors and national economies. The approach indentifies three key motifs: intensified rationalization, competitiveness, and resurgent firm power. The combination of these forces has generated a course of hegemonic political and economic rationalizations and firm interests in the practices of work and production. Chapter 4 explores the effect of an intensified economic incursion into the education sphere which has been facilitated under the public policy notion of the "knowledge-based economy" and the "learning society". It discusses the modern expansion of higher education and the current models of the learning society, the demand for higher-level skills and production of techno-scientific research knowledge. The chapter argues that vertical alignment of education with economy is achieved through demanding the reform of education, especially of higher education, toward the "scientific episteme".

Chapter 5 focuses attention on the level of the firm's organizational behaviour. Prevailing economic discourse on the knowledge-based economy projects that high productivity sectors requiring high levels of skills will successfully displace low productivity sectors that require low levels of skills and accrue low wages. Any gaps in this path are considered to be due to time-lags, structural inertia and other hindrances to perfect dispersion. The chapter examines empirical evidence from labour economics and organizational studies which reveals the persistence of deep contradictory tendencies in the knowledge-based economy path. It reveals that rational organizational action uses hierarchies and skill sorting systems that contribute to segmented and bifurcated labour markets. These apparent contradictions raise many concerns about the real extent of the knowledge-based economy and the promised generalized improvement in jobs and prosperity for everyone.

Chapter 6 addresses the overarching concerns of liberal marketization and scientific rationalization that critically connect education and work. Paradoxes of higher-skilled economies include degradation of quality of work, the loss of social and cultural capital and weakened participation and protection of workers. The privileged pursuit of higher-skilled jobs effects a disparagement of ordinary work – work that remains of moderate skill application and productivity – and which remains socially necessary in contemporary economies. Education faces dilemmas in regard to the rationale and quality of higher education and lifelong learning. The university's adaptation to the knowledge-based economy risks attenuation of classically valued conceptions of the university's role in the pursuit of higher knowledge forms beyond the instrumental and the material. Chapter 7 explores potential currents of response in regard to the prevailing corporate orders of society. It explores a reinvigorated philosophical interest in notions of social citizenship, in civic rights and responsibilities as well as of trust and solidarity in shared fate. The chapter argues for an innovative concept of citizenship, which includes sensibilities beyond modern humanism, and looks to a reformed role for universities in social citizenship education. Are there prospects for a revitalized university to foster "sites of citizenship" to assist people to gain renewed powers to act to protect society and non-market relations from the market? Can these endeavours forge new social capabilities beyond the economic, in the worlds of work and education?

1 Critical reflections on economy and society

INTRODUCTION

The elevation of neo-liberal economic discourse to a predominant place in social life appears now a normative condition, assumed as a *fait accompli* that defies serious criticism. Social life has accommodated to this economization. People are conforming, remarkably, to the behaviour expected of the economists' abstraction of *homo economicus*. More than ever, it seems, they are conducting their lives as rational, calculative and competitive individuals exchanging ever more goods through marketized relations with one another in the pursuit of the maximization of unrelenting self-interest. As well, it would seem, we tolerate with diminishing hesitation the incursion of economic logic into domains once thought of as properly protected from instrumental rationalities and market action. As more and more spheres of social life are brought under the sway of market action, and as individualized economically rational behaviour is widely sanctioned and rewarded, people can assume that particular, contemporary economic patterns and tendencies are self-evidently normative and irrefutable. Moreover, as the welfare state strains precariously under myriad social and economic pressures, many political leaders assume that market action provides an alternative, socially weak form of governance. Commentators and policy-makers can incline to the view that the neo-liberal economic dominance of society is now reasonably to be expected. Yet, of course, despite these powerful tendencies, *homo economicus* can never reflect the rich complexities of being human. It cannot account for, nor speak of, social and cultural values, motivations and bonds between people nor grasp the mysteries of the affective and interior life of persons.

Much critical concern has been raised in recent decades over the social and cultural consequences of the intensification of economic rationalization under a persistent neo-liberal political climate, which has scarcely altered since the 2008 financial crisis of capitalism. Prominent sociologists, including Pierre Bourdieu (1999) and Alain Touraine (1995, 2001) have railed against the tyranny of the market and the dispersion of society into asocial individualism. For Manuel Castells (1998), a virtually unrestricted market logic of technologically driven "global informational capitalism" forges the segmentation of societies into areas in which many people are structurally excluded from formal economies and globalizing markets and a minority of others are their beneficiaries. For Colin Crouch (2005a), a "resurgent capitalism" and the neo-liberalized recalibration of social relations that has dramatically tipped the balance in favour of capital effect an "entropy of democracy". We now witness marketized individuals retreat from a public politics that has degenerated into business-dominated demands on a compliant state. For Boltanski and Chiapello (2007), a "new spirit of capitalism" incorporates the emancipatory cultural movements of the post-war generation and directs their energies into capitalist legitimation and renovation.

The social prices wrought from the rapid uptake of neo-classical economics demanded by political and business elites and which legitimated the neo-liberal political turn away from a managed capitalism in the latter years of the twentieth century are immense. Even as a few economists, prominently Keynes (1936), Galbraith (1967) and Polanyi ([1944] 1957), noted in much earlier years that economic forces left to themselves do not work out for the best but rather for the interests of a powerful few, the prevailing political elites of recent decades took a decisive course. In opting for the business-elite demand for greater economic freedom for private action, a path to an economically rationalized and highly marketized social arena, with markedly uneven regulatory relationships and greater social inequalities, was set in place. The state, voluntarily weakened in response to business demands (including those for requirements to bail out the market failures of the corporate firm), has assisted a wide social and cultural accommodation to market economic rationalities that now shape society. Now, political efforts to challenge and mitigate the feral capitalism that neo-liberalism let loose encounter its institutional pathways and cultural accommodation which obstruct efforts for imaginative and widely innovative social action. For some, the prevailing conditions are appropriately described, following Polanyi, as "market society" (Slater and Tonkiss 2001) in which the market economy's triumph over social and cultural relations appears complete. Still others seek to understand sweeping currents of identity, expressivism, consumption, religious movements and post-materialist values (Beck 1992; Inglehart 1997; Taylor 1989) that interweave with market economic forces but which may variously contest or refuse them.

The spheres of work and education lie in the middle of these currents of market economies and cultural aspirations. It appears that work, most especially, and increasingly education have become ineluctably transfused with market economic rationalities. But the broader contexts in which education and work are embedded have historically been composed of richly varied social and cultural sources. Even as economic features have been prominent in both, they have never been exclusively so even in the world of work. Each of the spheres of work and education is now more than ever affected by particular configurations of capitalist economic imperatives and their institutional conduits, including, according to Boltanski and Chiapello (2007), their sources of cultural critique in the name of emancipation. The critical connections and degrees of autonomy of work and education in regard to economy have altered. That alteration is of profound import for society and citizens. In this introductory chapter I endeavour, from a sociological vantage point, to give an overview of the main currents and confluences of economy and society with particular attention to their contextualization of the spheres of work and education. In endeavouring to understand the political economic context, a clearer light may be cast on the effects and implications of neo-liberal political forces and economic rationalization on work and education. The context of the discussion is the decades at the turn of the twenty-first century.

ECONOMIC REASON AND TWENTY-FIRST CENTURY CAPITALISM

The decades following World War II set a particular historical context in which subsequent social and economic developments have frequently been reflected and compared. Those decades are characterized by social and political arrangements that may usefully be termed the mid-twentieth century social compromise, or Keynesian settlement, in the European model welfare states. Those decades, often glowingly referred to as "*les trente glorieuses*" (the "thirty glorious years") in the words of the French economist Jean Fourastié (1979), achieved in the post-World War II period of industrial growth and working-class advancement an unprecedented social redistribution and relative social cohesion. That period of socially managed capitalism was one in which the forces of capitalism were subject to forms of regulation that included effective roles for non-state socio-cultural institutions and democratic political actors. Institutional forces, as Emile Durkheim proposed, including especially those of the state and of civil society, managed, more or less, to constrain societal conflict and domination by particular powerful sectors, including of markets. That regulatory regime enabled the tensions between a capitalist economy and democratic polity to be recognized and institutionalized. It enabled advances toward forms of, or at least effective argumentation for, worker participation and democratization in the regulation of work and production that assisted the stability of the mid-twentieth century compromise.

The collapse of that regime's efforts to tame capitalism, through a series of experiences and narratives of crisis, opened the way to the new, or restored, power of elite interests. Those ideological interests, although particular and partisan, have been taken up in social discourse in ways that legitimate those interests as *necessary* economic and social rationalizations and, moreover, their realization as advancing the realm of freedom and autonomy in society more generally. The cultural promotion of neo-liberalism and competitiveness extends even to wage-workers who are encouraged to seize their market freedoms and be more entrepreneurial and competitive in taking up the exciting opportunities of liberated capitalism. The rise of such a powerful view of economic necessity was fuelled by new complexities and exogenous pressures on the Keynesian settlement that emerged after the 1970s as well as by elite demands for the retraction of managed capitalism. The new dynamic forces exerted intense pressure on political governance institutions and on the Fordist production model and accumulation regime.

Rapid technological advancement, the crisis of Fordist production and the high levels of industrial unemployment experienced in the 1980s and 1990s across most European welfare states unravelled the Keynesian regulatory regime. Economic models and policies that were relatively popular and effective in the latter half of the twentieth century gave way. A sea change in economic regulation occurred. Two main elements can be identified within this climate of heightened complexity and dynamism. These elements overlap and intertwine to the extent that they are often treated as inseparable or their coupling as co-determinant. One of these elements is the immensely influential turn – initially in the Anglophone countries in the 1980s – of neo-classical economics. The neo-classical economic turn intersected with a longer and broader cultural trend toward a cultural liberalization with an individualist character. The neo-classical economic influence was taken up in political and social arenas. It fuelled a wider project of neo-liberalism which may be understood generally as those political forms, institutions and sensibilities that assume the superiority of competitive markets, economic individualist action and minimalist social roles for the state. The other element, which, like the individualist character of neo-liberalism, emerged earlier than the current decades of its momentous impact, is the rise of advanced technologies of production, information and communication.

For many analysts, it has been the technological factor itself that is most momentously significant. The extraordinary growth of the ICT sector through the 1980s and 1990s wrought an immensely disruptive effect on conventional industrial production and jobs (which is discussed in Chapter 2). It led many, prominently Castells (1996), to view the technological expansion as revolutionary, yielding through its disruption and generation a new economy of the future. Many saw the globalizing expanse of production and markets as well as cultural interactions and mobility on a historically unprecedented scale as consequences of the technological acceleration.

Sociological theorizations of a postindustrial society and an information age regard the role of technology and knowledge as powerful transformation factors in socio-economic systems of the latter half of the twentieth century. The sociological account of the technological revolution, as exemplified in Castell's œuvre (1996, 1998), emphasizes its social effects and patterns. For Castells, we are living through a period of history that is "characterized by the transformation of our 'material culture' by the works of a new technological paradigm" (1996: 29). The "*core* of the transformation we are experiencing in the current revolution refers to *technologies of information processing and communication*" (ibid.: 31; original emphasis). Informational capitalism denotes a new paradigm and a global economy. Philosophers, too, took up these propositions as self-evident. Jean-François Lyotard's (1984) influential book, *The Postmodern*

Condition: A Report on Knowledge, confirmed the view that knowledge has become the principal force of production. Knowledge in the form of "an informational commodity is indispensible to productive power".

Economists, while generally more cautious in speaking about grand social patterns and societal change, but wildly confident in their deployment of abstract modelling of macroeconomics, entered the debates initially with critical concerns about the looming economic crisis effected by new production technologies and stalled accumulation. They found broad agreement with Castell's information age and ICT revolution thesis, and with Lyotard's commodification of knowledge. Many economic and social analysts agreed that the ICT revolution proposed developments of such magnitude that they indicated that a new paradigm in economy, with unprecedented effect, had emerged. The dynamism and excitement of these developments lent much weight to those voices arguing for the liberalization of constraint on markets and firms. The further development and exploitation of the ICT revolution required, its advocates insisted, a sweeping liberalization of managed capitalism. Governments, one after the other, took up a neo-liberal programme of reform. A "new capitalism" of the twenty-first century of knowledge and information and their market generation (Castells 1996; Sennett 2006) now permeates society and culture.

By the 2000s, promotion of the knowledge-based economy and exploiting its potential had generally become accepted. Robert Reich's (1991) popularization of the concept in the United States was echoed within the decade by European economists. For economist Dominique Foray, society as a whole is shifting to knowledge-intensive activities. The new knowledge-based economy "represents a qualitative innovation in the organization and conduct of modern economic life" (Foray 2004: x). Foray proposes that far-reaching conceptual and structural transformation of the economic activities of advanced societies has led to a shift to knowledge-intensive activities in which knowledge itself is principally an economic good. The knowledge-based economy characterizes a scenario of "structural transformations of economics".

Although Castells was careful to point out that all technological revolutions have knowledge development at their core, the predominant economic account emphasizes the pivotal role of new scientific and technological knowledge and higher order skills as the principal sources of economic development. They are, moreover, the core elements of *comparative advantage* and wealth creation which have come to assume the principal objectives of economic action. The greatly elevated role of knowledge in the production of the new technologies and in their subsequent commercial applications and potential for firm *comparative* advantage through the latter decades of the twentieth century gained wide policy consensus. The elevation of liberalization and competitiveness accompanying knowledge-rich production expressed a shift in political economy. Instrumental market action and private profit-seeking displaced substantive social ends of a socially embedded economy which saw the management of capitalism as a social necessity. A socially embedded economy included, alongside private profit-making, social institution building, economic distribution, and advancing cultural development toward a good society for the many. This was always a fraught and tense configuration. But relatively strong democratic institutions and participatory disputation constrained and utilized those tensions.

Some analysts in the 1980s saw a "disorganized capitalism" (Lash and Urry 1987) succeeding the organized capitalism of the Fordist-Keynesian regime. Certainly, the new dynamism and institutional breakages portended an end to managed capitalism. But the capitalism unleashed under that neo-liberal re-regulation has not substantively fragmented or dispersed its power. The new capitalism of the early twenty-first century has reconfigured itself to shape a powerful and strategic neo-organization. That neo-organization, as I elaborate in the following chapters, crucially includes heightened systems' rationalization of production, organization and work in accordance with the commands of accelerated competitiveness, and enabled by advanced information and communication technologies (ICT). Moreover, the dominant policy model of the highly liberal and radically marketized knowledge-based economy extends in reach to discipline or assimilate other domains of social and cultural life – prominently education. That ambitious reach appears as the overarching governance project of the reformed and flexibly re-organized capitalism we currently observe.

In the early years of the technological revolution some writers posited alternative scenarios of the social possibilities enabled by technological advancement. A more emancipatory vision was on the horizon. Some imagined the end of the working class and the tyranny of labour as postindustrial possibilities widened democratic participation and freed people from machine-bound labour and capitalist labour relations (Block 1990; Gorz 1982; Leadbeater 2000). They proposed that freedom from work and economic compulsion would enable greater cultural enrichment – more music, art, leisure and non-economic productivity.

A freer, more egalitarian and harmonious social life and a greener planet with socially tamed technologies were promoted as politically possible (Bahro 1984; Daly 1996; Méda 1995). Within the diversity of views, a general agreement that advanced technological change was revolutionary and socially irrevocable shaped the debates. There were profound political and social choices to be made. By the end of the twentieth century, however, the diversity of views and potential for wide visions of the technological and cultural shifts had been quietened.

Crucially, the definitive elevation of a particular form of knowledge, that of instrumental reason, of technological and scientific knowledge, which had long been criticized by critics of modernity certainly since Weber and Freud, achieved a great boon in the surge of the knowledge-based economy and its political facilitators. The triumph of techno-scientific knowledge inferiorized and marginalized non-economic reason. Capitalism is agnostic. Its liberalization strengthened its demand for concordance in a more general secular scientific reasoning. That proposed a fortuitous assimilation for business elites and a boon to profit-seeking action. The inferiorization of non-scientific knowledge extended to a further eclipse of sources of value and meaning beyond economic and material prosperity. Techno-science and market action converged as a triumphant instrumental reason. It ensured that the only forms of critique that could be marshalled against a neo-liberal knowledge-based economy rested primarily on a contestation of degree of liberalization or constraint, not its surpassing.

Still, some social analysts expressed little enthusiasm for the popular terminology of a knowledge-based economy. A singular "new economy" or a unifying model of a knowledge-based economy – especially one that requires a necessary and expansive liberalization – leading the march to prosperity is suspected of being a convenient political programme with an ideological agenda serving elite interests. Much political science and economic discussion has emphasized the varieties of capitalism. A diversity of institutional configurations in the regulation of economic forces is observed across Western countries and within Europe (Amable 2003; Esping-Andersen 1990; Hall and Soskice 2001). Against narratives of globalizing uniformity, these varieties of capitalist institutions, some propose, may offer sources of new governance practices. As well, cultural factors, which economists often overlook, affect socio-economic diversity (Keating *et al.* 2003) and may indicate challenges to monolithic economic discourses. For others, the search for a "third way" (Giddens 1998, 2003) has dented the hitherto unchallenged neo-liberal master discourse of the 1980s and 1990s. Nonetheless, that third way proved to be an expression of its neo-liberal parent far more than an effort to recreate political forms of constrained capitalism.

There may be much to offer in an emphasis on varieties of capitalism and a retrieval of elements of national and culturally diverse institutional approaches. Yet that scrutiny of institutional variety has been prone to an under-estimation of the occurrence of significant convergences. A striking uniformity of acceptance of the imperatives of liberal marketization, privileged knowledge-based production and accelerated competitiveness as the predominant forces of economic activity in the current decades is readily observed. For some analysts, the extent of the economic consensus suggests little variety of institutional forms and sources of renewed social governance, but rather a rapid globalization, for ill or good, extending a monolithic liberal and technologically rationalized capitalism across the world (Harvey 2005; Robison 2006; Stiglitz 2002).

A politically won consensus that holds that the turn of economic development is toward techno-scientific production now lends the new economy its description as the "knowledge-based economy". The knowledge-based economy, confident of its superior scientific episteme, requires an overarching policy model to disseminate its capacities and mobilize populations to its adaptation. That policy model gives synthetic policy expression to sociological theses of grand social changes described as postindustrial and postmodern, and to economic and technological accounts and projections of productivity growth and necessary market liberalization, and to government efforts to maintain sufficient levels of employment and social welfare provision. The elevated importance of both market economy and knowledge facilitates a public acceptance of – or at least compliance with – political economic demands on society and people to respond as required to the new regime of the extensively liberal, highly marketized knowledge-based economy.

The neo-liberal governance models that have facilitated the particular form of the knowledge-based economy modelled in policy discourse have elevated the role of the business firm to a highly powerful position in economic and social relations. neo-liberalism's central emphasis on market supremacy assumes that non-market institutions constitute performance-inhibiting rigidities. The logic of the priority of the business firm as the institution most effectively responsive to market dynamics and uncertainties has accorded to the firm considerable political and social power. The corporate firm has gained under neo-liberal governance regulatory environments favourable to private profit accumulation, and has forged a social acceptance of sweeping ideological demands. Over the past three decades it has achieved extensive recalibration of the power relations between capital and labour, the state, society and citizens of a general public, and among citizens themselves. The power of that success is witnessed even more surely after the financial crisis of 2008 which saw spectacular government bailouts of private corporate firms in the European states. No change to the entrenched power of capital has yet resulted and firm action has proceeded as business as usual.

As well as dramatic recalibrations of relationships and accelerated dynamism in work and labour markets, neo-liberal policies taking up the logic of firm interests and market expansion extend to an equally dramatic reorientation and reform of education systems.

Work has always been central to economic activity even as people have found various meanings and value in its activity beyond the economic and instrumental. Education, though, has long exhibited various and contested relations with economic action. It has maintained a cultural distance in its pursuit of knowledge and sources of human development even as it necessarily intersects with and depends on economy. In recent decades, education, like work, has come more intensely than ever under the influence of economic and market action.

The new economy of knowledge and competitive innovation requires components that Fordism did not require. Fordist capitalism demanded grossly under-skilled workers for highly routinized labour in mass production systems. Within a decade of the demise and mutation (but not obsolescence) of Fordist systems, as flexible specialization utilized the advanced ICT capacities for diverse commodity development, the new capitalism demanded a mass up-grading of workers' skill levels. These features, which are discussed more fully in the following chapters, saw in the 1990s a remarkable convergence of economic and educational policy among OECD countries and many other countries in the collective, competitive pursuit of a knowledge-based economy and learning society through the mass expansion of education and training systems.

The European Union most famously declared its ambitious knowledge-based economy agenda. The Council of the European Union at its Lisbon Summit in 2000 declared that the Union had set itself that now widely known agenda: "to become the most competitive and dynamic knowledge-based economy in the world, capable of sustainable economic growth with more and better jobs and greater social cohesion". The Lisbon Agenda, confirmed and reiterated in 2005 (European Commission 2005a), represented a culmination of policy intention evident in OECD countries through the 1990s. In 2010, the European Union launched its Lisbon successor which retains the crucial emphasis on the knowledge economy pursuit. The new policy, *Europe 2020*, acknowledges that more education has not matched skills with jobs and acknowledges the lack of "robust supervision" of liberal markets but essentially endorses the knowledge-based economy's extant directions and continuing liberalization. *Europe 2020* seeks "Smart growth: developing an economy based on knowledge and innovation". *Europe 2020* imagines no change to its conception of knowledge and innovation as a techno-science endeavour. The Lisbon institutional pathways appear firmly set.

The demand for a highly liberalized, marketized knowledge-based economy is accompanied by political calls for a "learning society" to be developed through the institutional settings of economic action – that is, through society, a context which has persistently refused recognition in classical economic models. The concept of the learning society has its earlier origins in social democratic movements for education expansion, notably the thought of the American philosopher, John Dewey ([1916] 1966). The learning society would learn, through expanded education in cultural and practical arts, to humanize and civilize its social and economic institutions, to fairly regulate its conflicts and develop its citizens.

The gradual expansion of education in the twentieth century saw a concerted and popularly welcome acceleration in the early post-war decades. The expansion of that period was marked by the prominence of a social agenda for wide population participation and democratization, and for the advance of social values of equality and human development through educational participation. In brief, the notions of a learning society that have been formulated in association with the knowledge-based, learning economy have taken a decidedly different character. Under the neo-liberal policy directives, the learning society is conceived simply as the auxiliary social arrangement that will generate and maintain the dynamic knowledge-based, continually learning economy of superordinate power. The learning society is depicted as comprised of lifelong learning workers seeking, gaining and updating employment skills in a techno-scientific knowledge-based economy. In collapsing notions of the knowledge-based economy and learning society into one general concept, policy discourse promotes a monolithic economic reason intricated with market imperatives. These forces are asserted as normatively legitimate and irrefutable. It is the task of the education sphere to generate the learning society for the economy. The implications for the education sphere of this techno-economic conception of education and the task of education institutions are immediate and immense.

Neo-liberal capitalism seeks unceasingly new markets, new products, competitiveness and profitability, and rationalization of systems to economize its costs. The rational subjugation of both work and education to economic reason and liberal market governance is achieved by rendering them subject to an overarching project of coordination under an assumed superior scientific episteme that obscures the force of ideological interests in their rationalization.

WORK

The world of work is enduringly more complex than the dimensions of work that are most saliently influenced by economic action and policy interventions. Undoubtedly, economic and technological forces have powerfully shaped the world of work through a long industrial history. But sources of social and cultural regulation, including those of mid-twentieth century accords and compromise, have also greatly influenced the practices, values, meanings and rhythms of work. The institutionalization of conflict negotiation in work and employment relationships recognized and endeavoured to regulate deep antagonisms in the capitalist economy. Collective participation in bargaining in industrial relations endeavoured to maintain a calibration between interested parties that hindered the dominance and pre-determined advantage of one party.

In recent decades we can observe a powerful recalibration of relations between employers and workers that is distinctly in the favour of employers. As an accompaniment, an intensified rationalization of diverse dimensions of work occurs. Socially dominant economic and technological modes of thought and practice in the shaping and regulation of work appear to have achieved a near exhaustive subjugation of human work to economic rationalities and capital interests in the advanced industrialized societies. Cultural aspects of work – that render work more meaningful, enjoyable and civilized, yet often less efficient – have become marginalized and compromised. The neo-liberal political climate, combined with elevated technological and economic reason, has enabled a managerial and shareholder revolution to extend a technocratic rationalization imperative not only over working-class work but over most professional middle-class work as well. The shareholder model of the firm holds that the central objective is to maximize profits for shareholders. That model overarches and penetrates all relationships and job directives within the organization.

The category of worker is displaced in managerial discourse in preference of an employer descriptor. The employee as a "human resource" subtly yet powerfully shifts the conception of the working actor away from the subjectivity of the working person to one of subordinated relationship and as resource for another's utility. The concept of the worker, as a person exerting effort of her/his being in productive activity retains, in principle, an irreducibility to market action or subordinated necessity. The employee, in contrast, is a categorical subject of a dependent, contractual relationship of employment. Now, in everyday parlance and as a consequence of successful managerial discourse, many prefer to avoid the term worker. Its respect of subjectivity has been eclipsed by a discursive association with industrial muscle and a prejudice of low skill. More educated and white-collar, as well as blue-collar, workers take up their employer-favoured post-Fordist designation as employee and human resource. However, throughout the discussions in this book, the category of worker is used to refer to the vast mass of wage and salary earners who are managed as human resources. Its use retains the implicit possibility of inalienable subjectivity and collaborative relationship beyond normative subordination and utilitarian reductionism.

Workers' efforts to counter the normative acceptance of instrumentally rationalized work and to culturally enrich the work performed in formal production systems do, of course, remain part of everyday practices of work. So too do the efforts of many workers and their collective organizations to participate in the regulation of their workplaces and work practices. But the recognition of these socio-cultural expressions and demands in current economic policy discourse is marginalized or trivialized. Efforts to exert forms of social regulation on modern rationalization imperatives, at least in the earlier post-war decades, brought certain pacts of compensation and worker-interested participation in the regulation of rationalization decisions and processes, including new technological applications and job design. European trade unions devoted much effort to workers' participation in the regulation of rationalization in order to mitigate its systems' imperatives and control over workers. By the 1990s, however, pacts of regulating rationalization and accommodating workers' socio-cultural interests in production were in crisis across many of the advanced economies. Influential efforts toward industrial democracy which were vigorously effective in the 1970s and 1980s have been systematically obstructed and attenuated in political effectiveness through liberalized regulation and reassertions of firm prerogative.

Capitalist tendencies toward increasing rationalization of production and workers, as Weber predicted and as long noted through the twentieth century, now extend to a hyper-rationalization. A definitive shift toward an exaggerated structural asymmetry of power relations between workers and employers has been wrought by the altered regulatory regime for workers and industrial relations. The deregulation of industrial relations, while variably introduced across European model welfare states and most prominently in the Anglophone countries since the 1980s and 1990s, has brought significant changes to the social and economic contexts of work. In sum, those changes have brought about for the majority of workers general patterns of altered and deteriorated conditions in employment practices, greatly diminished bargaining and representation capacities, much weakened workers' political power and a birfurcation of labour markets. Workers experience long-term stagnation of real wages (Streeck 2009), intensification of productive effort, heightened risk and insecurity, de-collectivization of their interests and alienation from intrinsic values.

The weakened position of labour and the re-regulated industrial environment now visible across Western countries more generally have further enabled a firm-led intensification of rationalization of production systems. ICT applications enable greater system complexity and dependency, with more information generated and applied to rationalize production activities. Rationalization enables greater efficiencies through tighter control, predictability and strategic utility of resources, including labour, and of systems and production processes. Intensified managerial and systems rationalization achieves, for the firm, greater productivity yields and controlled labour costs. Yet the pursuit of intensified rationalization, business economists argue, must be accompanied by the simultaneous and continual pursuit of innovation in order to maintain competitiveness. Innovation, which in its generation is wasteful and inefficient, must be strategically cost-managed and its investment carefully calculated. That strategic management of competitiveness through the simultaneous pursuit of rational efficiency and innovation prominently focuses on the utility of workers and skills. Corporate firm interests have confidently argued that those dynamic pressures on competitive firms (of intensified rationalization, cost effectiveness, innovation and competitive advantage) justify the firm's new pressures on work and employment relations. Those interests just as successfully have argued that the development of economically useful knowledge must be the principal task of society's education institutions. Governments, in response to these demands, have placed intense new pressures on education systems to generate mass numbers of skilled workers. As the world of work has become normatively subordinated to and regulated by resurgent elite interests and economic priorities, so, too, has pressure come to bear on education to yield to rationalized integration in the superordinate political-economic system.

For many observers, a comprehensive yielding of the world of work to instrumental economic rationalities is an ineluctable consequence of the advance of technologically sophisticated capitalism. The deployment of technological and industrial rationalizations, disciplinary and integrative practices, and managerial authority over diverse sectors of workers, including professionals, enables a comprehensive subordination to neo-liberal capitalist imperatives. The proposed alternatives to that subordination had, apparently, been defeated after the collapse of the Fordist-Keynesian regime. The incursion of economic rationality into the socio-cultural sphere of education is, however, a much more recent affair.

EDUCATION

Under the oft-repeated directives of the European Union's Lisbon knowledge-based economy agenda, education systems sustain continuing pressure to adapt to the requirements of a highly competitive economy. Education's adaptation requires large-scale, multi-level institutional reform of the education system, especially higher education, to the generation of advanced technological and scientific forms of knowledge and their application skills. Labour activists and employers had widely agreed in the 1980s and 1990s on the need for workers' education and training and the public has been persuaded of the general appeal of the notion of highly skilled, knowledge-based economy. But concession to that appeal has enabled, however unintentionally, the dominance of neo-liberal forces and of economic rationalization of diverse dimensions of education as well as work. The course of neo-liberal normalization has enabled an apparent acceptance of the singularity of the economic purposes of human work, and increasingly also of education. Elite interests in private wealth creation impose sweeping demands on public institutions to serve their objectives. These conditions pose an immense challenge for an alternative imaginary.

The economic rationalization of education is occurring less bloodily than it did in the world of work and the lives of workers, yet it nonetheless appears to be increasingly effective and generalized. Remarkably, many of the most influential commentators in Western societies on education are not scholars devoted to advancing education's contribution to people's social, cultural and personal development as they were a generation ago. The efforts toward greater equity of access to education, advanced quality of practice and curriculum enrichment, and broad distribution of the goods of education have taken a distant second place to an agenda set over recent decades by other, newly interested, parties. The renewed power of corporate elites freely extends into the sphere of education. They have won the ear of economists working in national and supranational institutions, notably the Organization for Economic Cooperation and Development (OECD), the European Commission and the World Bank. Government policies on education in OECD member countries, and those that wish to follow the OECD's development trajectory, appear more likely to be influenced by these supranational economic scientists than by political participation and argumentation among their polities.

Just as the state retreats from participation in the regulation of work and leaves de-collectivized and weakened workers exposed to the liberally restored powers of firm action, it increases its interest and attention toward education. The state, and in the case of the European Union, supranational policy-making bodies, extend an over-arching policy agenda toward education while rationalizing and retracting their financial investments in achieving that agenda. The earlier twentieth century expansion of education to a wider public as an essential development of modern democracies required extensive investment and involvement of the state. Mass compulsory education could not be achieved through private action. As higher education expansion eventually became part of the state's interest, it too required extensive public investment. Education's continued necessary dependency on the state carries, therefore, the disadvantage of being subject to changing state agendas. The political ideological shift in European model welfare states toward a liberalized, socially weakened state in response to elite business demands has in turn launched a new state agenda for education. That agenda is distinctly narrower than the agenda for education fostered under the mid-twentieth century ethos of Keynesian managed capitalism and socio-cultural demand. The new agenda forges a programme of rationalization of education in alignment with the neo-liberalized knowledge-based economy model and business demand for higher levels of skills among workers and commercially useful technological and scientific research products. Education, as a multi-faceted socio-cultural good that fundamentally includes forms of knowledge and ends beyond the utilitarian, is in a process of substantive reconstruction toward singular economically utilitarian objectives and the scientific episteme. In the course of these actions, the cultural goods of education, and not least the university, are placed at risk of marginalization and neglect or retrenchment for renewed capture by traditional elites.

The continuing expansion and modernization of education systems toward the improvement of skill levels in order to improve economic productivity and gain comparative advantage in a global economy are a major policy objective of governments in much of the world. The high convergence of policy intention and the general consensus on the value of expanded education and training is clearly evident. Their reasons have been compelling. Certainly, it is hard to be against "high skills" as though favouring low skills or cynically neglectful of human flourishing and people's need for employment.

There has been, of course, good reason to emphasize the links between educational improvements and economic performance. Especially evident is the development and influence of sectors of highly skilled and educated elite workforces at the forefront of technological innovations and new product markets. These sectors have produced increased national growth and highly successful technological products in global demand. Highly skilled workers in these sectors continue to accrue labour market advantage and competitive remuneration. Moreover, the general public appeal of the cultural and personal good of persons gaining further education and training lends popular support to notions of a learning society that is good for everyone. The learning society, with its emphasis on continuing, active, lifelong learning emphasizes the on-going changes in knowledge and skill requirements and the uncertain dynamism of economic activity both today and in the future. In its politicized iteration, and drawing on the residual moral basis of the normative personal and social good of education for mixed social, cultural and economic objectives laid down in earlier centuries, the notion of the learning society encourages individuals to adaptively respond to the dynamics of the advanced technological economy. It is a powerfully persuasive argument.

The policy attention to education occurs on multiple levels. It is prominently directed at the macro systems of education and training, involving the reform of school curricula and administration; restructuring and rapid expansion of tertiary education systems; strengthening efforts to align education and training systems with innovation and entrepreneurial development and labour market competitiveness; and the marketization and privatization of education provision. At a more intermediate level, and one that often escapes the attention of education researchers, is the intense interest by knowledge economists, business and management academics and technologists, on the development of "knowledge production" within the firm's organization. The extraction from education of what Foray (2004) calls "knowledge capacities" that enables knowledge to disseminate and generate innovation at the level of the production organization attracts increasing attention of a new branch of economics, that of economics of knowledge. It puts education at the very heart of the firm's interests and organization.

Extending the capacities of knowledge- and skill-acquiring workers is a key factor in organizational knowledge capacities. Lifelong learning models are invoked to accompany knowledge management models developed for application to business production. For knowledge economists, education is crucially a *subsystem* of the economy. The transmission of the goods of education into commercially productive knowledge is the substantive rationality of education. Understandably, educationists disclaim this reductionism. At the same time, however, they struggle to articulate a recognition and persuasive critique of the modern scientific episteme and an imaginary beyond it.

KNOWLEDGE-BASED ECONOMIES, WORK AND EDUCATION: LIMITS AND PARADOX

Governments around the world have adopted policy imperatives on education, training, lifelong learning and employment in accordance with policy models of a knowledge-based and learning economy. A decade or two ago there was some distinct national variation in that adoption. As Streeck (2009) recounts, the German case was often regarded as a non-liberal capitalist approach to a high skills economy. More recently, it appears that a general consensus on the optimal knowledge-based economy model, even in historically more corporatist Germany, favours neo-liberal regulation. That liberal consensus shapes the context in which the particular national and regional economies and societies adopt policies and implement strategies.

Talk of a new economy that is predominantly knowledge-based and liberally regulated permeates political, economic and social fields. Within this discourse is a general assumption that a trajectory toward a high-skilled economy is a singular one that involves an increasing elimination of low-skilled jobs in the advanced economies. This view assumes that the newly industrialized countries will generate high levels of low-cost production through low-skilled, low-paid jobs. Through the 1980s and 1990s, off-shore (from the advanced economies) relocation of many heavy industries, manufacturing operations and routine data entry work occurred. That massive out-sourcing of Taylorist-Fordist production alongside the growth of knowledge-rich production in the developed economies fed an assumption that low-skilled work would virtually disappear in the advanced economies. Workers affected by the loss of low-skilled jobs would need to develop higher levels of skills through education and training programmes in order to avoid unemployment. Their retraining for newly created jobs in the new knowledge-intensive ICT sectors, it was assumed, would deliver more highly skilled and higher paid jobs.

The attractiveness of the model of the higher-skilled, better-paid knowledge-economy worker encouraged a single-minded policy focus on the knowledge-intensive trajectory. In that single-minded zeal, the failure to take due notice of the effects of liberalized marketization, accelerated competitiveness and rationalization, and of the rapid development of the newly industrializing countries, occurred. Empirical discrepancies point to persistent contradictions in the optimally liberal knowledge-based economy model. Higher levels of post-compulsory school qualifications are undoubtedly being achieved across the OECD countries and by a wider social demographic in most societies (OECD 2008b). There are consequently many more highly qualified people working in the labour market. But equally undoubtedly, many of the new jobs being generated variably, or rarely, require the application of advanced skill in their performance. Privileged emphasis on the knowledge-based economy expansion ignores (as the following chapters discuss) persistent realities in the world of work. Work, for most people, even in the advanced economies today, is not in the innovative sector. Work, for most people, remains hierarchically differentiated, and the application of skills remains predominantly determined by the firm's managerial agents.

The retention and expansion of lower-skilled, lower productivity sectors in contemporary work, while frequently over-looked or trivialized as temporary imbalances in the knowledge-based economy expansion, present salient features of the current economy. It is more accurate to speak of a multi-level economy in the advanced industrial countries that contains significant sectors of lower and moderately skilled jobs. Such jobs, with limited technological applications and limited opportunities, remain economically viable. The social retention of a vast array of moderately skilled jobs which cannot be performed off-shore – such as hairdressing or cleaning office towers – or in externalized sectors of national economies although ignored or, at best, cursorily addressed in dominant economic models is empirically observable.

Many of the moderately skilled jobs remain *socially necessary* for most sectors of the economy – from bus drivers and couriers, security personnel and hospital aides, receptionists and care-workers, to car mechanics, construction workers, baggage handlers and many others. While all of these jobs are performed in industry sectors which integrate advanced technologies and knowledge-rich systems into their organizational design and management, the principal work tasks of these industries remain of modest skill level, low task complexity and routine productivity. Beyond a certain general improvement in efficiency and congeniality, most of these jobs do not objectively require skill up-grading. Their integrity requires a respect of a different quality than accorded to complex technological skills. The lower-skilled service economy occurs not just in popularly visible sites such as McDonald's-style fast and cheap service operations but as routine clerical and data processing services in offices everywhere. These services are typically neglected in economic models and policy. It is remarkable, for instance, that Dominique Foray's (2004) influential work on the economics of knowledge does not discuss the persistence of lower-skilled work, both as services in the wider economy and as necessary sectors within knowledge-intensive firms. The persistence of these sectors cannot be dismissed as though they are part of a technological lag that will eventually catch up with the expanding knowledge-intensive sectors in time.

Moreover, a sector of new lower-skilled jobs effectively restores the performance of a servant class to the middle classes in their provision of marketized domestic services. Services in child and elder care, house cleaning, food preparation, garden maintenance, shopping deliveries, and so forth, formerly provided within the middle-class household are now frequently provided by low-wage workers. Even as these private services – which are as gendered now as they were in the past – as well as moderately skilled, more socially necessary jobs are welcome, they are at once disparaged and inferiorized in hyperbolic knowledge-based economy discourse. That disparagement (discussed further in Chapter 6) expresses a sublimated denial of the limits of the knowledge-based economy and of persistent social necessity of lower-skilled jobs.

Policy discourse proposes that the exclusion of workers from knowledge-rich sectors is a consequence of poor skill acquisition among large sectors of the population. That view fails to take into account the roles that lower-skilled work performs in support of the infrastructure of the knowledge-rich, high productivity sectors. Ignoring or disparaging the retention of socially valuable work that is of limited skill and lower profitability, and in which significant sectors of the workforce are and will continue to be employed, worsens social tendencies of weakening cohesion, polarization, cultural poverty and exclusion. The assumption of a gathering momentum toward a high-skills, knowledge-based economy and learning society, alongside repeated exhortations from business leaders of the need for workers to keep abreast of the changing skill needs of industry – as unpredictable as these may be – continues to fuel demands for the considerable expansion of higher education, especially the university, of an economically instrumental, and corporate, character.

A generally favourable bias toward education and lifelong learning provides a certain public receptivity to the continued expansion somewhat in disregard or ignorance of the shaping and imperatives of the new education models. The dominant knowledge economy/learning society model appropriates and utilizes the moral imperatives of a humanistic heritage of education. It demands and assumes a popular acceptance that draws on a scarcely articulated moral premise that education is good and more of it must be better. It distorts those imperatives toward the aims of a reductionist, instrumental economic agenda that impoverishes education, diminishes culture and contravenes richer human flourishing.

The generalized policy drive toward a learning society of continually skill-acquiring workers in the service of the knowledge-based economy bears an agenda of even greater aspiration than that of fuelling competitive market advantage. That accompanying agenda is proposed to resolve persisting economic and social problems that have been exacerbated by the neo-liberal knowledge–economy distortions. That agenda proposes the neo-classical belief that market expansion will of itself resolve those social problems. It promotes an imperative for individual responsibility for one's economic and social fate and for a retraction of welfare state collective provisions and safeguards. The ambitious agenda to shape an economically individualized citizenry which is dependent on finding skilled jobs in capricious labour markets for personal social inclusion is highly problematic for education systems, and citizens. People are compelled to quicken their chances on the newly constructed education markets for labour market competiveness. Independent competitive individualism, transposed in expression under a more congenial rubric of a learning society, is imagined as the force that will forge the way out of macroeconomic crisis and fragmenting social redistribution of the welfare state. Governments are demanding as much compliance from working citizens as do their employers.

The functional relationship between education and economic activity at the level of labour markets and workplaces is fraught. Government policies on education and training that are heavily biased toward technological skills for high-value productivity and that prolong periods in individually funded education and training, especially for the vast majority of people in the mass of the working population, yield very disparate results. Large firms reap disproportionate benefits as working people bear heavy costs in gaining skills and the risks of their marketability. The social good of optimizing broad socio-cultural educational development and employability for workers and stimulating distributive productive conditions in society conflicts with private employer demand for specifically skilled employees – which includes flexibility, mobility and contingency – utilized for the firm's profitability. The deepened bias of socio-economic policy-makers toward action favouring the politicized economic interests of corporate business elites and shareholders has led to scant recognition of the realities of today's labour markets and workplaces.

A further social paradox that accompanies the rapid liberalization of markets and firms and more educated and skilled workers coming on the labour market is that of a rapid ascent of authoritarianism in workplace life. Internal organizational operations and employment relations (as Chapter 3 elaborates) enabled by ICT applications have been managerially tightened. Workers, including senior professionals, notwithstanding their higher educational qualifications, are more powerfully subordinated. Intensified vertical and horizontal systems' integration and control over workers provide organizational defences against market uncertainties and volatile competitiveness. More tightly controlled workers, managed through firm-demanded high-performance systems, flexibilities and contingencies, bear an insidiously unfair burden of risk and domination under the liberalized, deregulated conditions of new economy production and organization. Their higher-level skills are exploited just as their subjectivities are suppressed.

Universities have been quick to take up their new mission in providing mass quantities of higher-level skills and techno-scientific research for the utility of the knowledge-based economy. The entrenched bias toward business elite interests and public subordination to an economic authoritarianism that permeates state polities give rise to grave social concerns. As the university, increasingly governed by principles and agents of economy that were historically foreign to it, yields to neo-liberal capitalist imperatives, its role in the lives of the citizen-students it educates and the public goods it once espoused to serve fundamentally alter. In loosening and severing historical socio-cultural obligations and attenuating its cultural roles in pursuit of non-economic knowledge forms, the university's economistic orientation forms a different graduate. Young people, at once more highly qualified in techno-scientific skills yet frequently culturally under-educated and typically indebted, enter liberally regulated labour markets and tightly controlled production organizations. Prepared for competition, productivity and compliance, their lack of cultural education and democratic sensibility places a new generation of workers under the triumphant power of the corporate firm and governing elites. The limits of the neo-liberal knowledge-based economy, which are currently ignored or disregarded, are generating social problems of considerable magnitude for the European social model. In the long run, these limits and contradictions cannot be ignored.

ECONOMY, GOVERNANCE, SOCIETY

The neo-liberal political turn of recent decades has been a decisive one. From the initial systematic interventions to radically restructure industrial relations and to incontrovertibly alter the balance of power between capital and labour, to incursion into education spheres, neo-liberal effects are readily observed across diverse social arenas. In socially managed economies, inevitable forces against societies and publics – which include firm and market action – are recognized. Those forces and institutions which are capable of causing harm must necessarily be subject to efforts to constrain them. Yet, the turn to liberalization rejected or ignored that recognition. The social problem of the firm, neglected for three decades, has fallen from recognition. The rapidly successful uptake and expansive reach of neo-liberalism's competitiveness and neo-rationalization of production and work, and general worker compliance and acceptance, have been politicized. The rapid advance and globalizing expansion of advanced technologies without doubt fuelled new complexities in production and economic environments. But the liberalization of firm and market action and its consequent social problems for society cannot be attributed to technologically driven hyper-competitive and globalizing markets of an insuperable capitalist juggernaut. Strategic politicized action taken on the part of powerful interests played a decisive role in wilfully liberating socially harmful institutions from social controls. The reasserted and intensified roles of political interests unleashed the resurgent power of the corporate firm.

The politicized interests of the corporate firm – as private, collective, economic action – extend their influence and demands into remarkably wide social arenas. In addition to the extensive demands of work and education, firm powers have persuaded policy-makers and the public that business organizational forms and management practices are the best suited agents to act in consumer market economies in pursuit of competitive productivity and efficiencies. As the state retreated from spheres it had formerly protected from market action and facilitated vastly expanded market action, it enabled a shift in social valuing of the public sphere and its role of social protection against the forces of the market. The state has actively encouraged a lack of confidence in public sector capability unless it too adopts a business firm model and forms of governance (Crouch 2005a). Competitive and market models now permeate hospitals, schools, public services, and even religious organizations. A "new public management" (see Chapter 3) of market sensibility and rationalization applies and enforces that market model. The neo-liberal pressures variously effective across European model societies now permeate cultural fields and dilute their potential to assert the value of non-market realms and relations.

Notwithstanding the current disembedding of economy and markets from society, economies are always located in social and cultural institutions that enable and constrain them. This recognition, long noted by the classical sociologists Durkheim and Weber and expressed more latterly in Polanyi's influential essay ([1944] 1957), has been astonishingly ignored in the predominant economic and business writings on economy, including the so-called new economy. Attempts toward a "new institutionalism"[1] which recognize social and cultural contexts of firms, markets, governments and other actors, in economic analysis now make some headway, with Polanyi's theorizations now gaining wider attention. But a fuller recognition in the prevailing economic models of the social and cultural complexity in human behaviour and aspiration remains cursory. The prevailing neo-liberal view that only highly liberalized and competitive contexts will generate economic prosperity continues to demand market freedom from social and cultural regulation, and indeed to invert those relationships of constraint.

Society, conceived as a sphere of social action that is irreducible to economy or community, was, in classical sociological thinking, an accomplishment of civil, social action. Earlier patterns of modernity in Western societies described a modernity not only of rationalization but of cultural liberalization and individualization which was also accompanied by democratization and collective social actions. The struggle of persons for subjectivation, as Touraine (1995) describes it, refuses rationalization and elite dominion in the quest for emancipation. The late twentieth-century turn to a neo-liberal economic ethos quickened the cultural shift to liberalization and individualization that had been evident earlier (Taylor 1989). However, the shift toward neo-liberal market individualism simultaneously effects a distortion and weakening of political democratization and broadly shared, contentious civil society. Competitive individuals are absorbed in the business of assessing and taking their chances in the competitive arenas of education and labour markets and in commodity consumption. Disciplined at work and no longer expecting fruitful collective interest expression, they appear to have retreated, too, from participation in their polities and civil societies.

Across the European model welfare states, as liberal marketization expands, we observe an erosion of public participation and a much weakened role for civil society. We observe a state weakened in response to its *demos*, compliant to markets and business demands and strong in its assertions of increased expert policy-making and bureaucratic management at the expense of participatory democratic forms. In place of democratic forms of politically contested government, especially but not only evident at European supranational levels, we observe the rise of forms of government adapted to neo-liberal institution building. In order to stimulate market expansion and broader institutional homogeneity in socio-economic regulation, efficiency rationalizations in processes of decision-making are pursued. The rise of governance, in the form of depoliticized and technocratic decision-making, displaces cumbersome and messy democratic processes. Institution building is imagined, and promoted, as being a technocratic, rational process. Policy-makers adopt governance methods that promote non-adversarial, business-like processes of consultation and dialogue between non-state expert actors and government ones. Nonetheless, despite stated intentions to disperse the functions of governing and decision-making to wider social interests (European Commission 2001), the practice of governance limits governing action to elite experts. Expert knowledge sets the content and terms of participatory debate, of which the public is informed and consulted after the fact. Decisions are taken far from ordinary people and public voters are left with little capacities for organized opposition or contribution to contested issues. Technocratic governance normalizes the powerful roles of expert elites and effects a distinct and serious deficit of accountability, legitimacy and democracy (Offe and Preuss 2006).

Through the course of the neo-liberal political-economic action sketched above, critical connections between education, work and economy have been reconfigured. They are stripped of quasi-autonomous roles, values, knowledge forms and modes of interaction. They are connected in a chain of command, vertically integrated into economic imperatives and elite dominion. In addition to the direct reform of education institutions in rationalized alignment with the liberalized knowledge-based economy, the fruits of individuals' education are pressured into similar correspondence to economic productivity. A generally more highly technically skilled workforce that has been generated by the expansion and reform of education is not accompanied by equally highly skilled citizens capable of actively participating in society and polity. Education's potential to participate in the regulation of the economy through the socio-cultural development of learning citizens is thwarted. That potential is obstructed and circumvented, not only through the everyday enactment of authoritarian managerial workplaces but in technocratic political governance in the public sphere. That portends a grave failure for education in its classical historical and modern conceptions.

The dramatic decline of ordinary people's participation in a civil polity is replaced by increased individualized market action. Governed by neo-liberal markets and technocratic experts, citizens surrender identities, rights and responsibilities of political and social citizenship. They perform instead the roles and duties demanded of markets and consumption.

Neo-liberal capitalism has won new sources of wealth for elites and vast habits of consumption among the general population. In its course it has effected a melding of the actor of the worker and the consumer into one. A dynamic of continual capitalist reproduction seems powerfully probable. Certainly, it has achieved apparent legitimation, while obscuring its destructiveness, among the populace.

The crisis of egalitarian politics is accompanied too by a retreat into the private sphere or communalism. As others have noted (Lasch 1995), privatized forms of critique, of negation, irony and passive disdain, have for many supplanted active political participation. Furthermore, alongside the rise of neo-liberal political economies we observe the rise of neo-collectivist movements of identity, ethnicity, religion and self-expressivism. Their occurrence – which may be signs of a struggle to assert knowledge forms and values that transcend those of modern scientific and economic reason and marketization – suggests signs of a bi-polar societal tendency. That bi-polarity tends, on the one hand, to economic interests and economic thinking, with the market assumed as the dominant social agent relegating political action to response to market needs and failures. And, on the other, in the weakened social arena that has resulted from heightened market action, a turn to culture in its reduced sense: communalisms, familism, tribal loyalties and of unreasoned emotional imperatives and individualist self-interests. These polar trends signal a rejection of the social, of society, where a public life shared tensely and argumentatively, but widely collectively, has the potential to integrate and cohere in its transcendence of hyper-rationalized economics and unreasoned traditionalism. A politics in the absence of society serves either a politicized economic rationality, or a politicized communalist culturalism (Touraine 1995). Neither is good for society; both portend further social fragmentation and conflict.

In the face of these tendencies, vital non-market and non-state institutions in the regulation of economy struggle for survival. These socio-cultural forces, though weakened, retain resources and possibilities for intervention, political participation and popular governing action. The effectiveness of these forces in the socio-cultural regulation of economic activity may depend on their ability to claim sufficient autonomy of action and validity of political influence through non-economic discourse. Among these resources is a new interest in old ideas of social citizenship and civil society that is emerging in political and academic fields. The new interest seeks a revitalized role for the socio-cultural notions, values and practices of social citizenship in contemporary conditions (Archibugi 2008; Balibar 2004; Crouch 2000). As Crouch proposes, forms of positive citizenship represent democracy's creative energies (Crouch 2000) which may mobilize new sources of social innovation and forms of governance that are not yet on the horizon. The possibilities for innovative conceptions and practices of citizenship, of complex subject-citizens as Touraine (1995) proposes, are explored in Chapter 7. A consideration of social citizenship in relation to the problems and dilemmas for work and education is elaborated in that discussion.

Despite the trends toward market and expert authoritarianism governing economy, work and education, cultural interests for social and political action to shape the world remain active. Their practical arenas include, importantly, the world of work and economic production. While there is no question that the efforts toward an expansion of a democratic, participatory and distributive culture in production relations have experienced severe political defeat in recent decades as economic reason expands its dominion, these efforts are neither exhausted nor dismissible as rearguard residue. The long period of crisis and retreat has yielded new efforts to reconfigure a social regulation of work in postindustrial and globalizing conditions and in knowledge-based economies. These efforts draw on new possibilities opened up in the new conditions. In particular, they seek to utilize avenues made possible by the knowledge economy's search for innovation and knowledge dispersion that require renewed forms of social and collaborative relationships, and may yet recognize knowledge forms and sensibilities beyond the material and utilitarian. As neo-liberal orthodoxies will decay and give way, prospects for social restoration, in the longer run, can be imagined. They may draw fruitfully on diverse institutional and knowledge forms and their political recombination and negotiation in a considerable, collective, project of social renewal and innovation. Certainly, if the financial crisis of 2008 and its after-effects were not sufficiently shocking to stimulate serious social and government response, the environmental sustainability crisis may prove a more decisive one.

CONCLUSION

There is much to welcome in the broad-based, normatively popular consensual narrative of learning societies and knowledge economies. There is no question that the knowledge-based economy's accomplishments are significant and that the advancement of skill levels and general education across a wider population in society contributes much social good. But in addition to these features other, disparate, outcomes raise reason for serious concern. The real limits and structural inequalities of the liberalized knowledge-based economy model are scarcely recognized or interrogated. The cohesion and validity of an economic and social model that is highly dependent on increasing productivity and distribution of knowledge-rich production rest on adherence to core assumptions and a selective and stubborn ignoring of interruptions and contradictions. Those core assumptions of liberalized market action and techno-scientific reason have set neo-liberal institutional pathways that now exacerbate both constraining and socially innovative responses. The cultural integration of those concepts and values presents myriad challenges to a critical enquiry into the disparate social outcomes of the liberal knowledge-based economy. A close look at what is occurring in the spheres of work and education reveals that many economically unforeseen pitfalls of uncertain long-term significance, and unacceptable socio-cultural costs, have been incurred on taking the singular liberal path to a knowledge-based economy and its learning society.

For societies that culturally aspire to democratic, emancipatory and socially just regulation, neo-liberal economic governance generates untenable contradictions. Its advance has favoured the private collective interests of a powerful few and worsened the quality of life conditions for the many. A very considerable cultural price is being exacted through the prevailing policy agenda of recent decades to subjugate education to economic policy, and assert economic policy as social policy. This agenda has shown few signs of alteration. Work, long aggressively subjugated to economic rationalities, poses even greater challenges for re-imagination. In order to grasp the complex connections between work and education and to imagine innovative social responses, the following chapters explore more closely key aspects of neo-liberal capitalism on economy, work and education. The tasks of exposition and critique are enduringly necessary to the sociological imagination and its contribution to social renewal and development.

2 A liberal economy of knowledge

INTRODUCTION

Can we speak seriously of a knowledge-based economy in this historical moment that suggests something qualitatively more than a politically useful catch-phrase to encourage a popular conformity to the imperatives and demands of contemporary, liberally regulated, highly marketized economic activity? Knowledge has always been important to societies and economies throughout history. Is there a special, indeed crucial, significance to its role now? Is the "new economy", with which this knowledge-intensive production is invariably linked, a generalized phenomenon with a singular and sweeping path? Moreover, as Fordist capitalism only a generation ago demanded grossly under-skilled workers for highly routinized, command and control production systems, can workers take seriously the new demands for highly skilled work and the promises of education for all? These questions invite much caution in their consideration. A close look at the factors that have led the advanced economies to pursue a mode of production and exchange that privileges the role and impact of knowledge to an unprecedented extent can enable a sharper assessment of this policy pursuit and its effects. A critical inquiry seeks to probe both the possibilities and the limits of this economic policy model, and place under scrutiny the claims of singularity and inevitability so often made in its name.

Notwithstanding the patterns of unevenness in the labour market and varying features of skill utility, it is evident that the developed societies have embraced the idea of the knowledge economy with remarkable uniformity. The reception of the knowledge imperative appears also to have been extended to an accompanying acceptance – even more than of previous economic regimes in the West – of the emergence of a "new" economy and its politically attached neo-liberalism, reaching comprehensively over many other domains of life. This acceptance, although attracting much criticism from commentators across a spectrum of civil society groups including traditionally conservative and radical groups, religious and community interests, environmental and trade union interests, indicates the influence of a wider acceptance, or toleration, of a cultural liberalization accompanying the neo-liberal economy.

The European Union expresses continuing commitment to the broad objectives of the Lisbon Agenda into the twenty-first century. Its *Europe 2020* Agenda further endorses the liberalization of labour markets, the pursuit of competitive knowledge and innovation, and education expansion. The Lisbon strategy is a particularly prominent iteration of a general policy model of the knowledge-based economy. It is the ideal type that comprises the object of the discussions below. This chapter addresses the discourses of the knowledge-based economy, its liberalized institutional demands, and the knowledge or learning society promoted as its accompaniment. These discourses have over the past two or three decades profoundly influenced policy developments in wide fields in the OECD countries and those that would emulate them. Their influence in contemporary developed societies is wide-reaching and is likely to portend a long duration as institutional path dependence tendencies shape subsequent institutional scope and action.

The interplay of advanced technologies in production, the collapse of the Keynesian settlement through both exogenous and endogenous pressures, and the neo-liberal political turn reshaped the dominant political economy of the European welfare state model countries in the last decades of the twentieth century. The collective effect of these factors enabled a favourable receptivity of a new set of arguments and demands, finding expression as a "new economy", a "knowledge-based" and globalizing "learning economy" in advanced industrial societies. A view that the route to stimulating growth and regaining accumulation capacities would be found in strategies that were politically promoted as inseparable came to assume a generalized influence. The pursuit of those principal strategies of the new economy – of liberalization, competitiveness and advanced techno-science and innovation – further ensured that the Keynesian social regulation model would be discarded. The new economy, characterized by uncertain and accelerated dynamics of technological development, increasingly global competiveness and market expansion could not gain its momentum on technological innovation alone. It required particular macroeconomic policies and state intervention for its facilitation. It required major institutional alteration in the regulation of economy and attendant social institutions. In order to map out its implications and consequences a brief historical review is warranted.

AFTER THE CRISIS OF KEYNESIANISM

In much of Europe, the accumulation crisis resulting from the slow-down in profitability and rising inflation through the 1970s and 1980s drew much economic criticism of the macroeconomic policy arrangements of the Keynesian regime[1] that had been forged in the decades following World War II. Keynesian regulation and demand management saw an unprecedented role for the state in the social distribution of productivity gains. Under Keynesian regulation, the state's role as an economic actor involved central planning, macroeconomic steering and large-scale public investment. It also took a prominent role as employer and guarantor. The state acted as a mediator between the different economic interests of capital and labour, in regulating tripartite wage bargaining, arbitration and union recognition. The application of Keynesian policies stimulated increased productive activity and increased national growth rates. It achieved high employment of adult males and wage levels more or less supportive of dependent households. Large-scale public expenditure programmes included the maintenance of an expansive welfare state in redistribution, health care, education, transportation and other public facilities. The development of the institutions of the welfare state, with variations across different countries (Esping-Andersen 1990, 2002; Hall and Soskice 2001), premised on state demand management, social redistribution and social protection was a successful and popularly welcome achievement of the mid-twentieth century. As Wolfgang Streeck (2009) remarks, notwithstanding its crisis and reduction in recent decades, public desire for the retention of the welfare state and distribution of benefits remains high in the twenty-first century.

Keynesian-style policies, while not universal, were extensively adopted across Western European states. Their application attracted the reference of the "Keynesian consensus" (Jacobi *et al.* 1986) or the "social compromise" (Crouch 1999) of the mid-twentieth century in European model welfare states. The Keynesian model was regarded as managing, more or less, the contradiction between capitalism and liberal democracy. Keynesian economic regulatory models and welfare state development were accompanied with social demands of a social-democratic character.[2] The post-war economic growth, increased social provisions and relative social stability, also favoured the rise of social citizenship rights and participation. The rise of the political power of the working classes, assisted by their numerical size and expanding educational participation (including in voluntary adult and community education activities), stimulated a cultural climate in which expanded democratization and greater potential for human development were favoured. The expansion of social democratic institutions also favoured a climate in which the rise of the feminist movement for the emancipation of women reached critical heights and whose demands led to further significant socio-cultural changes in the following decades. The accelerated participation of women in the labour market and women's expanded social participation as a consequence were among the enduringly significant developments of the later twentieth century. Since the 1960s, women's rates of participation in the labour market have grown to reach significant levels, nearing parity with men in some member states of the European Union in the 2010s (EGGE 2009).

By the late 1970s and early 1980s, the Keynesian consensus, especially in the United Kingdom, was showing signs of breaking down. Influential economists, political leaders and business leaders argued that Keynesian protectionism had proved unsustainable after the exogenous shocks of the oil crises of the 1970s. The technological revolution had disrupted established employment models and the economic and industrial management models pursued in the mid-twentieth century. High unemployment and high inflation levels in Europe and other developed countries employing the Keynesian consensus indicated that the macroeconomic regime of demand management, full employment, substantive public spending and currency stability was failing.[3] Critics predicted depression and worsening depreciation and argued that regulated financial capital markets exacerbated the inflation and accumulation crisis. The continued application of Keynesian policies, it was contended, stimulated adjustments by firms and wage levels to anticipated inflation (Bonham and Cohen 1995) generating further inflation and higher unemployment. In other words, the behaviour of the firm was learning to find ways to escape the demand management of the Keynesian model. The macroeconomic system, critics pronounced, was in an intractable crisis. The crisis, depicted as a set of factors of slow growth and declined profitability, unpredictable advances in technology, rigid capital regulation, high wages, high inflation and of an over-burdened, publicly indebted state, required urgent and sweeping new interventions.

Other analysts, especially in the United States, conceived these developments as post-Fordist, emphasizing more particularly disruptions to the logic of mass production, relatively stable industrial hierarchies, and wage levels sufficient to generate increased purchasing power among – and relative harmonization of – the working class that had prevailed in the mid-twentieth century (Piore and Sabel 1984). The risk of social instability, fragmentation and division following the collapse of Fordist certainties portended a significant alteration in the social structures of industrial, Fordist societies. The technological acceleration and increasing education and skill levels among a wider population made possible new forms of production and new product markets and consumer demands.

By the 1990s, a view that Europe was in the grip of "Eurosclerosis" and required extensive deregulation (as had the United States a decade earlier) to remedy its situation was being taken up in policy programmes. The economic governance of developed welfare states had entered a new crisis for which it was structurally unprepared and unable to manage. Elite business leaders and politicians invoked the economic arguments of prominent liberal economists Hayek (1945) and Friedman (1953) in demanding a radical response to the crisis. The Chicago economist, Milton Friedman (1953, 1962), argued that the state's intervention in the market compounded market fluctuations and instabilities. He advocated a drastic limitation of the role of the state in favour of maximized market action. That view found a new and rapidly influential convergence with views emphasizing the uncertain dynamics of the technological revolution.

As well as the pronouncements of crisis emanating from corporate business interests, other voices raised concerns that featured in the multi-faceted crisis that was apparently in course. For some, the crisis was depicted as sourced in the decline of conventional industrial production and its consequences in high levels of unemployment caused by a deliberate political neglect of the

Keynesian model; as a crisis of political leadership in a "disorganized capitalism" (Lash and Urry 1987; Offe 1985); as a crisis of legitimacy in modern social and political structures (Habermas 1989); as a crisis of unprecedented social and environmental risk (Beck 1992; Harvey 1989; Gottdiener and Komminos 1989), and also as one aroused by a growing cultural disenchantment with capitalist materialism (Bahro 1984; Gorz 1989; Inglehart 1977). An excitation of crisis was politically exploited. Despite the differences among the perspectives on the sources and solutions, the consensus on a condition of crisis ensured an apparent normalization that in turn affected government and citizen responses. There are, as expected, country-specific variations on these complex movements but a general pattern of a post-Keynesian, post-Fordist shift in the European model welfare state is discernible (Crouch 1999; Esping-Andersen 2002; Streeck 2009).

The rise of neo-classical economic models and their accompanying neo-liberal policy applications, brought about (with national variations in pace and severity) through the 1980s and 1990s a systematic deregulation of markets and economic institutions. The return of classical economic ideas was expressed in large part in the form of an emphatically elevated role for the market and a much diminished role for the state. The state's management of capitalism in the post-war settlement had never been popular with traditional elites. As Crouch (2005a) points out, older, established business elites, notably the City of London, which had not been especially affected by the technological waves, stepped into the political and policy uncertainty, adding weight to claims that the Keynesian compromise was outmoded and ineffectual in the new conditions. A considerably more favourable environment of liberal competition to generate capital accumulation required a programme of radical reforms.

A pivotal aspect of that liberalization from its outset in the 1980s took the form of rapid deregulation and expansion of financial markets. Financial liberalization enabled freer currency and bond trading, freer flow of capital across international borders, new investment regimes and the stimulation of new financial products and markets. The deregulation of the financial markets was not only a boon to capitalism after its years of so-called crisis of accumulation in the opening of new markets and global expansion, it also brought to the firm a dramatic new set of freedoms and scope for political action at the level of its organization. Those new freedoms, which in the first instance were expressed as the firm's need to strategically diversify and compete, included a greatly elevated role of shareholders to influence management action in firms. Increased shareholder power fuelled a subsequent demand for deregulation of labour markets in order to accelerate flexible accumulation. These new, or restored, capacities of the firm, as Polanyi [1944](1957) theorized, decisively strengthened its demands for freedom of mobility of capital and production. The corporate firm demanded the ability to move into and out of national and global regions according to its perception of favourability of labour market and regulatory conditions, and it demanded that the state, and individuals, take up a range of costs formerly borne by the firm.

The erosion and dismantlement of the Keynesian model did not occur with a general consensus of collapse and inevitability. It required direct state policy shift and intervention to reorder political institutions, massively reduce public spending and transform public bureaucratic management. It also required an alteration in the legitimacy and role of labour in the configurations and application of state power. The new conditions, proponents argued, required dynamism in the market and in the firm and freedom from constraints. The old regulatory regime of the mid-twentieth century accorded labour institutions too much power. Trade union action was, in the neo-liberal view, essentially obstructive and counter-productive to profit-making by the firm. A dramatic alteration of existing industrial relationships was demanded. The United States was a ready model for alternative industrial relations arrangements to those generally practised in the European model countries (Heckscher 1988; Kochan *et al.* 1995). The US model of industrial relations, it was argued in the 1980s (Crafts 1988; Metcalf 1989; Peters and Waterman 1982), had achieved successful productivity growth and market expansion through its liberal, business-favoured approach and strong containment of organized labour.

The United Kingdom, led by the outstanding economic radical in Europe, Margaret Thatcher, was the first to introduce a radical programme of deregulation. The active weakening of trade union power in relation to employers took the form of labour legislation designed to diminish the role of wage bargaining and conflict expression and, moreover, to reduce the legitimacy of trade union participation in national political life (Crouch 1986; Jacobi *et al.* 1986). Direct attacks on organized labour and its political role with the state occurred, prominently illustrated by the defeat of the British miners' strikes in the 1980s. In many instances, previously lawful trade union action became unlawful as new sets of constraints and penalties were rapidly instituted.

The sweep of deregulation of industrial relations institutions was of such magnitude, initially especially in the United Kingdom, that industrial analysts refer to the launch of a "new industrial relations" (Beardwell 1992; Nolan 1996) in the United Kingdom and a grave crisis in trade unionism that influenced similar paths of change across other European model welfare state countries. The legislative changes quickly exerted effects on workplaces, workers, trade unions, and labour markets. As Beardwell (1996: v) summed up, in the 1980s and 1990s: "There can have been few decades in which so much has happened to, and in the name of, industrial relations reform in so active and fundamental a manner." Defeating or neutralizing workers' collective associations effected a de-collectivization of workers' interests and negotiating power. De-collectivization eroded notions of solidarity and resistance to employer action. Union representative and negotiating power in regulating the social relations of production has dramatically declined. Industrial analyst, Heery, concludes that this period "has witnessed a long retreat of organized labour across the developed world" (Heery 2001: 307).

These events, which were initially most prominently influential in the Anglophone countries, are now similarly observed in the always more corporatist German and Scandinavian models (Bordogna and Winchester 2001; Dribbusch and Schulten 2007; Streeck 2009). The course of the neo-liberal turn favoured by elite interest groups succeeded in achieving public acceptance of a key set of assertions and representations. With workers' institutions weakened and increasingly excluded from effective political participation, corporate elite-led arguments persuaded policy-makers that technological reason and necessity required accompanying social conformity and acceptance of new institutional arrangements in the conduct and regulation of work. The imperatives and unpredictability of technological change and of continual innovation necessitated, its advocates persuaded, a neo-liberal economic policy environment dispersed throughout economic and industrial institutions and accompanying social institutions. It required an expert managerial action with increased authority of regulation exercised over re-subordinated workers and acquiescent citizens. These assertions, further accompanied by excitations of turbulent, unpredictable and highly competitive markets increasingly reaching around the globe, effected a new normative public compliance with business and employer interests. The successful application of neo-liberal policy demands altered the regulatory conditions in which the advanced industrialized economies operated. For Boltanski and Chiapello (2007), the changes that resulted were of such magnitude to signify a "dismantling of the world of work" and socially established role for trade unions and worker representation in the regulation of work.

A NEW ECONOMY: POST-FORDIST HUMAN CAPITAL

The neo-classical turn in economics did not propose the adoption of classical economics with conventional industrial organization. Rather, the new turn of thought sought theorizations that would reinvigorate the political demands of classical economic models – although these political elements are classically refused recognition – in relation to the new forms of technological development and demands for innovation that were evidently expanding through the 1990s. The new economy was modelled as technologically expansive, highly competitive and demanding vastly expanded markets and liberal regulation. And it was modelled, crucially, as "knowledge-based". Further technological development, through knowledge application and product innovation, a powerful lobby argued, required not only a liberalized, highly flexible, regulatory regime (Fourcade-Gourinchas and Babb 2002; Gadrey 2000; Coutrot 1998) as the optimal form of governance, it also demanded a significantly new recognition of the role of knowledge and skill levels among wider sectors of workers.

Economists investigating the dynamics and drivers of the technological expansion and the occurrence of variable growth rates across countries and regions observed the role of knowledge and skill – as measured by qualification levels of the working population – as key elements in the variable growth rates. Those countries like the United States which were generating higher levels of skills through expanding education and training systems were producing higher quality goods and sustaining competitive market positions. Economic attention to knowledge and information, just as the post-industrial sociologists of the 1970s had proposed, as the key element for generation and exploitation in a new economy, gained increased political attention. The development of knowledge required a vast new set of demands on the working class whose skill levels had been systematically constrained under Taylorist-Fordist production organization. It required a new economic conceptualization of workers' role and value in production. The turn to new models of economic growth utilized the Chicago School's free market theories and took up "human capital theory" as the conceptual framework for popularization.

Ideas on the value of human capabilities, which, if appropriately developed, would yield economic and social benefits to individuals and societies, derive from older philosophical traditions. Philosophies of education have long held conceptions of education and human development in which persons are enriched by learning and knowledge acquisition and their applications. While these typically remained the preserve of elite classes, progressive democratic philosopher, John Dewey ([1916] 1966), argued that these educational ideas ought also be utilized in the worlds of play and of work. For Dewey, the importance of learning and skill development was so vital to human life that he considered work which was degraded into "uncongenial labor for the poor" indicated "false economic conditions" that education in society ought to improve. In the 1960s and 1970s, just at the very moment that many educationists influenced by Deweyan, and radically humanist philosophies, were expanding education and human development to the working classes, the notion of developing human capabilities and propensities found formulation in economic thought. Those ideas became known as "human capital theory". Mainstream economic thought had conventionally conceptualized labour as aggregate and homogeneous. Workers expend and trade their labour power motivated by the assumed rational interests of *homo economicus*. For employers, labour is typically regarded as a cost factor of production and a drag on profitability. The supply, malleability and low cost of human labour, rather than its quality, were regarded as principal factors in economic growth. In a radical departure from the classical view, human capital theorists (Becker 1964; Dennison 1962; Schultz 1960) refocused attention on a much wider range of capacities and potential resources possessed by the worker. Human capital theory proposed that a broader concept of capital includes workers' knowledge and skills, and the education required to acquire them. This expansive reconceptualization drew direct and heightened attention to education.

Theodore Schultz succinctly expressed the key proposition: "education is an investment in man … its consequences [are] a form of capital. Since education becomes part of the person receiving it, I shall refer to it as human capital" (Schultz 1960: 571). Human capital proposes that aggregate education and skill levels are the most important determinant of economic growth. Human capital theorizations have been widely taken up in policy development in the OECD countries. Despite an initial general attractiveness of these ideas, critics argue that human capital ideas exaggerate the economic profitability of the formation and application of skills. Critics claim that measuring the productivity yields attributable to human capital at both personal and social rates of return is fraught with difficulty (Hartog and Van der Brink 2007) and highly controversial (Wolf 2002). But human capital theory has achieved the role of a received view. It has fuelled the rapid generation of Human Resource Management theory (HRM). HRM initially proposed a positive value on the role of labour as resource, rather than as conventionally calculated as cost. In its initial conception and positive view toward the development and application of workers' intelligence and skill, it found favour with educationists and worker-interested bodies. In its normative practice, however, HRM is more prosaically a form of utility management in which humans as economic resources for the corporate firm are managed in accordance with generating greater productivity yields and profitability. (Chapter 3 develops a closer scrutiny of HRM as a managerial technology.)

Economic theorizations on "new growth" and the "new economy" took human capital premises as fundamental. Prominently, Romer (1986, 1990) proposed a "new growth theory" that regarded growth as being strongly correlated to the development and application of knowledge. For Romer, as for many others (Drucker 1993; Eliasson *et al.* 1990; Freeman and Lundvall 1988; Lucas 1988; North 1981; Reich 1991) knowledge has now become the *basic form of capital*. Romer's new growth theory views economic growth as being driven, and may be sustained, by the accumulation of knowledge and the continual generation of innovation. The creation of technical platforms based on the accumulation and sharing of knowledge stimulates innovation and ensures the conditions for further innovation. These dynamics, the new growth theorists argued, render traditional economic cycles of expansion and recession obsolete. The "new" economy regenerates itself through knowledge development, application and continual innovation. The technical platform therefore is the key driver of economic growth. That technical platform requires two powerful ingredients: a continuous supply of greater skill levels and worker competencies; and a liberalization of constraints, regulation and institutions. The proposition that cycles of expansion and recession could become obsolete in a new form of economy was, and remains, hugely attractive to governments. The attraction of a new growth theory premised on a continuously developing knowledge economy convinced many regarding the demands for education reforms that would ensure that new economy.

Economic theory had importantly developed human capital theory which formed a principal premise in policy models of the knowledge-based economy that emerged in the 1990s and 2000s. But economics is hampered in its consideration of social theories by its predominant methodological device. The penchant of economics in recent decades to shape its discourses through the device of the formal abstract model has yielded mixed results. Economics as an academic discipline had predominantly opted by the 1980s for mathematically sophisticated models as the favoured method of its scientific pursuit and form of knowledge. Grand social theoretical propositions, along with qualitative research methods which inform much sociological research, are considered extraneous to economic theoretical models. Disciplinary and methodological differences, and their tendencies toward enclosing debate among their own cognoscenti, continue to hinder and distort the advancement of knowledge and comprehensive policy development. The predominance of economic theorizations, quantification and modelling in conceptualization of the knowledge-based economy and their uptake by political advocates exert inordinate power. Their effects are most especially evident in education and work.

A NEW ECONOMY: KNOWLEDGE AND INNOVATION

Political and corporate advocates of the new growth theory and new economy argued that the liberalization of economic and industrial institutions was necessary for the development of the conditions of knowledge-rich production and innovation. Liberalization stimulates competitiveness in the unpredictable dynamics of the new economy which in turn further stimulates development of the technical platform necessary for innovation to occur. Competition pressures corporate firms to expand and intensify market action and fuels the growth path. An implicit alliance of many economic and technological analysts produced a persuasive view of the necessary political management of the new economy. The general appeal of the combined economic and technological argument for the validity of a model of a regenerating, continually innovating economy that is liberally regulated and globally expansive found a wide policy-making audience. The acceptance of that model rapidly influenced a new turn of interest in education. The policy assertion of the knowledge-based economy as the political economic project of the present and foreseeable future by the European Union, like other OECD states, proposes that educational institutions are now ineluctably made to submit to the over-arching umbrella of economic policy. The new economy, despite its liberalization and invocation of Hayek's (1945) "invisible hand" of spontaneous order of market society, requires the state to actively stimulate a rapid increase in the supply of new skills for the new, technologically-rich, innovation-seeking post-Fordist production regime.

By the 1990s, the "new economy" model of a technical, educational, and economic coordination had permeated education and academic institutions, as well as government policy-making arenas. The persuasive power of these economic conceptions and their political effect has forged a new course in economic governance and increasingly in educational governance into the twenty-first century. A view of an inseparable intermingling of the advanced technologies – which are accorded revolutionary effect – with particular economic and political strategies favouring their investment and expansion and liberalized governance has gained common acceptance. A general convergence of conviction among leading economists and business agents on the new centrality of knowledge-rich production in the economy generally is captured in the OECD's influential 1996 definition of the concept of the knowledge-based economy. A knowledge-based economy is: "an economy in which the production, distribution and use of knowledge is the main driver of growth, wealth creation and employment across all industries – not only those industries classified as high-tech or knowledge intensive" (OECD 1996c). While the rate of movement toward a knowledge-based economy differs across the developed world, all OECD countries, the OECD confidently reports (OECD 1999: 7), are moving toward the knowledge-based economy. National education and training systems including lifelong learning are emphatically brought into service of this goal.

Prominent EU advocates portray these developments in emphatic and near prophetic terms. For Rodrigues (2002), it is necessary to distinguish the knowledge-based economy from vague discussions of the "new economy" and to point to much wider and enduring social changes that are occurring at all levels and across all sectors of society. For Rodrigues, invoking Polanyi's ([1944] 1957) well-known term of a "great transformation", this new great transformation involves all the social processes of knowledge production and utilization: "The organization of the cyberspace is re-organizing the existing world, shaping its economic, financial, political and cultural exchanges. Cognitive capacities, connectivity and cultural identity become the key instruments for survival in the new world" (Rodrigues 2002: 5).

Along with excited enthusiasm for the new knowledge-based economy, a tendency in the economic and policy literature to elide descriptive analyses and prescriptive injunctions to adapt to the requirements of the new economy is readily apparent. As one business economist opined: "Flexibility, adaptability, responsiveness and a capacity to innovate rapidly – these are coming to be seen as the elements of "best practice" organizational architecture in the knowledge-based economy." These are the attributes of successful firms "which can bring new products to market swiftly, which can draw on the skills and knowledge of their workforce in effecting continuous process improvement" (Matthews 1998: 165). Others, too, quickly saw the market implications and potential for education:

> The development of the knowledge-based business is a reflection of an even larger transformation occurring in our society. The market for learning is being redefined dramatically to encompass ... lifelong learners. A new meaning of education and learning is bursting on the scene.
>
> (Davis and Botkin 1998: 163)

While the neo-liberalization turn in economic and social policy took effect through the 1980s and 1990s most visibly, and painfully for many, in the

United Kingdom, the wider world influence of the policy drive toward knowledge-based economies was led by the OECD and the European Union Commission. Both of these immensely influential policy-making bodies have provided the principal forum in which the political consensus and policy drive toward a knowledge-based economy have taken place. They have also provided the basis of a very effective, near global, dispersion of particular conceptions and models of the knowledge-based, new economy. Key European Commission documents through the 1990s including the influential White Paper, *Teaching and Learning: Towards the Learning Society* (European Commission 1995) had earlier emphasized developments toward a learning society and of lifelong learning in relation to labour market participation. These papers were accompanied by a number of OECD documents including *Measuring What People Know* (OECD 1996a) that stated that: "OECD governments are strongly committed to improving the skills of their citizens as one of the principal means for dealing with economic uncertainty." This series of documents brought together current ideas about economic growth and competitiveness as increasingly reliant on the knowledge and skills of the workforce. They culminated in the Lisbon Agenda of 2000 and its latter iterations. A virtual general consensus regarding the imperatives of learning societies to generate learning workers engaged in the pursuit of product and process innovation and adaptation for competitive economic advantage appeared to have been achieved (e.g. European Commission 1993, 1997, 1999, 2001; European Round Table of Industrialists 1994; Lundvall and Borrás 1999; UNICE 2003). As the World Bank succinctly expresses it: "lifelong learning is education for the knowledge economy" (World Bank 2003).

The European Commission's conception of the knowledge-based economy endeavours to give practical expression and delimitation to the "new economy", the post-Fordist regime, the technological expansion, and the "high skills" conceptions that had emerged as preferences in the latter two decades of the twentieth century. This conception of the knowledge-based economy is a particular political and economic project yet one with a far-reaching effect. The systematic application of knowledge to an ever expanding range of production practices and production factors entails the dispersion of knowledge-intensive activities into all industry sectors. As analysts, including Drucker (1993), noted, there had been earlier twentieth century efforts to apply knowledge to production and work practices which stimulated much managerial attention on manual labour productivity, skill development and efficiencies. But these efforts, ranging from Taylorism and Fordism to Human Relations School interventions, yielded improvements largely only in industrial processes of mass production and some mitigation of worker exploitation. These were important, but the post-industrial economy requires much more. The post-industrial economy, in which the ICT revolution generates new products, processes and markets, requires both intensified and extensive systematic application of knowledge in the generation of new knowledge and further innovation on a continual basis.

The pursuit of the scientific application of knowledge to knowledge production itself intensifies as the technological advance accelerates and the economic value of education and skills attracts excited interest. The growing influence of the new field of the economics of knowledge places much emphasis on "knowledge activation". Knowledge activation refers to the ways in which production and organization systems, including education and training systems, can facilitate the dynamics that optimize the generation, flow and dispersion of knowledge. The numerous grand assertions of the compelling forces of technological innovation in producing the new economy, generating wealth and transforming education and other socio-cultural spheres continue to find expression in the policy documents of the OECD and the European Commission, as well as at national levels. The now routine assertion in economic policy literature that the knowledge economy is empirically demonstrated and rationally pursued in the developed countries is illustrated in Steinmueller's view that:

> The term "knowledge-based economy" captures a qualitative distinction in the organization and conduct of modern economic life ... The determinants of the success of enterprises, and of national economies as a whole, are ever more reliant upon their effectiveness in generating and utilizing knowledge.
>
> (Steinmueller 2002: 142)

He adds:

> To say that an economy is "knowledge-based", therefore, is a simple recognition that the content and structure of economic activities, as well as many of the social foundations of industrialized countries, may be distinguished from their historical antecedents by the rate and extent of knowledge generation and use.
>
> (ibid.: 141)

Soete (2006: 194) provides a further iteration: "For high-income countries, the only input factor which promises long-term sustainable output growth is, ultimately, knowledge accumulation in its various forms: embodied in more efficient capital goods, in human capital, in organizational methods, in new production techniques or products."

Many analysts, policy-makers and commentators in the 1990s agreed on the basic premises that the knowledge-based economy proposes a systematic development of knowledge-intensive and innovative production of goods, services and processes. There was broad agreement on an intense new emphasis on education and training systems that was also generally welcome to educationists. But there was less agreement on the strategies undertaken in pursuit of those objectives. There were national variations in the pursuit of these objectives and alternative models of high-skilled and high-waged economies (Brown *et al.* 2001).

CLASSICAL MODELS OF "HIGH SKILLS"

An economic interest in education had long been evident as Hayek's (1945) propositions made clear but the new interest drew more explicitly on propositions that human capital development was needed across a much wider population base than in Fordist mass production economies. An acceleration of a general movement toward education expansion and higher-level skills formation has been, since the 1990s, observable across the European model welfare state countries. Patterns of this movement in the decades prior to 2000 showed national variations more prominently than a clear pattern toward convergence around a singular and liberal model that is currently dominant. Debates in the 1980s and 1990s frequently emphasized the term "high skills economy". The debates, prior to the popularization of the term "knowledge-based economy", reflected the institutional diversity and different national strategies toward raising general skill levels, facilitating greater economic efficiencies and redistributive policies in different European countries. That diversity of policy implementation, many analysts observed, occurred along the axes of diversity identified in the "varieties of capitalism" literature (Esping-Andersen 1990; Hall and Soskice 2001). Debates continue on the extent and relevance of that diversity. More recently, however, analysts observe patterns of increased convergence toward a general liberalized model promoted in current European Commission policies as well as in OECD discourse (Streeck 2009).

It is helpful to review the approaches which were especially influential in the 1990s in which analysts distinguish two main types of approach toward a high skills and knowledge-based economy (Green 2001) One of these, identified as a classical political economy model, emphasizes both social and economic dimensions of the high skills economy. It seeks the distribution of more highly skilled work across a much wider population and across more industry sectors that would in turn maintain lower levels of social inequality. This approach is presented in the work of Albert (1993), Crouch *et al.* (1999), Finegold and Soskice (1988) and Streeck (1992, 1997). The classical political economy model was especially evident in the 1980s and 1990s in the Nordic countries and Germany. Germany, an exemplar of this approach, as Green (2001: 67) summarizes, "exhibits a relatively even dispersal of skills throughout labour market sectors". Importantly, the German and Nordic cases show that the drive toward "equality of productive capacity" is regarded as an essential basis of social solidarity and economic competitiveness. Streeck (1992) emphasizes the role of economic and industrial institutions, importantly German neo-corporatism, which refers to the involvement of collective actors: trade unions, firms, industries and governments, in shaping the way that skill formation systems and skills dispersal occur across society.

The classical model sought to distribute the benefits of higher-level skills and increased productivity to a collectively more highly paid workforce. As Brown expresses it: "the development of a high skills society clearly depends on a model of human capability based on an assertion that all have the potential to benefit from skills upgrading and lifelong learning" (2001: 40). The emphasis is on all people. For supporters of this classical model, there is shared agreement on the need to develop a "high level of human capability through education, training, and lifelong learning". Brown outlines a model of "the seven C's of high skill formation" with consensus listed as the first.[4] That proposed consensus is needed to occur between "the major stakeholders, government, employers, and trade unions [who] are signed up to a commitment to upgrade the skills of the workforce" (ibid.: 35).

The classical political economy model of higher-level skills as described by Brown *et al.* (2001) that pursues higher-level skills, high value-added and wide distribution endeavours to integrate a humanistic educational agenda with economic objectives. It proposes an intermediary path between the human capital models and the radical educationists of the 1970s. Brown and colleagues' study (ibid.), undertaken from an education vantage point, exemplifies this effort. In recognizing the immense economic policy interest in education for higher-level skills these researchers argue that, "Education and skill development are as central to social policy as they are to competitiveness strategies" (ibid.: x). For them, the "high skills society" which they, like many economists, advocate, is an "ideal". It is "the best means for achieving economic and social progress" (ibid.: 261). Moreover, for Brown and many other educationists, expanding human capability and ridding ourselves of a "dim view of intelligence" is an unequivocal social and personal good. In this way, the humanistic academic and social democratic view finds agreement with neo-liberals and business economists on increasing investment in education. Education is at once socially and personally valuable and economically useful and profitable. Both the richness, and risk, of the broad consensus on the value of further education and skills development continue in tense conflict in the midst of the pursuit of education expansion.

Frequently posed in dualistic opposition to this classical model and more evident in Anglophone countries is what is typically called the Anglo-Saxon model. That model favours a liberal approach to capitalist market economies in the generation and utilization of higher-level skills. The model, in according primacy to market action and to business and shareholder interests, omits emphasis on a wide social distribution of higher-level skills and higher wages. It favours liberal and flexible employment relations and high levels of market and individual competitiveness. It also favours tolerance of higher levels of unemployment, more polarized labour markets and social inequalities. The Anglo-Saxon model requires lower rates of social expenditure, greater demand for individual risk-taking and investment in skills development, and reliance on free market mechanisms of distribution.

The Anglo-Saxon model of high-skilled production took up themes around notions of the "knowledge worker" that had gained popularity most notably in the United States. The notion of the "knowledge worker" had been sketched in earlier sociological theorizations (Bell 1973; Touraine 1971) and found a renewed emphasis with the work of economic analysts Peter Drucker (1993) and Robert Reich (1991) in the 1990s. The emphasis in these latter works, respectively, lay principally on the rise of highly skilled workers in technologically intensive fields and their influence on economic production and competitiveness. A wider distribution of higher-level skills across all economic sectors and low wage inequalities was scarcely prominent in these theorizations. For Drucker and Reich, knowledge workers are crucial to the development and expansion of the knowledge-based economy. But they were not imagined to necessarily encompass all sectors of the workforce. Knowledge workers were depicted as being the most successful and high-status workers in a highly competitive knowledge economy environment, which for Reich, was a global one. In order to join their elite ranks in the knowledge-rich sectors, individual workers must gain higher levels of skills and personal competitiveness. A wider distribution of skills may occur through workers' general skill upgrading and competitiveness with one another. But that wider distribution was not modelled as a policy intervention.

The highly liberal knowledge economy model favoured among many US economic policy thinkers is not a general one with wide population participation. There were, and remain, extensive debates over skills development and reform of education among social and educational analysts through the 1980s and 1990s (Goldin and Katz 2008; Popkewitz 2000; Rifkin 2000). Critical analysts in the United States and elsewhere observe that the high competitiveness model has exaggerated the polarization of US labour markets. Large sectors of low-waged workers and high levels of poverty among sectors of the national population are widely noted in economic and social analyses of the United States (Kalleberg, 2009; Levy and Murnane 2004; Mishel *et al.* 2005; Tilly and Tilly 1998).

The United Kingdom has similarly demonstrated a case of a lower generation of higher-level skills and uneven productivity levels. Lower rates of capital investment in plant and equipment, as well as weak distribution of general education and technical skills in the United Kingdom, have affected its lower productivity in comparison to other Western European countries (Crouch *et al.* 1999; Finegold and Soskice 1988). The United Kingdom's economic competitiveness has relied heavily on the competitiveness of its financial markets, the capitalization of asset sales, mergers and acquisitions, and the invention of new ICT-enabled financial products in the 1990s. The expanded financial sector generated considerable private wealth but low distribution of both its advanced skills requirements and productivity gains. Analysts conclude that a "low-skills" pathway with a limited distribution of skills throughout the workforce may achieve competitiveness and persist alongside knowledge-rich sectors (Finegold and Soskice 1988; Green 2001; Streeck 1992). The United Kingdom has sectors of highly skilled elite workers in classical professional occupations and in newer occupations such as ICT professionals, financial and marketing and design professionals. But it displays a lower distribution of general education and post-compulsory education and training participation in comparison to the social economy model of corporatist Germany and Nordic countries (Green 2001; Lauder 2001).

Overall, analysts find much evidence for a distinctly uneven uptake of the high-skills, high value added, higher wages model that Brown *et al.* (2001) and Green *et al.* (2006) elaborate as the classical political economy model. A variety of models of skills development, distribution and utilization (Green 2001; Crouch *et al.* 1999) have been pursued across the different countries and regions in the latter decades of the twentieth century. For some analysts, that diversity remains important and may offer sources for the development of new and alternative policy pathways in the future. Yet, it appears that the diversity in national models has diminished. Recent research finds that even the Nordic countries, formerly an exemplar of the social-democratic high-skills education model, have now similarly embarked on a neo-liberal course of reform. As Fagerland and Stromquist's (2004) extensive comparative study of five Nordic countries demonstrates, reforms to higher education show a similar pattern toward rationalization and economically oriented skills and research applications. The adoption of policies of market liberalization and labour flexibility and increased migration flows brings a powerful disruption to classical models of workers' education and training. Streeck's (2009) detailed study of the German case reveals the erosion of its former non-liberal capitalist institutions, neo-corporatism and low inequalities and the increased convergence toward a prevalent neo-liberal governance order.

The policy movement toward an overarching model of the knowledge-economy and learning society was consolidated in the European Union in its 2000 Lisbon declaration. At its launch, the Lisbon Agenda favoured a conceptualization of the high-skills economy that endeavoured to bring together various notions and models of high-skills productivity, distribution and comparative advantage at transnational levels. The promotion of high level skills, and better jobs was intended to foster a wider distribution of higher-level skills, higher productivity and higher wages across the European Union economy as a whole. The Lisbon 2000 Agenda sought, in the process of developing the knowledge-based economy, to also maintain the European social model and promote social cohesion. But an accompanying strategy of market liberalization made those two-fold aspirations increasingly ambitious. The 2005 review of the Lisbon Agenda announced a further strengthening of neo-liberal competitive strategies and further labour market modernization accordingly. The Lisbon Agenda in its relaunch in 2005 steered convergence toward the pursuit of the objectives of a liberalized knowledge-based economy as an overall economic policy. It strengthened demands for continual innovation, for knowledge management, and dispersion of learning. It also emphasized increased individual responsibility for gaining higher-level skills and maintaining employability in the highly competitive and flexible labour markets (these points are discussed more fully in Chapter 4). The launch in 2010 of the Lisbon Agenda's successor, *Europe 2020*, endorses the broad economic programme of Lisbon and proposes further education expansion and labour market flexibilization.

THE "LEARNING ECONOMY": CONTINUAL INNOVATION

A key element in the successful rise of the knowledge-based economic (KBE) model was the theoretical influence of evolutionary and neo-institutional economics *vis-à-vis* classical and neo-classical economic models. Much neo-liberal theorization, certainly at its inception in the 1980s, readily invoked classical liberal economic models. Yet other economists argued that classical models could not adequately take into account the crucial importance of innovation, as well as the inherent dynamism and instability of markets. The development of evolutionary and neo-institutional approaches[5] to economic theorizations seeks to redress these omissions and to draw particular attention to the dynamics of change and innovation. The "new institutional" economic theorizations direct attention to a variety of aspects for which the classical economic models, and assumptions of rational calculative behaviour between economic agents, are unable to account. They address factors in institutional change and the roles of multiple actors in the social and political context of economic activity. Technological advancement involves unknown and uncertain elements that cannot, by their very nature, be pre-known and calculated.[6]

The ICT revolution, as Castells (1996) theorized, launched in its first waves a vast expansion in productivity and disruption to conventional modes. Many economic analysts argued that the route to successfully competing in the dynamic new markets of "informational capitalism" was to generate continuous innovation capacities. Innovation involves elements of the unknown and the uncertain. Innovation-based growth is risky. Exploiting these dynamic features requires a liberalization of institutional environments including those of the firm and labour market. The firm's attempt to strategically manage knowledge production and application toward the generation of innovation requires it to be able to deploy labour and resources on a more contingent basis. Knowledge creation, dispersion and flow need appropriate management, and variable financial incentives, in order to convert them into innovation. The elevation of innovation – which results from creative and *strategic* application of knowledge – into a crucial factor in the new economy swiftly followed the crucial pairing of advanced technologies and institutional neo-liberalization. The knowledge economy requires institutional change to match the dynamics of change, competitiveness and innovation that are at its core.

An illustrative and highly influential contribution to the development of the knowledge-based economy theorizations is the work of European Commission advisors, economists Bengt-Åke Lundvall and Susana Borrás. The influence of these theorizations warrants a closer look at the model. Lundvall and Borrás describe a model of a learning economy that requires the development of continually modernizing, rationalizing and innovating strategies. They, like many others, propose that a "new society" is on its way – a "society based increasingly on knowledge and learning capacity of its citizens" (Lundvall and Borrás 1999: 3). A "learning economy is an economy where the ability to learn is crucial for the economic success of individuals, firms, regions and national economies" (ibid.: 35). The transformation puts pressure on national and firm levels of the economy toward technological change, and organizational adaptation and innovation require the intensified learning abilities of workers. "The economic future of Europe will reflect, above all, the learning ability of its citizens" (ibid.:160).

The ability to innovate depends on "the development of human resource policies, labour market policies, new forms of organization, building innovative networks, and integrating research institutions into the innovation system" (ibid.: 160–61). Knowledge "as an economic resource ... determines the context in which the dramatic changes in knowledge generation and use" occur (ibid.: 32). The ultimate aim of innovation, which is both the imperative and the outcome of worker and organizational learning and knowledge, is "the shaping of institutions and structures of production so that the innovation system becomes better suited to future market developments" (ibid.: 164).

To underscore the crucial emphasis on innovation Lundvall and Archibugi (2001: 1), in their Introduction to their book: *The Globalising Learning Economy*, quote the CEO of Rank Xerox: "Both the pace and the acceleration of innovation are startling; nay, terrifying ... no-one can predict the ... range of skills which will need to be amassed to create and take advantage of the next revolution."

The unpredictable nature of innovation requires that the firm develops a capacity for a continual dynamic of learning. Innovation within the firm and its organizational forms is crucial to operationalizing the knowledge-based economy (Coriat and Weinstein 2002; Kahin and Foray 2006; Whitley 1999). The "learning economy", which economists propose as the refined concept, points to processes in which various types of knowledge are gained, and some knowledge becomes less important or redundant. Following Schumpeter's notion of creative destruction, they argue that there is a process of knowledge destruction in the dynamic learning economy, and that enables innovative new knowledge to be generated. As economists Conceicao and colleagues summarize: "innovation is really the word that best fits with the idea of the knowledge economy understood from a dynamic perspective" (Conceicao *et al.* 2003: 4).

Knowledge economists assume that the relationship between knowledge and development is universal and unidirectional. Their efforts for the most part, are to contribute to richer understandings of the innovation process in order to advance economic growth. These have led to considerable contributions and advancement on classical and standard economic approaches. Classical and linear models of innovation are criticized for their insufficient description and account of the complexity and contingency of the innovation process. The attention to innovation systems, Lorenz and Lundvall (2006) argue, has drawn much greater attention to the role of history and institutions in shaping economic action and policies. An emphasis on the interactions of people, firms, regions, and countries shows the complexity and diversity of national innovation systems, and shows the inadequacy of linear models of innovation that focused on the productivity of research and development (R&D) and knowledge generated within the firm. A significant difference, they argue, between dynamic knowledge and learning is that these cannot be measured or predicted in conventional linear models of innovation.

This argument, with earlier iterations by Freeman and Soete (1997) and Nelson and Winter (1982) among others, attempts to develop alternatives to microeconomic foundations of classical modelling. The principal focus in this attempt to develop richer descriptions of the innovation process is attention to the link between the complexity of the innovation process and the specific characteristics of knowledge and learning. As Lundvall and Borrás (1999) argue, analyzing the specific characteristics of knowledge and its accumulation and dispersion, allows knowledge management to facilitate innovation processes. Other analysts, notably Nelson and Romer (1996), argue for the nonrival nature of ideas and the rival character of tacit knowledge. Again, as Lundvall and Borrás argue, an emphasis on open discussion, the importance of interaction and communication between knowledge holders, and the role of organizational structures and processes are seen as crucial to understanding the organization's part in stimulating or hindering innovation.

The new knowledge-based economy contains an increasingly important role of change as an economic activity in itself. The new economic regime replaces the former regime that combined brief periods of construction of new capacities with longer periods of exploitation of those capacities. The new regime is "one of constant innovation" (Foray 2004: 38) that requires higher levels of education and training, specific skills, and transferability of knowledge. Priority is given to adaptability, mobility and flexibility. Constant innovation requires constant efforts to develop the product and organizational form that will successfully disrupt the market in its favour. Innovation, thus conceived, is the strategic application of knowledge and change toward the development of products that are successfully taken up in competitive markets, and of processes that render knowledge creation and management more efficient and productive. Creativity, although gaining some recent attention in organization studies, is not in itself the harbinger of innovation. It is the application of science, planning and learning by doing that achieve constant innovation. And it is the fuel of competition that drives it.

For Foray, "the advent of the knowledge-based economy is manifested less in the continuous expansion of a specialized sector than in the proliferation of knowledge intensive activities throughout all sectors of the economy" (ibid.: 8). Consequently, social institutions need stimulation for the dispersion of knowledge to generate new knowledge and further innovation. The knowledge-based economy experiences, through the general trajectory of ICT and highly skilled workers, constant waves of innovation. These constant waves of innovation, while they can and do generate successful developments, are also sources of endless turbulence. Such economic and organizational turbulence carries considerable risks and unpredictability for the firm and for economies. These factors (Foray 2004; Foray and Gault 2003) may lead to a paradox of the new economy. An economy of perpetual and radical change can undermine the bases of productivity gains. Therefore, to manage this paradox, constant efforts at knowledge management become a crucial new organizational capability. The expansion of research programmes in economics and business research institutes to analyze knowledge and to find optimal methods of its production and strategic management is precisely devoted to that task. At a more macro level, attention to the demands of institutional and organizational change stimulates intensified attention to social systems of education and learning. The generation and management of knowledge, it is argued, require institutional and organizational change and continuous learning.

KNOWLEDGE MANAGEMENT AND ORGANIZATIONAL LEARNING

A business discourse promulgated through especially North American and Anglophone university business schools over the last two or three decades encourages attention to the knowledge economy at the level of the firm's organization. A key component of that attention took, in its first forms, the development of management practices to pursue a notion of the "learning organization". The learning organization, its prominent theorists Argyris and Schön (1996) and Peter Senge (1990, 1999) argued, could accomplish both the necessary adjustment to organizational restructuring and reconfiguration demanded by heightened competitiveness and could utilize human capital more efficiently. Borrowing much from literatures on adult and lifelong learning of the 1970s and 1980s (discussed in Chapter 4), the notion of the "learning organization" is conceived as a crucial dimension of the "learning economy" of the 2000s (Archibugi and Lundvall 2001).

The concept of the "learning organization" has developed from the general premise of knowledge assuming the role of the principal productive force of contemporary capitalism. Human capital can be generated and reproduced at the organizational level of production, and utilized to gain further production innovation and/or efficiencies and profitability for the firm. Just as "new growth" economists had recognized that workers' skills and knowledge are resources, the notion that organizations as collective practices can learn new processes and responses to production environments has gained much attention. The development and utilization of the intellectual capital of the firm are a key source of its comparative advantage. Organizations and employees can actively learn new ways of doing things and forge institutional changes at the coal face of production. They can collectively learn to generate innovation in processes and in product development. Learning organizations are the operational agents in the generation of technological innovation and competitiveness.

A literature on learning organizations promotes a general model of the learning organization as an interactive system of continuous learning by doing, of reflection and refining practice according to what has been learned and judged beneficial or inefficient (Boisot 1998; Easterby-Smith and Lyles 2003; Senge 1999; Stewart 1997). Learning and adjustment take place at all levels from the individual worker to systems levels. The model emphasizes strengthening learning capacities, the management of knowledge for business decision-making and for strategic exploitation of the knowledge capital within the firm. Learning capacities and dynamic knowledge flows comprise the vital "social capital" of organizations (Cohen and Prusak 2001) that are essential for innovation and the comparative advantage of the firm. That social capital comprises trust, mutual understanding, shared values and behaviours that make cooperative action possible and sustainable through organizational changes. These additional competencies to those of formal skill and qualification formed in education and training systems comprise vital factors in the recruitment of employees, as Brown and Hesketh's (2004) study demonstrates. Once again, these factors of learning and development present both rich promise and risk for workers.

For knowledge economists, as Lundvall and Borrás (1999) illustrate, worker and organizational learning and knowledge development in the learning economy are for "the shaping of institutions and structures of production so that the innovation system becomes better suited to future market developments" (ibid.: 164). It is the aggregate effects of organizational learning and of their inter-organizational interactions on the functioning of economic institutions, particularly industrial organization that are regarded as the substantive measure of the learning organization and the learning economy. Organizational learning focuses on learning directed to the tasks of selection, coordination and retention of practical and theoretical productive knowledge. It includes the extraction and codification of workers' personal capacities, tacit knowledge and affective creativity in order that these knowledges may be shared and regenerated. It also includes strategic containment of worker knowledge, and the elimination of redundant (inefficient or undesirable) knowledge.

The codification of knowledge plays a vital role in production and in competitiveness. It extends capacities for innovation, and it also enables the commodification of knowledge to extend system controls, to outsource knowledge (as it can be bought) and to sort internal operations according to routinized knowledge and non-routine tasks. For knowledge economists, these capacities are accomplished through the organization's utilization of education and training systems – both those provided externally to the organization through schooling and tertiary education systems and the popular cultural formation of today's workers as lifelong learners, and the organization's internal learning and knowledge management system. The utilization of education and learning is a highly rational strategy for organizational advantage. For Foray: "the internalization of ... external knowledge cannot rely on the spontaneous actions of people but requires ... explicit practices of knowledge management" (2004: 212).

Knowledge economists argue that organizational learning and knowledge management, as well as workers' skills and learning capacities comprise the principal competitive advantage in globalizing production and trade environments. Those knowledge requirements irrefutably confirm the need to expand education and skills production and to disperse knowledge-sharing activities throughout the economy and society. Research at industrial organization level finds that the rates of failures and disjuncture between new technological applications and human misunderstanding and errors in their use are high (Rooney *et al.* 2005). These "human infrastructure failures" do not reflect simple human error, but rather the "miscalculation of the educational, cultural and institutional requirements needed for creating and enacting knowledge" (ibid.: 2). To reduce the rate of "human infrastructure failures" organization scientists and knowledge economists pursue optimal systems of knowledge codification from skilled and expert workers for future dissemination.

Knowledge scientists identify the problem of the viscosity or "stickiness" of knowledge and the persistent difficulties in generating efficient diffusion. These are vital issues in applications of knowledge science to production organizations. The efforts to develop and apply scientific methods to knowledge production and dissemination indicate management science efforts go much further than the popular appeal of the learning organization. The management of knowledge has now arisen as a principal new competence of strategic organizational management. The extraction, codification and transmission of tacit knowledge into knowledge products that may be exchanged are crucial tasks in the knowledge management of an organization. These competences are of further significance to the new scientific management of knowledge in that they can enable improved performance, continuous innovation, and greater efficiencies. These advantages can occur even as employment relations in flexibly structured organizations display lower employer commitment to workers and higher rates of staff turnover.

Close scrutiny of contemporary organizational and employment practices reveals that outcomes of management utility of intensified learning and knowledge systems are more mixed than the model purports. For workers and wider end-users of organizational productivity, the increased capacities for knowledge generation and transmission increase skill levels and stimulate production of higher value goods. These are typically welcome outcomes. However, despite its persuasiveness in the apparent generation of more highly skilled jobs and more varied work for employees, the rationalization of organizational and worker knowledge brings other consequences and problems.

Management of knowledge generation, flow and utility accrues to management greater sources of power and control and generates new sets of problems for workers. It delineates a crucial juncture in the role of learning at work – that between worker interests in wide use of their fruits of education and lifelong learning and production-relevant knowledge, and management interests in the strategic utility of all of that knowledge toward organizational objectives.

The learning organization, undoubtedly, contains immense potential for workers' learning to be utilized for diverse purposes, and for new conceptualizations of management to be the herald of new collaborative practices (Casey 2004). These may variously benefit both workers' and company objectives, and the benefits may extend beyond the immediate pragmatics of knowledge sharing and job development. There is potential, for example, as some recent Italian and German studies have shown, for worker learning to significantly affect the development of new forms of organization and quality of workplace life (Garibaldo and Telljohann 2006; Whittall *et al.* 2007). But the typically prevailing economic model of the ideal learning organization developed in business literatures proposes a rational and subordinated alignment of knowledgeable workers with the organization's strategic techno-economic imperatives. The organizational level of learning in the managerial perspective requires institutional reform toward facilitating the strategic selection of innovative ideas, knowledge pursuits, technological developments and ways of doing things in the midst of firm-favourable flexibility and contingency of employment relations.

Knowledge science and knowledge management now more systematically conceptualize, and seek to operationalize, the popular concept of the learning organization. The learning organization, ideally modelled as comprising learning and collaborative workers and dynamic systems organized toward the objectives of product and process innovation and cost efficiencies, makes concrete the learning economy/learning society model of the grand policy conceptualization. However, despite the convictions of knowledge economists and scientists that the development and dispersion of knowledge-rich and learning systems will lead to their continual self-regeneration, we observe significant social problems in the policy adoption of this model. The first flaw is observed in the conceptualization of the idealized knowledge-based economy and learning organization model itself. That conceptualization, which occurs in abstraction from real-world conditions and effects, generates and fuels a principal technocratic orientation – one that views knowledge as synonymous with science and technology – which the dominant model is unable to reflexively interrogate.

Diverse, culturally valued forms of knowledge scarcely feature in the dominant, liberalized knowledge-based economy model and, when they do, it is to the extent to which they may be incorporated in knowledge policy conceptualizations as useful to innovation or market efficiencies. Under a liberal market political governance regime, that techno-economic conception of knowledge and learning gains a hegemonic effect. It effects a subordination, neutralization and assimilation of cultural aspirations for education for diverse non-economic ends. It marginalizes forms of social knowledge and their contribution to the regulation of economic and social life. In the workplace, collective knowledge of the risks of exploitation and degeneration of human spirit which arise under organized system action, which Weber recognized as domination, is marginalized or lost. The social regulation of those organizational tendencies of domination and exploitation requires much more than techno-scientific knowledge and elite insistence. The following chapter reveals the effects of these forces on work and production at the current time.

CONCLUSION

Earlier policy pursuits of "high skills" economies displayed national variation in strategies and outcomes. Much of that variation, which included non-liberal capitalist paths, has now substantially given way to a pattern of convergence toward a neo-liberal policy model of the knowledge-based economy. The assertions and demands of powerful interest groups, most especially of corporate firms and their associations, have persuaded governments that the optimal course of action is the pursuit of a liberal, highly competitive and highly marketized knowledge-based economy. General policy discourses of the OECD and the European Commission encourage the adoption of neo-liberal macroeconomic strategies at supranational and national levels. Their encouragement of expansion of education systems, of labour market flexibility and organizational restructuring occurs within that overarching liberalization framework. Yet the policy enthusiasm for that liberal regime and its facilitation of dominant techno-scientific model of a knowledge-based economy conceals the role of those politicized corporate interests. Instead, the dominant policy conception of the knowledge-based economy proposes a universally desirable and singular model of economy.

The adoption of a generalized knowledge economy model belies a vastly overstated promise of advantage and benefit for the many. The limits and contradictions, the biases of advantage, and the inherent and predictable inequalities consequent of highly marketized action are ignored. Those limits and contradictions, observed in the unevenness of its application and practical exclusion of many sectors of jobs and workers, are accompanied by further social and cultural costs. They include consequences for the sphere of education and its cultural repository of non-economic values which contribute immeasurable qualities to persons and society, matters which are taken up in following chapters. And they include the unleashing of forces which now shape the world of work in ways that risk new forms of exploitation and degradation of workers and their work. The actual picture of current directions in the structures of organizations, work arrangements, and employment relations poses a disjuncture of the correlation between education and employment opportunity, between higher skill levels and workplace harmonization, between a more educated workforce and higher wage levels. The generalized utilization of skilled labour in the generation of innovation and profit growth is in practice a far less than ideal representation. It is, more accurately, as the following chapters reveal, a virtual contradiction to the ideal model.

The policy emphasis on expanding a highly competitive, liberally regulated knowledge-based economy in the 2000s has fuelled a market economic incursion into many social and cultural spheres, especially education. Education is being actively remodelled in correspondence with macroeconomic policy. Its institutions are being reformed to serve the economy's demand for techno-scientific knowledge and lifelong learning workers. In the course of that major social project, little attention is accorded in education policy to the realities of the world of work and production to which education is pressured to correspond. Despite the oft-repeated assertion of the knowledge-based economy expanding and creating more opportunities for more highly skilled and better jobs, empirical realities indicate otherwise. A close look at the effects of the neo-liberal forces of production and the organization of work reveals many practices and trends that pose gaping contradictions. Chapters 3 and 4 examine generalized imperatives and thematic patterns in the world of work and education in the European model welfare states. Chapter 5 explores more closely the interactions of labour market dynamics and education at the organizational level of the labour market – a level of practice too often overlooked by economists and educationists.

3 Work now

The forces of production

INTRODUCTION

The forces of unleashed capitalism are far-reaching in their effects. The world of work has experienced their full brunt. Work has historically been understood and experienced as a complex arena of social and cultural practices as well as of economic action. Workers produce sociality as they produce goods. Contestations over the regulation of work; over the interests, rights and duties of its actors and stakeholders have long been fierce even as working-class interests were equally long and violently suppressed. In the mid-twentieth century those contestations reached unprecedented settlement. The social institutionalization of deep conflicts mitigated their antagonisms and enabled movements toward fairer, and more rationally legitimate, negotiation over the relations of production. The industrial relations systems of Western European countries more or less instituted practices of collective bargaining, of representation, of more social regulation and distribution of work and production. The pressures of neo-liberalism have now fractured and dispersed those institutions and obligations in the social regulation of work.

The institutional reforms brought about by the neo-liberal macroeconomic policy turn that began its sweep in the 1980s and 1990s very specifically targeted the activities of production, organization, management, employment relations and labour organization. The reforms, in sum, demanded and achieved a powerful *recalibration* of capital and management relations with labour and a wide-scale reconfiguration of the world of work. The subsequent institutional arrangements currently set the prevailing contexts of work and labour markets and conditions for workers. There is little doubt that the technological acceleration has been of immense influence, especially in the 1970s and 1980s. The Fordist production regime appears ineluctably to have buckled under that tide of change. But what is often accorded less salience in the forces of change and recalibration of production relations is the role of the firm: its shareholder interests, its managerial agents and its organizational prerogatives. The collapse of the Keynesian compromise was abetted and succeeded by a resurgence of private, collective interests in economic institutions, most saliently those of the corporate firm. The technological acceleration, the restored powers of the firm to exert its privileged interests in organizational practices, employment relations and labour markets, the political-economic liberalization of financial markets, the drive for a highly competitive knowledge-based economy in order to stimulate the innovations conducive to new profit regimes combine to set the political economic context of contemporary work.

This chapter examines more closely the economic and political forces that shape the dominant conditions under which work and production occur in contemporary advanced economies. Aspects of national varieties of capitalism still do remain visible and effective. But within that variety general trends of increasingly convergent neo-liberal forces of production and work are observable across industry sectors and national economies. A vibrant field of scholarship discusses many aspects of contemporary practices of production and work. My approach in the following discussion casts a sociological gaze over key overarching patterns and imperatives generally occurring in work and production organization. An analytical approach that focuses on general patterns and trends always runs the risk of inattention to specific national or regional and industrial sector institutional variations, pace of change and degree of counter-movement to general trends. However, in order to delineate and explicate significant general elements, patterns and responses, that risk is cautiously taken here. The approach taken is also necessarily limited in its attention to other important levels and concerns[1] in working life and to industrial and employment legislation.[2] It must further be noted that a critical analytic view of the overarching power relations to which workers are subjected does not, of course, ignore the irrepressibility of the human spirit that inspires people to make the best of their work and job situations. But neither, of course, ought a spirit of amelioration be expected to acquiesce to an elite expectation of toleration of new, quieter, forms of exploitation and injustice.

The discussion below identifies three clusters of imperatives. Discussion of these imperatives takes as extant the technological acceleration that has been extensively discussed in the literature. These imperatives occur in interactive and intertwining rather than clearly sequential ways. It is the combined effects of these imperatives and their institutional effects that produce the particular dominant patterns and forces of work and production in the advanced economies observable in the early twenty-first century. Had any one of these elements been subject to substantially different political and social forces, a different pattern of consequences might well have resulted. The forces described are not of themselves able to include limits to their action. They cannot, without social and civil intervention, deliver the qualities of fairness, respect, justice and society-building solidarities and reasoned contestation.

CURRENT PATTERNS: COMPETITIVENESS, NEO-RATIONALIZATION, AND RESURGENT FIRM POWER

The changes of the later decades of the twentieth century brought considerable disruption to the social institutions and regulatory compromises achieved, more or less, for some thirty years under the Keynesian-Fordist regime. Certain features of the collapse of the Keynesian settlement, the crisis of Fordist production and accumulation, the technological acceleration and corporate business interests interacted with sufficient political force to dramatically alter the social and economic institutions formed in that period and to launch new conditions of economy, production, and work. For many analysts, prominently Castells (1996), the overarching force appeared to be the technological one. But others observe (as also does Castells) the elements of what may usefully be described as *strategically combined* forces were already visible and effective in mid-twentieth century social and economic conditions. The neo-classical sweep in the late twentieth century enabled the uptake of those elements to form a powerful convergence.

The first of these imperatives, which I describe with emphasis on its *intensification*, is that of *technical rationalization.* Increasing rationalization ("*zweckrational*"), as Weber ([1922] 1978) identified, is a characteristic feature of societal modernization. The occurrence of *zweckrational* action increasingly apparent in all spheres of social life gave rise, Weber observed, to social consequences. Increased instrumental rationality is especially effective in economic action. That economic rationalization which we have recognized since Weber has incurred a distinct intensification. That intensification occurs through a combination of two key factors: *the technological acceleration* fuelling expanding production capacities and, *an expansion and intensification of competitiveness.* Techno-economic rationalization, following Weber, comprises instrumental and deliberative action toward economic ends abstracted from substantive socio-cultural values. The stimulation of competitiveness may further be understood as instrumentally rational action in response to uncertainty and unpredictability associated with the technological acceleration. An assumption of *de facto* heightened competitiveness concomitant with the technological acceleration is often invoked as the compelling reason in policy discourse for the sweep of neo-liberal institutional reforms instituted across the formerly managed capitalist economies.

Many analysts regard the current features of heightened competitiveness and intensified rationalization as an ineluctable course following dramatic technological development, especially that of new information and communication technologies (ICT) (Drucker 1993; Castells 1996; Reich 1991). Manuel Castells' extensive investigations certainly address the complex interplay of technology, economy and political interests. In describing the "new informational economy" he recognizes the powerful roles of political-economic elites in its course. Yet he nonetheless accords to advanced technologies an emphatic role. He notes that capitalism is "alive and well despite its social contradictions" (Castells 1996: 195) but his focus is on "informationalism" as a new dominant mode of development of capitalism. As he succinctly puts it: "New information technology is redefining work processes, and workers, and therefore employment and occupational structure" (ibid.: 251).

Castells' weighty emphasis on the technological imperative in organization and production change has been widely influential. For Castells, the "extraordinary increase in flexibility and adaptability permitted by new technologies opposed the rigidity of labour to the mobility of capital" (ibid.: 278). Productivity and profitability have been enhanced as labour loses its institutional protection and bargaining capacities. "What made possible this historical redefinition of the relationship between capital and labor was the use of powerful information technologies and of organizational forms facilitated by the new technological medium" (ibid.: 278). For Castells, informational capitalism generates a new "unit of analysis" which he calls the network. The network is made up of various subjects and organizations in continuous dynamic interaction. Castells' network enterprise is undoubtedly important. But his schema has influenced a tendency to overestimate the loosening of vertical integration, hierarchical management and internal organizational rationalization. Politically networked action by firms won institutional liberalization to enable the firm's new relations with labour and its new flexible organizational forms. At the same time, the firm retained and strengthened its vertical, and horizontal, integration, as I endeavour to show below.

Elements of the features outlined above, especially of rationalization, were observable, as Weber had earlier noted, during the earlier stages of modern industrialization. Forces of rationalization were further accompanied by the technological acceleration through the post-industrial, post-Fordist transition. These more well-known patterns affected organizational practices and workplaces. They were variously managed under the Keynesian demand management regime. But the interplay of a third factor: *a resurgence of politicized private economic interests,* especially in the form of the firm (including its network of shareholder interests) took a decisive role in fuelling and capitalizing on a drive toward highly rationalized production systems, ICT-enabled flexibilities and new sources of competitiveness and accumulation. Closer attention to the role of the firm and its organizational practices adds further aspects to the general analysis. Elite business interests have won an apparent public acceptance of the institution of the firm as the legitimate predominant actor in contemporary economic organization. The firm,[3] it has been widely politically asserted and appears normatively assumed, is the best-placed actor to succeed in conditions of accelerating international competitiveness and marketization. The asserted authority of the firm under the guise of an assumed necessity of a neo-rational model of organization accords to the firm and shareholder interests extensive powers. A strategic combination of interests has enabled a resurgent power of the firm to capitalize on the technological acceleration and to win institutional liberalization. The intensified competitiveness and further forms of rationalization that result powerfully shape the world of work and production in the advanced economies. The following discussion addresses each of them more closely.

INTENSIFIED COMPETITIVENESS

Classical industrial economics assumes that the reduction of production costs is a principal factor in the achievement and maintenance of accumulation efficiency and competitiveness. The rationalization of all production components – including wage costs, innovation costs, materials sourcing, manufacture and/or delivery of production and performance of services – is sought through the reduction in their costs to the firm. Wage bargaining strategies reflect this assumption, with employer trade-offs only conceded in order to maintain production efficiency by workers whose wage levels are sufficient to retain their labour as contingently required, or to avoid strike action. In periods of greater worker collective power during the mid-twentieth century, systems of trade-offs and participatory regulations relatively managed the imperatives to lower wage costs and displace other organizational costs incurred in production uncertainties onto workers. Furthermore, Fordist production efficiencies enabled higher wages for mass production workers in order to stimulate mass consumption of their steadily rising production output. But competitiveness on costs including wage costs reduction remained the orthodox position in labour economics.[4]

Some more recent economic approaches, especially those associated with the new institutional economics, argue that achieving greater efficiencies is not unilaterally associated with reduction in all costs, especially labour costs (Foray 2004; Lorenz and Lundvall 2006). Analysts now argue that competitiveness is a composite outcome of increased efficiency measures, product quality and quantity, and market strategy (Durand 2007; Kahin and Foray 2006). Firms need to stimulate competitiveness through a combination of strategic measures: principally of costs and of innovation. A key reason for the imperative of intensified competition, as Durand (2007) argues, arises as an effect of post-Fordist production practices and advanced ICT applications in commodity production in the developed economies. By the 1970s, the rapidly expanded capacity to produce goods and services in many basic product ranges had generated a situation in which not all goods produced in mass production systems were sold. In some key sectors the production of consumer items, such as household appliances, furniture, cars and clothing, which until that time had been objects associated with some scarcity, as a delayed or permanently deferred purchase by a mass public consumer base, now exceeded market capacity to absorb. Mass product markets of abundant goods generate an unpredictability of consumers' purchasing desire and behaviour. The unpredictability of consumers' purchasing desires has not, however, had the effect of reducing supply. Importantly, it has had the aggregate effect of intensifying competition among suppliers. These suppliers now compete on price, quality of goods and services, appeal of product variety or novelty and power of marketing pitch.

Market saturation and the subsequent unpredictable purchasing behaviours among consumers in the developed economies were accompanied by another significant factor. The expansion of advanced technological applications in manufacturing and organizational processing to the newly industrializing countries (NICs) of Asia further intensified competitive conditions. The rapid expansion of lower-cost production of basic manufactured goods – clothing and apparel, toys, plastics, non-durable electronics, and more recently more highly skilled service work in data processing, print and media, telecommunications and call-centre functions – to the newly industrializing countries enabled considerable acceleration of international production and trade. That acceleration and expansion now characterize the globalization of the competitive market economy and its uncertainties, risks and institutional fragility.

Further added to these competitive production factors is the strategy of market construction. The rapid growth of marketing – as strategic action to generate consumption – in the latter quarter of the twentieth century has significantly fuelled the climate of intensified competitiveness. Marketing is a practice that aims to produce and engineer markets, customer demand and consumption. Contemporary marketing practices intensify the search for new commodities and services. Intensified marketing, which marketing designers explicitly term "aggressive marketing", strives to generate product markets where none previously existed, and to maximize potential customer exposure to those products. Aggressive marketing stimulates desires, simultaneously transformed into needs to be gratified in purchased consumption. It achieves the normalization of market action in the public's consumption of wider varieties of goods and services. It functionally implements the neo-liberal elevation of market action through the encouragement and normalization of the conduct of more and more human exchanges via market action. Human exchanges formerly excluded or protected from market action are depicted in marketing discourses as traditional and inferior cultural practices.[5] Heightened marketing activity fuels a generalized public acceptance of higher risk-taking in production and market action as well as higher levels and shorter cycles of product consumption, which further accelerate market action.

A currently highly favoured route to comparative advantage is through innovation. Knowledge economists argue that the pursuit of knowledge-rich innovation in products, processes, market strategies and relationships can yield significant competitive advantage. Innovation, which may be understood to include the development of a novel good or successful variant of a product or process, involves risk and chance. It incurs higher risk in the ensuing uncertainty of its market adoption, and the potential of wildly successful outcomes, e.g. mobile phones, micro-fibre materials, widely prescribed drugs. In practice, aggressive marketing strategies may be utilized in the promotion of innovative products or just as readily they may be utilized to yield competitive advantage for imitative or repackaged existing products. Innovation can yield a competitive advantage but it is not in itself a driver of intensified comparativeness. The generation of innovation is, in essence, inefficient. It incurs the costs of risks and unpredictability of investment in activity for which the outcome is a calculated guess. The off-setting of those inefficiency costs and risks must be borne in some other sectors of the production enterprise or displaced onto other parties. The market strategy may assist the off-setting of innovation costs but the firm may adopt a further, often less well-noticed, measure in its competitive strategy.

The intensification of competitive environments and the uncertainties of consumption markets demand other accompanying measures on the part of the organization. In response to heightened competitive pressures the firm pursues organizational practices aimed at maximizing efficiencies and reduction of uncertainty costs. The organization, whether of the explicitly business firm or of other forms of enterprise such as public sector agencies or companies which are similarly influenced by market pressures and adoptive of market behaviours, pursues an intensification of organizational rationalization. Its pursuit of cost-management efficiencies through intensified rationalization involves a powerful reassertion of the firm's managerial power. The uncertainties of production in highly competitive environments require, according to the orthodox argument, intensified rationalizations in the form of re-establishing managerial prerogatives and authority over the organization of work and production.

Organizational neo-rationalization

The intensification of competitiveness crucially influences another core feature of rationalization at the operational level of production organization. The *intensification of production rationalization and efficiency* in the organization is a highly salient feature of contemporary firm practice across diverse industrial sectors. Organization scientists have long noted that organizations avoid uncertainty (Cycert and March 1963). Organizations impose "uncertainty-absorbing contracts" on their environments. Firms attempt to devise and negotiate an environment to eliminate uncertainty. Turbulent environments, such as those generated by rapid liberalization and heightened competitiveness, expose the firm to exogenous shocks. Liberalized institutional conditions, demanded by elite business interests, simultaneously prompt the firm to take action to reduce the new waves of uncertainty and dynamism of market-intensified action. The firm acts to displace uncertainty onto its workforce. The uncertainties and shocks of liberalized exposure can be managed through the adoption of strategically flexible organizational structures and contingent employment relations.

Fordist-Taylorist work organization had earlier enabled distinct rationalization of work processes which included simplification of work tasks, high routinization, and strategic application of skill (Bendix [1956] 1974; Blau 1965; Casey 1995; Durand 1994). However, the character of the new forms of rationalization, in contrast to linear intensification and efficiency through rigidities, is a multi-faceted one. It presents both flexibility and heightened managerial control. The organic-sounding notion of flexibility, favourable in the early days of post-Fordist movement to flexible specialization (Piore and Sabel 1984), is utilized through ICT systems to bring more factors of production – especially those pertaining to workers and the utilization of skill, and the utilization of quasi-organic, semi-autonomous team working arrangements – to be brought under an overarching rationalization programme. The new programme for organizational rationalization contains not just the conventional cost-reduction measures, and "lean production" of the 1980s, but a new emphasis on variety of response to heightened competitiveness. Since the 1990s the favoured route to competitiveness is now seen as residing in the development of innovative products and new forms of work organization (Best 1990; Dosi *et al.* 1998; Foray 2004; Teece 1987). Both of these routes require much more strategic utility and exploitation of human capital within the day-to-day operations of the organization.

Through the 1980s and 1990s, organization and management science literatures promoted theories of *strategic* organization models and management practices and a practical hybridization of rational and "organic" systems' rudiments. This strategic, neo-rational organization theory (Casey 2002) recognized the unstable character of organization structures. It sought to take into account both the limits of rational action, as often overlooked in classical Weberian models of bureaucratic organization, and the overly organic systems theories favoured by Parsonian-derived, structural functionalist models. Moreover, theorists proposed, a rationally contingent organizational model enabled faster response in a rapidly changing institutional environment and conditions of intensifying competitiveness. Programmes of organizational reform and restructuring toward more flexible, contingent and efficient organizations and strategic, neo-rational management introduced in recent decades have had extensive effects. A significant aspect is the development of new organizational forms especially those that alter conventional bureaucratic structures of hierarchy and linearity and which develop flexible, ad hoc and multi-stranded forms of relationship – the notion of the network organization.

These far-reaching developments predominantly took the form of internal organizational changes: the reduction of bureaucratic structures, wider and looser spans of control, the formation of project groups including semi-autonomous teams, matrix management structures and reporting relationships, and flexible structures of employment relations. The newly conceptualized hybridized model with its anti-hierarchical theme and promise of more respect for individual liberties contained much potential for development of new forms and practices of organization. De-hierarchicalization and adoption of a more organic structure could have favoured more truly collaborative and negotiated forms of organization. The turn toward a new valuing of workers' skill and participatory contribution could have opened paths for a radical humanistic conception and practice of production organization. Certainly, many labour-interested commentators in the 1990s hoped that the new organizational forms and processes, which contained distinct possibilities for post-Taylorist models of work organization and social integration, would bring greater benefits to workers as well as organizational management. The development of teams and project configurations intended to facilitate knowledge-sharing, problem-solving and creative ideas for production and process improvements also contained the potential for job enrichment among diverse moderately skilled workers as well as more highly skilled workers.

Dubois and colleagues (Dubois *et al.* 1995), for instance, in concluding their cross-national study of Italian, French and German manufacturing companies, point to the increasingly "indeterminate, flexible task structures" that do not facilitate the continuation of the "old top-down forms of organizational coordination":

> Post-Taylorist models of work organization and social integration will … be characterized by broader task structures, a higher but controllable autonomy of employees, an increased participation of employees in politicized, communicative processes of rationalization, [and] a reduced importance of hierarchical forms of coordination and control.
>
> (Dubois *et al.* 1995: 313)

These reforms promised much greater opportunity for formal equality and mutual respect in the organization of production. Jenkins (2000: 46–50), in reviewing the 1980s and 1990s, observed the potential for organizations to offset the "human price" of intensified demands for "constant innovation" and process efficiencies by seeking new ways to improve the quality of working life and to maintain widespread employer–employee negotiation. Sandberg's (1995) studies of Volvo's automobile manufacture, furthermore, saw the capacities in organizational change for more extensive and effective forms of worker participation and for the potential for unprecedented partnerships between workers, management and employers. Volvo's Uddevella plant famously demonstrated an exemplary case of management and worker collaboration in the operation and work design of the car manufacturing site. It was short-lived.

Despite these prospects and the rich potential for improved socio-technical and humanistic practices in the organization of production, and for more democratic regulation of work and economy, the hybridized, organic-rational model of organization predominantly favoured a distinctly privileged role for management. By the end of the 1990s practices known as "lean production", first deployed in manufacturing as crude cost reduction measures, had found further utility. Their principles were adapted to a new requirement of liberal dynamism. The principles of lean production require tight management of resources – including human resources. Management learned that pressures for intensification of worker effort and continuous improvement of performance could be coupled with new organizational ventures in team-working and horizontal networking (Durand 2007).

A key component of the re-intensification of rationalization against organic quasi-autonomous organic forms is an emphasis on "knowledge management". The strategic management of knowledge – its legitimation, dispersion and utility – is a prerogative of management. Its application demonstrates the neo-rationalization of management action. Rather than permitting flexible, semi-autonomous and quasi-organic team working behaviours, a highly elevated and determining role for strategic managerial action endeavours to master the design and integration of more contingent and flexible structures and network relationships of the organization. The management of knowledge and information flows (i.e. the diffusion of productive and profitable knowledge) and technical systems' intensification enable a greater vertical integration of the power of the firm in governing the relations of production and organizational arrangements.

Far from specific to manufacturing and heavy industry, a managerial strategy that combines the principles of tight process flow, continuous improvement and constrained employee involvement extend widely across industry sectors. Their application is evident in myriad processes in service sectors including hospitals and health services, banking and finance services, utilities, transportation, delivery, retail, catering, entertainment, public administration, and in often less noticed sectors of education and justice (Boltanski and Chiapello 2007; Clarke and Newman 1997; Durand 2007). The rationalization drive, which has brought many now standardized features, such as the managerial technology of HRM (Human Resource Management), ICT-enabled system integration, and flexibility of labour, shows a high convergence across most industry sectors in the advanced economies. Disorganized capitalism is, at the level of the firm, neo-rationally organized to encompass flexibility and dynamism.

Flexibility: new organizational behaviours

The restructuring of production organization beyond the Taylorist-Fordist model and classical bureaucratic forms to new forms occurred through the latter decades of the twentieth century. It is characterized by the developments of flexibility and contingency. Flexible and contingent practices are intended to enable quicker organizational response in the dynamic and uncertain environments of liberalized markets. Liberalized institutions, post-Fordist production systems, the search for product and process innovation and for sources of competitive advantage and increased profits demand organizational forms and management practices capable of implementing rapid, strategic contingencies for opportunity maximization.

Flexibility entered into the discourse and practice of organizations, initially in the United States, in the 1980s and 1990s. Piore and Sabel's (1984) influential work championed flexible specialization and institutional reform beyond Fordist mass production regimes. The notion of flexibility – in contrast to being rigid, static, unyielding and obstructive – has attracted a powerful connotation of being a normatively good state for organizations to pursue. Business management literature in the 1990s popularized notions of post-bureaucratic and ad hoc organization structures that were capable of "thriving on chaos" (Peters 1989). This notion regarded large bureaucracies as "dinosaurs" (Kanter 1989) that would quickly become moribund in the new conditions. Organizations were extolled to restructure toward more flexible configurations and processes in order to simultaneously pursue the divergent goals of dynamism and competitiveness, and efficiency and innovation. As that strategic flexibility also required intensified system integration and intensification of process, business advisors further extolled a new emphasis on leadership. Under the rhetoric of leadership, cadres of senior managers were further assimilated into the firm through their enhanced roles as leaders and "change agents" of the sweeping programme of organizational and employment relations reform. The spectacular success of that business campaign has ensured that in the 2010s employers can rely on the effectiveness of that hegemonic power. Workers, in European countries as in the United States, have internalized a normative expectation of their compliance with the managerial requirement for flexibility as a personal characteristic and rudimentary skill for labour market participation.

In general terms, intensified organizational rationalization in the form of flexibility of structure and processes has been more readily observed in the form of employer-initiated employment flexibility. The various types of flexibility[6] can be distinguished as occurring on two principal dimensions. Analysts Boltanski and Chiapello (2007) identify these dimensions as internal and external, with the latter referring to the consequences of the firm's actions in comprising aggregate effects in the institutional environment of organizational behaviour. Internal flexibility can be recognized as taking three main forms: *employment and wages flexibility, numerical flexibility, organizational and functional flexibility*. They are closely interrelated.

Employment and pay flexibility refers to the ability to vary the rate or tenure of the employment contract and rate of pay in relation to individual performance or in response to particular market conditions at a given time. The use of flexible or variable remuneration includes greater use of bonuses, non-monetary rewards, elimination of overtime rates or rates for shift work (as these are rendered "normal" hours of work). Employment flexibility includes job structure and design flexibility with changes in job content, titles, team working, and reporting relationships. It includes the use of broken shifts, variable hours of work, variation in holiday times, variable locations of work, and of deployment of workers to tasks.

Numerical flexibility refers to the ability to adjust the numbers of workers and/or the terms of working hours. Numerical flexibility enables a firm to hire and retain workers on a basis that is contingent on the organization's immediate requirement for particular skill sets. The use of temporary and agency workers, semi-dependent workers, and fixed term contracts on intermittent or terminal arrangements enables the firm to exert greater short-term control over its labour deployment and labour costs. Numerical flexibility requires employment contracts that enable the firm to retain individual workers for positions that may require variable hours of work and that may be temporary, intermittent, or contingently continuous. Business management literature argues that these measures indicate rational managerial responses to market uncertainties, heightened competitiveness and unpredictable dynamics incurred in the search for product and process innovations. Adoption of these forms of flexibility enables the firm to displace risks associated with retaining costly labour under variable rates of profitability in dynamic markets. Workers' insecurity of tenure individualizes and disperses that risk. The eventual socialization of that risk has found some policy response in the state subsidizing of employment in certain categories and in arrangements for "flexicurity" (discussed in Chapter 6).

The third main form of internal organizational flexibility refers to operational and functional flexibility. In the first instance, organizational operational flexibility refers to the employer's ability to deploy workers to various tasks, teams or units in the relatively de-hierarchicalized workplace. It also refers to various contingencies of the integration of system functions into the core organizational structure. A rudimentary form of operational flexibility includes job rotation, task variety and team working. The use of project teams or temporary structures for particular organizational objectives can stimulate greater knowledge flow, skill complementarity and increased worker participation in determining the organization of work. Organizational flexibility also includes flexible use of plant and material resources with, for instance, the variable use or temporary occupancy of buildings, rental of technology and provision for some categories of workers to work from home or use temporary, virtual office space. It also refers to contingent relationships with clients, suppliers, workforces and communities.

Looking more closely still, organizational flexibility can be seen to also involve components which at first glance may appear a hindrance to, or even a contradiction of, flexibility. The factor of functional integration, which emerged in the 1980s and attracted much excitement for its capacities for accelerated productivity, now enables greater facilitation of innovation. Functional integration refers to the ability of the organization to bring together, in a dynamic but controlled manner, core aspects of the system and production relations that were formerly, under typical Taylorist-Fordist systems, separated by linear structures and knowledge flows. The early developments in post-Fordist production exhibited a number of intermediary interventions, including the well-known "just-in-time" and "continuous improvement" programmes and semi-autonomous teams influenced by Japanese management and operational practices. However, the substantial shift occurred with the adept utilization of advanced ICTs *and* the flexibilization of job structures and employment relations enabled by a political liberalization of the regulative regime. A fully integrated production system radically changes the linear sequence and irreversibility of Fordist production. It simultaneously enables flexibility and horizontal as well as vertical control. Its successful operation more deeply integrates workers into the firm's managerial systems' governance of the production system.

Functional integration removes internal barriers between departments that under typical Fordist organizations were set up in large and medium-sized organizations, and often imitated in small organizations as well. Functional integration, enabled by ICT applications and the flexible deployment of workers, contributes a new capacity in interrupting the conventional timelines of linear, vertically integrated production.[7] It enables continuous feedback, simultaneous design and production, rapid attention to perceived market preferences or manipulations, and greater general capacities for knowledge and innovative interventions across the contributing divisions or teams in product and services development. In sum, the probability of identifying, and intervening in, design flaws or intended market pitch at any stage of production is much greater than under linear production systems. Functional integration is now regarded as a vital platform for a radical expansion in the capacity for knowledge sharing and innovation stimulation. It facilitates knowledge management and simultaneously enables unprecedented further forms of flexibility. It has considerable normative appeal and undoubted potential for new forms of organizational participation and governance. But its deployment reveals a distinct system of power. There are undoubtedly many continuities and extensions of Fordist and Taylorist methods that remain effective in contemporary production systems (Doogan 2009; Lomba 2005; Williams 2007). But crucially important innovations have achieved at a macro level substantive alteration to this regime. Now, the sophisticated, liberalized firm uses both neo-Fordist and highly flexible operation systems simultaneously and strategically. Tightly and vertically integrated production organization enables an intensification of managerial power under the guise of rational system governance. The current sets of practices and relations of production have wrought an immense post-Fordist effect for workers.

Internal flexibility in the firm is accompanied by external flexibility, or broader labour market flexibility beyond the firm. Labour market flexibility refers to a wide variance of employment relations, the rise of "atypical work",[8] and the erosion of collective labour institutions and occupational identities. The efficiency drive exemplified in the lean production principle of flexible specialization stimulated in firms a concentration on core competences and key profit-maximizing activities, popularly expressed as core business. This development indicates a further distinct feature of organizational flexibility with a considerable external reach. The firm's reform of conventional organizational structures toward flexible and highly rationalized forms enables the firm to strategically alter its external boundaries and to develop still further new forms of organization. These take the form of networked relationships in partnerships, alliances, subsidiary relationships, franchises and client dependencies. These arrangements frequently blur organizational boundaries (Grimshaw *et al.* 2006; Marchington *et al.* 2005) and incur consequences for employment relationships. The firm's increased engagement in networks of enmeshed activities blurs the existence of more typical, formal boundaries in regard to what belongs to the firm and what does not. The formation of subsidiaries and quasi-independent but subordinate business units and cost-centres, cross-shareholdings between suppliers and distributors, and the mixing of financial trading activities with material production enable new capacities in the pursuit of profit. Networks are conceived as displacing hierarchical and market institutions. They are permeable, looser structures that emphasize collaborations and synergies between firms (Di Maggio 2001; Rubery *et al.* 2002).

The blurring of organizational boundaries in the firm, the emergence of hybrid forms of organizations, and of networks of inter-organizational relationships enable diverse forms of flexibility and at the same time a transfer of integrated systems. That is, the interchanges between these forms enable an exchange and generalization of functional integration and flows of knowledge. Yet the hybrid and network organizational forms also enable, and demand, tightly managed human resources. Workers' flexibilization and contractual individualization facilitate that. Organizational configurations of core and peripheral activities, with multiple subsidiary units, require strategic sorting systems of workers' deployment. These arrangements reveal the particular, rather than the generalized, utilization of integrated teams of multi-skilled workers which require high trust and collaboration. Such collaborative teams of knowledge-sharing employees certainly are in evidence, but their generalized deployment across all sectors of knowledge-rich production enterprises, let alone the knowledge-based economy itself, is not evident and not required by the firm. The crucial point I wish to emphasize in this explication is that these intricate practices of extraordinary flexibility and system integration effect a strategic and structural birfurcation of skills utility. That point anticipates discussion of organizational skill sorting practices discussed in Chapter 5.

The deployment of flexible and contingent organizational structures saw, as mentioned above, the widespread introduction of team work. Team work, which often brings many benefits to workers, encourages the explicit sharing of knowledge among other skilled workers in order to diffuse knowledge and problem solving and make "in process" interventions. The potential advantages and satisfactions of teamwork, for both employers and workers, however, are typically distorted in teamwork's instrumental utility in the achievement of functional integration. Intensified organizational rationalization, functional integration and flexibility demand and achieve a mobilization of employees toward an intensification of productive effort and an elimination of non-productive time and behaviour from the workplace. Workers' ability to find loopholes in order to self-regulate pace and flow and enable self-styled breathing spaces and sociality is systemically intercepted.

Durand's (2007) term "tight flow" appropriately illustrates the process of intensification that has occurred through the sum of the mutations in production and organization which I have described above. Lean, integrated, ICT-rich production systems require tightly streamlined operations, workers' maximized effort, and accountability to other workers in the functionally integrated organization. Tight flow, as Durand demonstrates, requires a reorganization of labour and the re-prioritizing of its "collective nature", that is, its aggregate productivity (Durand 2007) – even as workers are increasingly de-collectivized and individualized. The firm-oriented collectivization of labour involves not only team and group work of knowledge sharing employees, but the "guaranteeing" of human resources – in other words, the provision of appropriately acculturated employees engaged in on-going skills formation, flexible utilization, and normalized compliance. Employees in today's highly modernized organizations find themselves in a situation in which they are, as Durand (ibid.: 205) puts it: "obliged to adapt, imbibe and adhere to the culture and objectives of the enterprise". This point introduces a further key pillar in the transformation of work under neo-liberal capitalism: Human Resource Management (HRM).

Human Resource Management (HRM)

The managerial technology of Human Resource Management, which has been widely, comprehensively applied in diverse industries in private and public sectors across much of the developed world, has been immensely effective. It is now normatively assumed as an unremarkable structure of contemporary organization and work. Its deployment has oiled the wheels of substantial organizational reform and intensified rationalization in the interests of the firm, or the "new management" of the public sector. It has established the managerial prerogative as the normative vantage point in the determination of employment relationships and of organizational actions. Human Resource Management (HRM) was developed originally in the 1970s and 1980s in the business schools of US universities in partnerships with large corporations and consulting firms. Programmes of Human Resource Management advocated a comprehensive and efficient approach to worker management that offered a different approach to that conventionally held in industry and labour economics. Workers are to be conceptualized as a resource of production rather than as a cost. That different conceptualization, promoted as highly favourable to workers, has brought two significant consequences for the definitively employer-advantaged recalibration of employment relations.

In its earlier iterations HRM found some popular reference to humanistic and paternalistic interventions derivative of the so-called Human Relations schools of management, which had emerged as early as the 1930s and 1940s, notably in the Tavistock Institute in London and the University of Chicago. The Human Relations school of thought emphasized psychological approaches to the management of workers. It encouraged management attention to workers' personal needs and roles in the workplace, including rest breaks and good lighting. The promotion of more humanistic, even if paternalistic, treatment of workers in comparison to the highly instrumentalized approach of Taylorist, scientific management found some favour in the expanding fields of management and organizational research. Taylorist scientific management famously focused on efficient extraction and utility of labour power of recalcitrant workers in routine production. But under those regimes employer recognition, even if reluctantly accorded, of workers' collective associations and trade unions enabled a distinct recognition of the contested nature of workplace relations and of managerial power. The subsequent development of Human

Resource Management usefully retained some of the favourable connotations of the human relations approaches in regard to workers' well-being and workers' personal needs. But it was essentially a political and simultaneously directly practical development in management arising from the application of Human Capital Theory in economics.

HRM develops strategies designed to accomplish more than the expected tasks of personnel management: of recruitment, remuneration, training and employment relations. HRM endeavours to acculturate employees into the objectives and priorities of the firm. As human capital resides in people who may express and pursue contrary and often inefficient desires – as many mid-twentieth century organization and industry analyses demonstrate – the management of human capital resources requires strategic attention to maximize extraction and productivity and minimize costs. Workers' recalcitrance and competing interests distract from production activity and weaken organizational efficiency. The depiction of workers as resources, similar to the way that material, plant and capital are regarded, facilitates recognition of their value but also their constitutive role in the organization's pursuit of functional integration. The attractive proposition of resource as value rather than simply as cost sought to win workers' identification with, and even a sense of family belonging to, the firm (Casey 1995). In the course of promotion of the caring employer of the valued resource of the worker, the firm discourages or refuses recognition of collective worker associations and trade unions, and of professional identities.

The active integration of employees into managerial practices that simultaneously foster job insecurity and flexible opportunity structures and the promotion of network organizations required a shift in the mindsets and behaviour of workers. Through the 1990s and 2000s, empirical research studies revealed the ways in which corporate firms develop and enact corporate cultures as devices to integrate employees into the activities and rationale of the firm yet retain prerogatives in uncertain labour markets (Casey 1995; Durand 2007; Jenkins 2000). Extensive hierarchical forms of control within the organization have observably decreased. But new forms of ideological control in organizational cultural integration, normative and peer control, and micro-systems management have enabled a more subtle intensification of managerial rationalization.

The new organizational practices have succeeded in generating greater levels of productivity and company profitability through more efficient and responsive organizational structures and have demanded greater levels of worker compliance with managerially designed work practices. The changes to the internal organization of work have been accompanied by increased psychological attention toward workers. Workers are selected for jobs on bases that include more than their technical skills and ability to perform the job. HRM in its integrative intent selects employees on the basis of psychological criteria. The use of psycho-technical tests in the recruitment and retention of staff has become a widespread, often taken-for-granted, practice of contemporary management (Brown and Hesketh 2004; Boltanski and Chiapello 2007). Psycho-technical tests include tests for personal dispositions such as social skills, ability to get along with others, self-composure, good humour and "openness" which refer to the character of the person and to their propensity to "fit in", to comply with the managerially determined organizational culture. Employees' capacities for commitment and adaptation are essential to a logic of flexibility that requires moving in and out of engagements, job tasks, even locations of work. My own empirical studies in the 1990s (Casey 1995) showed at a micro level how employees learned to become the adaptable, flexible, congenial team-player. They were required to perform the character qualities desired by the company and to encourage those traits in others. Under these company requirements there is little accommodation of competing professional loyalties and power bases of trade unions.

The firm's active erosion of workers' attachment to trade unions and occupational identities undermines sources of workers' power. De-collectivization of workers enables their smoother integration as resources into the managerial utility of the firm. That integration further enables a normative acceptance of intensified power of the firm. That normative acceptance obscures the use of HRM integration against the interests of workers in terms of their collective power in the workplace, their security and conditions, their application of knowledge and skill, and their intensification of effort without recompense. HRM wins a comprehensive set of requirements of workers: of acculturation into the company, yet dispensability and insecurity, of detachment from collective associations yet willingness to engage in team work and collaborative system integration and knowledge sharing – now known as "groupware". HRM's individualization of workers in regard to their employment contracts and utilization by the firm is simultaneously accompanied by the activation of firm-oriented collectivization of workers' effort and engagement. Research routinely reports that good HRM relations with staff, including reports of "being nice" (inter-personally) to employees generates higher work satisfaction scores on employer-designed satisfaction measures (Green 2006).

Programmes of human resource management are now routinely practised across the developed world and across diverse industrial and organizational activity. They are deployed in private sector businesses, public and governmental organizations, in trade union organizations, in not-for-profit and civil society organizations. The successful incursion, and embeddedness, of HRM – in its various forms of flexibility and contingency, integration and intensification, discipline and compliance – across diverse industry sectors in the twenty-first century are scarcely challenged even by trade unions and worker-interested bodies.

The neo-rational management practices described above, in the form of organizational rationalization through flexibility, of system integration and intensification and of HRM, comprise pivotal factors in the forces of production today. Organizational rationalization in the form of flexible organizational structures and relationships may have held, and indeed may still hold, the potential for new sources of worker autonomy and agency in collaborative production enterprises. But the concrete forms of organizational restructuring and radical management interventions toward intensified organizational rationalization have severely delimited those prospects for collaboration and democratization. These concrete organizational changes have gained for the firm distinct advantages in production proficiency, re-subordinated workers and increased profitability. The weakened condition of labour has enabled a regression of labour standards and conditions achieved by workers' associations in previous decades of the twentieth century, and a long-term stagnation of real wages for workers (Frege and Kelly 2004; Glyn 2006; Streeck 2009). These forces of contemporary work exhibit and enact the new spirit of capitalism with little impediment. Yet they have required, as they at once attest to, the resurgent power of the firm.

THE RESURGENT POWER OF THE FIRM AND THE DECLINE OF LABOUR

The imperatives toward intensified production and comprehensive organizational rationalization that we currently observe were given their decisive power by the dynamics of a liberalized, loosely regulated capitalism and accelerated competitiveness. The climate of accelerated competitiveness brought about by the ICT revolution, the unpredictability of production innovations and of global market expansion, and pressure for increased rates of profit made possible further demands of capital interests. Those demands, aggregated at the level of the firm and shareholders, sought a definitively altered pattern of relationships with workers and the extensive exploitation of workforces. Business management and popular media literatures since the 1990s have predominantly depicted the demands of firms as necessary and legitimate actions of profit-seeking enterprises in response to the ineluctable forces of capitalism. But the factors of technological advancement, intensified and uncertain competitiveness and their sensible firm management responses were, on their own, of insufficient force to have brought about the new order of organizational arrangements and the current structures of work and employment we experience today. The resurgence of capitalism and its new forms of rationalizations and worker subordination were far from inevitable developments.

The dramatic shift to flexible organizational structures and a re-mobilization and new compliance of labour required a recalibration of political forces in the world of work and production. Neo-liberal institutional reform enabled the firm to break free of former institutional constraints on its actions. A pivotal aspect of the liberal institutional reform was the promotion of the shareholder conception of the firm. That conception proposes that the role of senior management is to ensure maximization of return to shareholders. The interests of other stakeholders, prominently workers, are relegated or eliminated from the model. Shareholder and investor interests powerfully pressured firms to restructure organizations and to rationalize and intensify managerial control of production and workers. Management forged a powerful alliance with shareholder interests and broke former efforts to collaborate with organized labour. Senior managers and more highly skilled employees were actively drawn into the firm's and shareholders' interests through incentives in the form of stocks and shares and bonus payments. Firms reduced investment in production and organizational activities that incurred costs, including those of infrastructure, long-term planning and employee development. Cost reductions in the form of reduction of the permanent workforce and of employee wages and benefits and the expansion of competitive market structures within the firm intensified the firm's economic and political position in regard to production and workforce relations. Flexible liberalization brought the firm new capacities in its relationships with labour. These events – of both retraction of commitment to labour and intensified demand on labour – occurred at the same time as the new demands for "human capital" and higher skilled workers were being loudly raised. In the firm-won liberalized climate, the confidence of the firm soared to demand at once re-subordinated *and* higher skilled workers.

The resurgent power of the firm has seen its demands accelerate and extend broadly. It has moreover won an apparently normalized acceptance of its privileged interests in society. The political role of trade unions in the social regulation of production and work, while by no means ineffective today, is manifestly subordinated to the power of the firm. Variations in the fortunes of trade union activity across industry sectors and countries undoubtedly remain. But there is, it appears equally undoubtedly, a pattern of convergence in the occurrence of systematic political efforts on the part of firms in gaining a restoration of their powers. The much debated crisis in trade unionism has, in the first decades of the twenty-first century, congealed into a persistent condition for trade unions and worker-oriented political activism.[9]

The mid-twentieth century normative and institutionalized relations of work and employment afforded unprecedented protection to a majority of workers. Those institutions established a regulation of labour and employment that included not only the more commonly noted condition of continuity (or security) of employment contract but also qualities in regard to benefits and conditions, the design and conduct of jobs, agreed norms regarding satisfactory effort and limit of management demands on productivity of labour, and collective protections from exploitation. These had been substantively won through systems of collective wage bargaining and greater worker participation in production relations in previous decades. Their systematic retraction and replacement at varying pace across national contexts, including in Germany and Scandinavia, places long noted for corporatist and social democratic traditions and co-determination of workplace and employment relationships (Heppel and Veneziani 2009; Streeck 2009; Upchurch *et al.* 2009), have placed labour in a regressive condition of subordination.

Core features of neo-liberal regulation depict a fundamental alteration in the conditions in which employers and workers negotiate a compromised settlement on unequal interests and outcomes. The steady disestablishment of institutions of regulation and behavioural obligations has accorded to employers capacities of engagement with workers that systematically and dramatically favour employer interests. Employers have actively sought to move away from building collaborative relationships with unions. They actively pursue a policy of marginalization and disempowerment of unions and toward developing direct links between management and employees. The application of the philosophy of Human Resource Management enables the practical forging of an individualistic approach to the relationship between employer and employee at the workplace level. The initial moving away from collaborative relationships, while initially most effective in the Anglophone countries had, by the 2000s, accelerated into a systematic de-collectivization of workers.

Individualization of employment contracts, of employment rights, and of recourse to grievance manifests a highly significant factor in the recalibrated firm–labour relations. Individualization is evident at formal institutional levels in regard to labour and employment law (Avilés and Vina 2009; Hepple and Veneziani 2009), at the organizational level of the firm in regard to management accounting systems and numerical flexibility, and at the everyday workplace level for workers. Individualization at the workplace level is expressed in the everyday application of HRM to employment relationships and its direct, efficient means to union exclusion. Individualization refers to forms of employment relationships in which the wage payment system shifts from a collective approach to a system based on appraisal and remuneration of individual employees. It includes management communication systems which directly bypass union representation, including in regard to job design and deployment, and employee psychometric testing in the workplace. These direct actions of management reduce unions' knowledge of what is going on in workplace life and marginalize their relevance to employees' workplace experience and employment conditions. HRM promises to take care of employees and diminish sources of conflict that have tended to be politicized by unions. Workers placed on individual contracts with employer-initiated flexibility in hours of work, tenure of job, wage rates, performance-based pay, and education and training opportunities forge differential relationships among workers on the same site. Individualization undermines workforce bases of solidarity and organized contestation to managerial prerogatives. The overall effect is stronger managerial control and a generalized contraction in the role of unions across most European countries.

The rise of flexible and weakly unionized workforces has become a highly significant factor of contemporary work.[10] As Gallie *et al.* (1998: 152) remark: "the rapid expansion of a flexible or peripheral sector of the workforce" has formed a central theme in the changing structure of employment. The evidence for that rise through the 1990s in the numbers of workers on flexible and fixed term contracts (OECD 2004) shows national variations in the use of flexible employment, and in the quality of jobs such workers hold (Gallie 2007). In the early decades of the twenty-first century, the majority of workers in European model countries evidently remain employed on continuous full-time contracts (Doogan 2009). But the proportional rise of flexibility and its spread across industry sectors heightens the visibility of insecurity and contingency. It contributes to altered relations in workplaces where permanent and temporarily employed workers work alongside each other on different conditions and relationships with their employers.

Flexible enterprises structured with various subsidiary or subcontractor configurations with various competitive quasi-separate business units and profit centres with legally distinct employers allow for considerable variability in the employment conditions of workers. The firm is able to disperse its employment relationships through establishing multiple legal employers even as the parent company may own the subsidiary enterprises. This step enables the decentralization of collective bargaining. The firm arrangement of multiple employers reduces the collective bargaining capacities of workers as they are placed in smaller units with bargaining processes and outcomes specific to each unit. This process enables employers to contract workers according to differing arrangements, wage rates and conditions.

Multiple employer relationships, with their variable wages and conditions, can occur among workers working on the same enterprise sites (Marchington *et al.* 2005; Rubery *et al.* 2002; Plasman *et al.* 2007). Boltanski and Chiapello (2007: 229) provide a succinct illustration in their report on a case in France. An enterprise employing 500 wage-workers in the late 1990s configured its organizational forms and employment relations in a manner that divided the workforce into sectors with multiple legal employers. The legal employment status of its 500 wage workers, working on the same enterprise site, came under ten different employers, each able to vary the contractual arrangements of its employees. The researchers show that this occurrence was historically recent in that ten years earlier the same enterprise employed 400 wage-workers under a single employer.

The use of multi-employer relationships disrupts established practices, and assumptions, regarding a bounded relationship between an individual employer and employees. The development of complex inter-organizational relationships alters the institutional arrangements in which the employment relationship was formerly regulated. Liberal regulation has enabled a widening of the firm's scope of action and facilitated new network configurations of capital interests. The flexibilization of the firm, combined with its tightened organizational integration, enables the firm to mobilize its interests in the deployment of resources, including labour, to reduce costs and displace risk onto other parties. The "farming out" (Castells 1996) of individual workers in flexible networks of multiple employers produces a segmentation of labour markets with further extensive implications (discussed in Chapter 5).

Liberalization, HRM and de-collectivized, flexible workforces have gained, for the firm, powerful advantages. They have enabled a re-institutionalization of powerful managerial systems of control and exploitation. They have enabled higher levels of corporate profitability yet stable or decreased average wages in the 2000s. They have won a workforce increasingly tolerant of insecure and contingent employment. Firms have tolerated increased senior managerial costs for an overall reduction in labour costs obtained by both greater flexibility in retention and dismissal of workers and variable wage and conditions contracts. At the same time production and profitability uncertainties, fuelled by highly competitive and volatile market dynamics, have been increasingly shifted onto workers. Individualized and de-collectivized workers are increasingly likely to experience less secure and more fragmented employment contracts and working lives.

The rise of flexibility, volatile competitiveness and individualism has seen a rise in types of jobs that indicate employers' low cost strategies toward competitiveness. We observe a rise in the numbers, and expansion of breadth of occurrence, of new jobs often critically described as "McJobs". These jobs, noted for their low pay, low quality, high routinization and low commitment are largely exempt from former norms and institutions of employer obligation to provide sufficient wage sustainability and decency. As many studies report, an expanding *précarité de l'emploi* (Barbier and Lindley 2002) raises serious concern for workers shunted into precarious work and lives. Their risk of social exclusion through insecure employment is further noted by European Commission policy-makers. Even as the majority of workers in European welfare states are employed on continuous full-time contracts, their range of protections, avenues of participation and effective political voice in the regulation of their work and production are evidently considerably diminished. The resurgent power of the firm, with its organizational systems and managerial commands, has brought about, for large sectors of workers, what may fairly be called a social regression in terms of protection, representation, quality of work, opportunity for development and even of dignity and respect.

The resurgent power of the firm has enabled still further, and often less visible, advantages and adaptations to its demands. The state's move to defer to the demands of the firm in its adoption of neo-liberal macroeconomic and governance strategies has seen the firm's *modus operandi* extend beyond private sector domains. The firm's forms of organization and employment practices have been taken up as the ideal model in the public sector. A "new public management" (NPM) is in the course of implementation in European welfare state countries. Analysts observe international varieties in the course of implementation of these practices, which were first noted in the 1990s in the United Kingdom (Clarke and Newman 1997; Rouban 1999), are being pursued in the 2010s by contemporary governments in Europe (Weishaupt 2010) and elsewhere. New public management pursues efficiency reforms, marketization and competitiveness, and more broadly "governance modernization" in direct emulation of firm-style business models and organizational forms and employment relations. The bureaucratic form is retained in its elements of administrative hierarchies, rationalization and systemization. But it is reduced and modified in regard to its professional elements and private sector neutrality. A diminished professional authority and discretion concede to an increased managerial prerogative and line management. Increased efficiency accountability systems, structural flexibilities and contingencies are introduced which include ad hoc project teams and internal competitive markets for operations and employees. These firm-style organizational practices also include new business relationships with private sector firms in the provision of public services. Public–private partnerships engage both parties in market behaviours that adopt the regulative norms prevalent in the broader market economy.

Debates on various aspects and particular national conditions and experiences of these measures continue. They reveal advantages and problems associated with NPM and more generally focus on its practicalities. My point of emphasis in this note is not in regard to NPM's practical utilities. It is rather to point to the convergent aspects of new public management which lie in the public sector's general pressure to adapt to neo-liberal environments, reduced state welfare expenditure and greater alignment with market action with other market actors. These are patterns of response to the hegemonic demands of firm institutions for liberal state facilitation of extended and comprehensive market action.

Much debate on work and employment relations over the last two or three decades has emphasized the problem of flexibility – flexibility of firms, organizational action and of labour market dynamics. Those debates have focused concern about trends toward greater employment insecurity, coerced mobility and even precariousness of life conditions in the advanced economies. In addition to a popular focus on job tenure or on risk of vulnerability to precariousness for sizable sectors of the workforce, the overarching course of effects on workers of the reconfigurations and reassertions of capitalist forces poses even more serious and far reaching concerns. Whether or not workers are employed on continuous full-time or part-time employment contracts, whether or not they are secure and well-paid, they are overall subject to the re-privileged and normalized prerogatives of the firm. They are, at the aggregate level, re-mobilized for the liberally encouraged interests of the firm to set a wide social influence.

RE-MOBILIZED WORKERS

The forces of work and production today reveal a grossly distorted and weakly contested power of corporate interests. The combination of forces of competitiveness, rationalization in its complex forms of system integration, organizational flexibility and HRM as sanitized worker domination, and the institutionally enabled privileging of the interests of the firm and market action has immensely powerful effects on work and workers. Of course, the forces of capital domination over human interests have long been effective in industrial capitalism. They were, in the historically recent industrial conditions of the mid-twentieth century more socially managed. Workers had some social protections from the rationalizing search for profit maximization and won protection from historical exploitation. The crisis in trade unionism and the de-collectivization of workers extend into a less well-articulated crisis of worker interests in everyday organizational and workplace relations, and for their welfare in marketized society. Workers' individualization renders them subject to the coercive effects of authoritarian managerialism and rationalization. At the same time, it renders them subject to coercive marketing pressures that simultaneously add workers' consumption behaviour to the fuel of production. That market subjugation decays democratic values and viabilities.

The resurgent power of the firm has achieved for the interests of the firm substantial gains which pose potentially long-term advantages. Yet, still further, the forces of production discussed above require now, even more than did the Fordist regime of mass production and mass consumption, the participation of workers as consumers in the generation of continual cycles of production and increasing profits. Workers under Fordism fuelled production through the consumption of mass produced material commodities. To motivate consumption beyond satiation of Fordist goods, marketing and advertising ideologies stimulated new demand. Post-Fordist workers must learn, through the imbibing of relentless marketing ideologies, to intensify their consumption behaviour. The force of consumption in fuelling production includes the maintenance of unsatisfied desire for new products – including products far beyond the purchasing power of wage workers (a truly post-Fordist phenomenon) – and the shifting of utility of product to include symbolic and status value. The intricate entanglement of intensified production effort with intensified consumption further mobilizes workers into subjects of exploitation by the firm and the market. In the course of this mobilization, workers have learned to tolerate a general stagnation of wages *and* accumulation of their own private debt to maintain their consumption desires. The massification of debt, a construction of the firm and the market, fuelled wild innovations of new financial products and their immaterial trade into the 2000s.

Consumption of more complex, higher-value and higher-priced goods requires competitive innovation in production. Of crucial importance to the pursuit of innovative production is the knowledge-economy's ideal firm's demand for more highly skilled and lifelong learning workers. Government policy pursuit of the knowledge-based economy, in tandem with liberalized firms, exerts further and considerable pressures on workers. As well as bearing the demands of flexibility, risk, managerial compliance and relentless marketing, workers are further expected to conform to the firm's demands for aggregate higher levels of skills. Firms, having depressed workers' skills development for most of the twentieth century, now protest that a "skills deficit" obstructs economic growth and profitability. Liberalization won a de-collectivized and re-subordinated workforce and, as Crouch (2005a) demonstrates, it has broken the institutional arrangements that had more adequately provided negotiations for industry skill development. The institutional arrangements for the provision of industry-needed skills had comprised industry and education and training bodies assisting in the provision and calibration of needed skills. These institutions broke down as deregulation fuelled further production uncertainties and undermined skills planning provision. Nonetheless, firm interests claimed, the demands of high value-added, knowledge-intensive production in globalizing markets required vast numbers of more skilled and educated workers. The demand to redress the "skills deficit", for the "activation of knowledge", for the maximization of human capital exploitation, requires of the state a comprehensive new policy programme of education and skills formation.

The forces of production and work described above are observed in the political-economic context of liberal regulatory regimes and widely expanded markets. These forces have re-mobilized individualized workers disciplined and more or less compliant to their course. That re-mobilization is enacted at multiple levels: at the level of institutional change in labour law and at the organizational level of the firm in the decentralization of collective bargaining, at the everyday workplace level through the construct of the human resource, and at the level of consumer behaviour and indebtedness. The firm's "human resource" plays a multifarious role as the character of the new mobilization.

The mobilization of human resources is not that of the old regime's efforts to mobilize workers. The human resource is not the worker with an inalienable subjectivity and with legally protected boundaries between the qualities and foibles of personhood and the performance of her or his work. She is individualized in a manner than ignores her personhood and yet that demands her diverse human qualities and abilities, her emotional intelligence, adaptability, receptivity and congeniality be brought to production effort. These qualities of character and diverse skill are re-collectivized and aggregated for their utilization in the generation of innovation *or* new efficiencies and rationalizations. Innovation is a collective development dependent on knowledge flows as a collective, collaborative endeavour – even as collectivity in redistribution of profit, in shared reward, and shared fate is refused. Moreover, the diverse qualities of character as further capacities for productive effort are developed outside the firm. The worker's investment in the development of these qualities is excluded from wage calculations.

The re-mobilization of human resources requires of workers currently in and preparing to enter the labour market to invest more extensively than ever in the development of skills, particular character qualities and modalities of self. The demands of the re-mobilization find further and immense connection with the reshaping of institutions and practices of education. Education systems are directed to reform toward the provision of multi-skilled and congenial human resources. Policy pressures intent on stimulating and expanding a knowledge-based economy propose that employers express an aggregate demand for higher levels of education and lifelong learning employees. Yet the behaviour of the firm readily contradicts the economic models of widely expanding knowledge-based economic activity and utilization of higher levels of skills across a wide population. Structural and resource rationalizations incurred in the search for innovation and cost effectiveness enable new systems of skill and labour differentiation – that is, new sorting systems and knowledge hierarchies – to be established as the firm pursues a knowledge-based economy agenda. These practices, which are discussed in Chapter 5, pose a crucial new set of critical questions for the knowledge-based economy.

CONCLUSION

The power of resurgent elites, combined with technological reason and expansive market liberalization, has sweeping effects on the social organization of production, the regulation of work, and the conditions and experience of workers. Those forces have won a dramatic re-subordination and re-mobilization of workers to the interests of firm, shareholder and managerial power. An economic authoritarianism under the guise of a sweeping economic, industrial and social liberalization effects a crisis, not only for workers in the social regulation of work but of social and cultural domains more broadly. None of the prevailing imperatives of contemporary work substantively recognizes, let alone celebrates, non-economic virtues and motivations in human work. An economic authoritarianism subjugates, indeed silences, imperatives for self-expression in intelligent or soulful craft, in creativity, in sensitive attention to presence, detail, care, and in due pride in good effort. Imperatives for service, development, honour, contribution to a general social good beyond one's own productive effort and remuneration are frustrated or refused in an exaggeratedly market-rational condition. Values of shared pleasure, of gift, of self-surpassing hope for social and planetary sustainability and for future generations, which people quietly speak of, and yearn for, find no room for expression or integration within the daily labours of intensified productivity that characterizes contemporary work.

The reach of techno-economic rationality beyond the more easily impoverished world of work into the education sphere is currently in course. Having recalibrated the relationship between capital and labour, between business and society, between workers and firms, the politically liberalized governance policies spreading across European model welfare states since the 1990s have extended crucial new attention to education. A humanistic education reform movement of the latter decades of the twentieth century encountered a resurgent capitalism. The interests of the firm, fuelled by liberal regulation, heightened competitiveness, flexible organizations and human resources, searched for new sources of accumulation in the exploitation of advanced technologies and innovation capacities. Education systems, business interests decreed, were not up to the task of delivering technically skilled and individually competitive employees said to be needed by the new industries and by the demands of globalization of neo-liberal capitalism. They required institutional reform and reconfiguration on a vast scale. The turn of political and economic attention to education continues. Chapter 4 takes up that exploration.

4 A new economy for education

INTRODUCTION

Education, unlike modern work, has been much less directly shaped by capitalist forces of production. It has long been an arena of intense philosophical, religious and familial influence. Economic interests, though important, have more typically been constrained by those more primary cultural interests. The subjugation of work to economic reason appears now to have been normatively accepted. For education, that subjugation is a project still under way. Education, most particularly post-primary education, had historically predominantly served the interests of elites. Its historical governance under elite powers obscured the role of economic power through the guise of more overt cultural power and privilege. Education in Western countries was brought predominantly under public and professional governance during the mid-twentieth century. In that course, it was necessarily brought into close relationship with the state and public funds, but education retained effective plural interests in its institutions and socio-cultural roles. Programmes of reform and expansion of education in various national contexts during the twentieth century, most especially in primary and secondary education, saw a broad democratization of participation and distribution of many of the benefits of education. Expansion of higher education followed. Education's classical *raison d'être* for human development and flourishing, certainly for elites, generally ensured its maintenance of plural interests and curricula in the course of the twentieth century expansions.

Nonetheless, education now shares with the institutions of work a subjectification to concerted neo-liberal political efforts for systemic reform. In the European model countries, and elsewhere, the macroeconomic policy agenda in pursuit of a knowledge-based economy of continual innovation contains an immense project for education institutions. That project intends the reform and re-orientation of education toward a seemingly singular political-economic rationale. Education in all its forms, especially at post-compulsory levels of higher education and lifelong learning, and all its personnel, are targeted. Education has always been associated with economic interests. As state involvement in public education vastly increased in the twentieth century, governments encouraged the involvement of industry in education, especially in contributing to the skills formation of secondary and technical school students. These collaborations appeared of mutual benefit and readily involved educationists and trade unionists in their promotion. Education institutions had maintained degrees of autonomy and pursuit of varied curricula for most students. However, the character and intensity of the new association of education with economic interests appear distant from the memory of relative collaboration. It may more accurately be described as an economic incursion with colonialist intent. Education is to be re-imagined as a subsystem of economy. Educational and social critics have protested against these developments that have been underway in recent decades. The subjugation of education to economic rationalizations and elite interests is a project that portends far-reaching social and cultural consequences that contradict and undermine other cherished social aspirations in European societies. Nonetheless, that project appears strengthened in the early twenty-first century.

The institutional reform of education takes a two-fold trajectory. The first, more readily visible, is for the generation of higher levels of skills across a mass population and production of advanced techno-scientific research and knowledge. The second is for the rationalization, or "modernization" in policy language (European Commission 1998), of education in subordinate correspondence with the "scientific episteme" of neo-liberal governance. These developments, and the critical concerns they raise, are the subject of the discussions below. This chapter, in tracing the rise of a powerful economic conception of education in relation to the liberalized knowledge-based economy that is now generally in course, endeavours to inquire into the effects of economic reason and techno-scientific knowledge legitimating the ideological project of reform. As part of that effort, the discussion opens with a longer view in an exploration of the social institutional context of education in modern society more generally. That discussion focuses on two key features of the context of recent decades: that of the modern expansion of education and social-democratic notions of education for all, and the current feature of politicized economic interests in education, growth and wealth. The fields of education especially in mind are those of higher education and lifelong learning.

THE MODERN EXPANSION OF EDUCATION

Like all social and cultural institutions, education is embedded in a complex web of influences and demands, including those bequeathed from earlier centuries. For some sociologists it is useful to depict the development of socio-cultural institutions as occurring in an ethos, as Crouch (1999) describes it, of sociological liberalism – a form of liberal forbearance and relative autonomy between institutions such as the family, religion, economy and education in western modernity. But the relative autonomy of education has always been weaker in comparison to the relative autonomy of family, religion and economy. Education in modernizing societies has been more effectively constrained by keen vested interest from other social institutions which often compete for influence over education. Most especially the effective interests of family and religion in the socialization of the young and in cultural reproduction have seen the role of educational institutions gain only a limited institutional autonomy.

Until modern times, participation in forms of formal education remained the preserve of the wealthy and privileged. Even after the expansion of education in the nineteenth century to the provision of primary education to most children of all social classes, and the eventual rendering of its participation as compulsory until at least mid-teenage years in the post-war decades, the expansion of tertiary education is historically very recent. The history of post-compulsory education and training, typically in the form of young workers' formal training and apprenticeship programmes, displays considerable national variation. That national variation greatly diminishes, however, in the experience and character of the expansion of higher education which has been a dramatic feature of more recent decades in the European model countries and more generally across the OECD countries (Delanty 2001; Mazza *et al.* 2008; OECD 2008a; Trow 2006).

As modern social relations and institutional arrangements expanded, education, by the mid-twentieth century, had achieved relatively stronger institutional autonomy in relation to other socio-cultural institutions. The decreased effect of religious institutions in shaping education – although this has by no means been rendered ineffective – has been observed through the twentieth century. Public provision of education and the increased influence of professional practices and specialist expertise in schooling and curriculum design brought a reduction of direct religious influences in shaping education. The effect of family, however, appears to be more enduring. Families continue to pass on their cultural advantages, or disadvantages – their "cultural capital"[1] – to their children. The effect of family privilege continues to exert significant influences over the shaping of educational systems as well as affecting individual success through the course of participation in a particular education system.

The continuing influence of family and the social reproduction of privileged groups' interests led some sociologists to caution against views of a generalized, uninterrupted course of modernization. The persistence and reproduction of unequal outcomes of educational participation indicate that education did not achieve autonomy from the family. Rather, the differences between families are reinforced through educational systems still strongly shaped by traditional cultural elites. As Bourdieu (1998) argues, families' use of education produces and reproduces social inequalities. Education is a source of inequality even as much social democratic policy seeks greater equality of opportunity through expanded participation in formal education. Moreover, occupational institutions and employer behaviour also exhibit mixed relationships with education system outcomes. Even as the expansion of educational and skills formation systems presents employers with more formally qualified workers, educational qualifications are variably utilized in the gaining of advantageous jobs. Family and ethnic loyalties persisting in modern societies play roles that may outweigh the value of formal educational qualifications in the gaining of desirable employment positions (Brown and Hesketh 2004; Crouch 1999; Dronkers 2008).

Nonetheless, the relative institutional autonomy of education from the family advanced as modernizing processes in society continued. The social expansion and practical organization of education which increasingly came under the charge of educational professionals enabled greater and wider participation from traditionally under-educated sectors. The growing political influence of the working classes, long excluded from influencing policy-making, saw some concessions toward working-class interests in education structures and practices. These, along with cultural changes including the further emancipation of women and the decrease in many once-powerful traditions in some social structures, exerted pressures on the education system to accomplish changes toward greater social equalities and distribution of power. Progressive educationists championed and led programmes of egalitarian reform and wider participation in education.[2]

Post-war political movements favoured an expansion of democratization and social participation. These movements reflected the increasing demands of the working classes, especially those expressed through organized labour movements in much of Western Europe. They gained a wider cultural accommodation of efforts toward further educational expansion and professional influence in its institutional governance. The educational expansion was evidently uneven (Crouch 1999; Floud *et al.* 1956; Halsey *et al.* 1965). But a social democratic character fostering human development and wider social and cultural freedoms promoted overall increased equality – certainly an equality of opportunity if not outcome – as a definitive social good. An important platform of the social nature of the educational expansion was the adoption – already evident in the United States (Grubb and Lazerson 2004) – of a general commitment to policy programmes of equality of opportunity. A liberalizing reform of school structures, of programmes and curricula, although to widely varying extents, accompanied the social expansion. The participation of girls and working-class children in post-compulsory education began its unprecedented expansion in the early post-war decades. By the 2000s, participation rates in post-compulsory education for girls and young women had reached near parity with male rates in most Western countries (OECD 2008a). As well, the expansion of educational provision to adults of any class and age was a signal feature of the variously constituted but generally similar social democratic programme toward a more equal and participatory society evident in the Western welfare state democracies.

The cultural freedoms increasingly sought in and of the education sphere won wide popular support. For many educationists, the educational expansion was viewed as predominantly a cultural one. But the cultural expansion of the education sphere did not, however, render it free from economic interests.

First, the public expansion of education necessarily required the support and funds of the state. Second, while many of the tasks of the education system involve preparation for family roles, they include, as Crouch (1999) points out, even more so the preparation for adult life, of which a major component is the world of paid work. That association with the world of paid work limits education's scope for relative autonomy. Economic interests appear not only through business and employer pressures and demands but through the interests and demands of parents and students for prospective employment-relevant components to, and outcomes of, education. Economically-oriented concerns have gained in the course of the expansion of education a greater influence among various parties and participants in education. As family and religious influences have diminished across the breadth of public education systems in the face of modern professional and social democratic imperatives, economic interests have gained increased influence.

The semi-autonomy of education became a key target of the post-war reformers of education. The first prominent wave of reformers sought more societal influence in education. This is exemplified in the influential Swedish educational reformer, Torsten Hursén's, insistence that education must be viewed in a "wider social context" (Hursén 1974) and therefore socially governed. The reformers were interested in bringing education into social rather than private service. The education reforms of those decades took a predominantly social democratic character oriented toward social and cultural development of people for participation in democratic societies. Yet these movements also opened the path to much greater involvement of economic and technological interests in educational institutions and practices, a point discussed further momentarily.

The social democratic reforms launched an array of innovations, and interventions in various aspects of education ensued. These included changes in school curricula, in teaching practices, learning experiences, in the expansion of sites of learning and education, and in people's access to further and continuing education. The changes included attention to child-centred pedagogical approaches, curriculum innovations such as the "new mathematics" and "new science", and the professional formation of teachers. While these broad developments, it must be stressed, occurred with much variety in national contexts, as well as in application, style and pace, as national education literatures illustrate, their general trend toward expansion, wider participation and humanistic reform is evident across the European model countries. Importantly, the expansion enabled an unprecedented attention to adult and post-compulsory education. By the late 1970s in some sectors of education a notion of lifelong learning for human development was being promulgated as the enduring progressive form of education. At the same time critical commentators pointed to persisting class and gender inequalities in quality, experience and outcomes of education, and the role of education in the reproduction of class structures (Bernstein 1975; Bourdieu and Passeron 1977; Bowles and Gintis 1976; Karabel and Halsey 1977). They argued that the deep endurance of social class structures pervaded education systems and outcomes and subverted the democratic reform movements. They sought still more radical reforms of education systems.

Sociologies of education, especially those of the 1970s and 1980s, focussed much critical attention on class and ideological forces in education,[3] and, especially in the United States, on the role of economic factors. Those economic factors were typically viewed through a focus on abstract macro-economic forces, as aggregates of private business interests and their demands on educational policy-makers. Critical sociologies of education in the United States criticized the rise of business interests in the educational expansion and curriculum reforms taking place in that country. As corporate business interests took a keener interest in school curriculum, schooling quality and even in teacher formation (Grubb and Lazerson 2004; Newfield 2008; Popkewitz 1987), American academic critics saw little prospect for a sphere of education that maintained some semi-autonomy from economy and private elites. The culturally liberal agenda of wide participation, equality of opportunity, and promotion of liberal arts subjects in higher education programmes was weakening against the tide of corporate interests. Critics contended that corporate business power exerted hegemonic influence over education in society (Apple 1979; Aronowitz and Giroux 1986; Wexler 1987). Yet, the relationship between industry and education, especially higher education, in the economically liberal conditions in the United States had always been a significant one. Scientific and technological research in large university research institutions benefited richly from extensive grant funds, endowed laboratories and research facilities, and funded scientists (Grubb and Lazerson 2004). While critics had pointed to the controversial aspects of these relationships, there is little question that higher education and scientific research in the United States has maintained and courted these relationships. Pursuing those relationships has, until recent times, been rare in European model welfare states.

Alongside the concerns of critical sociologists of education, especially in regard to the persistence of social class inequalities and the power of corporate interests, other commentators pointed to additional outcomes of the education expansion. Some commentators, especially adult educationists who had witnessed the considerable expansion of adult and working-class education in the post-war decades, drew attention to evidence of greater occupational and class mobility, advancement toward gender equality, and an expanded and richer curriculum for more students. The expansion of adult education, increasingly conceptualized as lifelong learning, provided learners from social sectors that historically had been excluded from all but the most minimal education provision with greater opportunities and improved life chances across a range of measures. These unprecedented social developments raised prospects for a new social vision to be worked out. The vision and promise of a broad social democratic expansion with its favouring of a humanistic, emancipatory character and civilizing role for education were on the horizon. By the 1980s, radical ideas of a comprehensive "learning society" to which European model societies were advancing were entering popular parlance among adult educators (Boshier 1980; Hursén 1974; Hutchins 1968). Advocates of the "learning society" claimed that immense personal and social benefits were to be gained from population-wide and lifelong participation in education and learning as a distinctive feature of social democratic society.

By the 1990s, international agencies were promoting policy programmes advocating "education for all" (OECD 1996a) which included fostering a role for adult education in promoting human development, cultural emancipation and political participation. These ideas of a learning society gained popularity just as another new set of ideas was emerging at the same time. Notions arising from the technological expansion especially those of an "information society" and a post-Fordist "knowledge economy" were also arousing much interest among economic and political leaders and policy-makers of a more liberal and business-minded persuasion. These were rich conditions for much agreement among social democrats and liberals, educationists and economists, on the value of education and its further expansion in welfare state societies. The character of that expansion, and the aspirations its various advocates held for its accomplishments, however, sparked much disagreement and led to disparate outcomes.

EDUCATION FOR ALL: VISIONS OF THE LEARNING SOCIETY

In the 1970s and 1980s, many educationists in the European model welfare state societies may have readily argued that an emancipatory vision of a learning society was on its way to realization. Such a learning society, founded on post-war prosperity, the growing political power and numerical size of the working classes and a cultural sensibility toward expanded democratic governance under the mid-twentieth-century compromise, envisioned an enduring expansion of diverse educational activities. Earlier twentieth century attempts at adult education, including prominent examples of worker and folk education movements such as that of the Workers' Education Association (WEA), had been led by advocates in civil society and workers' associations. By the 1980s, lifelong learning advocates had succeeded in bringing the notion of further education and continuous learning to general policy recognition.

The policy discourses of the 1970s and 1980s expressed aspirations toward an inclusive "learning society" of lifelong learning citizens. The inclusive model favoured continuing education provision for diverse humanistic and economic ends and wide democratic access to participation. Proponents shared the view that an "historic transformation to a new form of society",in which learning was a key process in achieving successful transformation, and new social cohesion (Hayes *et al.*1998: 89) were underway. Notwithstanding persisting class and gender inequalities, many educationists saw a grand vision of social transformation that would overcome those inequalities. It would be achieved through the creation of a learning society. Form them, the creation of a learning society is "the constitutive condition of a new moral and political order" (Ranson 1998: 29) that would lead to a profoundly different kind of society in the future. The new moral and political order in this vision was one in which all members of society are learning. The character of that transformation would be one of human development, egalitarian citizen solidarity and participation, and cultural enrichment.

For the learning society advocates, diverse and multi-textured learning and education would be socially provided and partaken of from cradle to grave to enhance human development, quality of life, civil society and economic and production governance. Progressive and emancipatory practices of education and learning involved Deweyan educational philosophies of "learning by doing", of "self-directed learning" (Ball 1993; Hutchins 1968). Learner-centred pedagogies were much advocated and experimented with. These ideas, skilfully melded into the widely influential UNESCO Report, *Learning to Be* (Faure 1972), imagined that education and learning would be universally available, democratic in its provision and at the same time malleable to the individual needs and abilities of all citizens. *Learning to Be* (1972) emphasized learning as involving all of life and occurring throughout the life course: "Every individual must be in a position to keep learning throughout his life. The idea of lifelong education is the keystone of the learning society ... The lifelong concept covers all aspects of education, embracing everything in it" (ibid.:181, 182). It is "the principle on which the overall organization of a system [of education] is founded".

The humanistic and egalitarian character of this grand and ambitious vision reflected the moral ideals that helped to meld the practical arrangements of the mid-twentieth century social compromise and manage their always tense dynamics. The promise of an expanding and emancipatory learning society inspired fresh approaches to design and practice across various social institutions. As well as lifelong learning individuals, learning organizations and institutions were imagined (Argyris and Schön 1978; Schön 1971; Stewart 1997). For Schön, whose early theorizations of systems and organizational levels of learning helped expand the focus on education beyond formal educational systems to multiple sites of on-going learning, the task facing advanced societies in the 1970s was to become "adept at learning" (Schön 1971). The pervasiveness and frequency of technological change make it imperative for persons and institutions to learn how to manage the processes of transformation and to welcome lifelong learning as the means of achieving that. Efforts to imagine the "learning university" (Duke 1992) extended these ideas and sought practical redesign of established ways of providing education. These promised extensive systematic changes.

Lifelong learning proposes a rich conceptual and systems innovation to conventional educational conceptions and practices. It proposes three key principles (Schuetze and Casey 2006). Lifelong learning is lifelong, life-wide, and centred on learning rather than on education and the latter's assumed formalities and established institutions. Lifelong learning recognizes and promotes learning that takes place beyond formal schooling systems and which occurs in various places of adult life, especially the workplace and in communities. The concept of lifelong learning promotes the idea of "learner-centred" learning and teaching. Beyond the early childhood years, the proposition is that what, when, where and how learning occurs should be determined, in principle, by learners themselves. Learner-centred agency entails greater responsibility for taking action and making meaningful choices among the various options. Learner-centred learning poses a more negotiated power relationship among learners, teachers and institutional providers. It opens a wide course of options for persons and institutions and democratizes power in their pursuit.

Lifelong learning advocates have succeeded in bringing the notion of further or continuous learning after the phase of initial and compulsory education into general policy recognition. The conceptualization of lifelong learning used in European Union policy discourse focuses predominantly on post-compulsory or post-secondary learning activities. However, as lifelong learning scholars have consistently argued, the extent and quality of education and learning during the formative years are of crucial importance for the ability and motivation to engage in further learning later in life. Therefore, a strategy of lifelong learning must genuinely span the life-course and include early childhood. Lifelong learning scholars and activists have promoted these considerable innovations to, indeed radical departures from, conventional models of education.

It may well have been the moral vision of the egalitarian humanists – which appeared at least for a time the ascendant model – that enabled a new discourse on the learning society that accompanies the knowledge-based economy to gain a wide popular appeal. But the new model took a decidedly different turn of value and perspective. There remains much national variation in education and training systems and in visions of a learning society. But notwithstanding that variation, there is at the transnational policy level, especially in European Union and OECD discourse, a politically favoured model of education with clear general characteristics. That model of education, along with its accompanying set of moral imperatives regarding the value of education and learning, is the key component of the macroeconomic programme of neo-liberal reform toward accelerated economic growth and competitiveness.

The new dominant imperative for lifelong learning is that of skills acquisition for labour market participation privileged above all other roles of adult life. The moral and practical terms of that conception of lifelong learning are set by governing policy bodies in the facilitation of economic interests for the aggregate generation of higher skill levels and dynamic competitiveness. Lifelong learning, in its humanistic and egalitarian conceptions for human development and active participation in shaping the conditions of one's life and communities and in broader affairs of civil polity, has been supplanted. In its appropriation for economic knowledge and higher skills development, the economic model of lifelong learning has categorically ignored the antecedent lifelong learning model and its inclusive attention to early childhood.

EDUCATION FOR ECONOMY: FROM LEARNING SOCIETY TO LEARNING ECONOMY

Earlier reform movements in education had, until the crisis of Fordism, typically focused on schooling. During the post-war period of expansion and social reforms of education, professionals and government officials variously differed and converged over particular objectives of the reforms. But there was little interruption through the 1960s and 1970s of the general imperative of reform and modernization of curricula and teaching practices, initially especially evident in the Anglophone countries. The social reformers had sought the wider involvement of society in education, which was intended to increase education's autonomy from family and religion. The widening involvement also opened education to much greater involvement of economic and political interests. Intersecting with, but largely successive to, the reforms after the 1970s was a new tide of interest in and motivations toward educational reform and expansion.

The new interest, while initially appearing to share some of the core ideas of the learning society imagined by many educationists, came to adopt a distinctly different and singular objective. It also placed higher education and universities clearly in the spotlight. Economists and business interests had begun to take a strong interest in education's role in generating new economic growth. Economic and political attention to education and skills as significant economic factors arose from the influence of the notions of human capital and new growth theory in economic thought. The notion of human capital (discussed in Chapter 2) which first emerged in the 1960s in economic theory, was taken up to a critical degree only in the 1980s and 1990s. Fordist capitalism had required only a sector of educated and knowledgeable workers to achieve its principal endeavour of mass production and mass markets. The vast majority of workers were required to have only basic education and high tolerance for under-skilled, highly routinized mass production jobs. The discovery of the utility of higher levels of education for application to post-Fordist advanced technological and diversified production saw human capital theory come into its own. The recognition of human capital as an economic resource and vital component of innovation fuelled the economic and political interest in generating a wider population distribution of higher levels of education and skills.

The spill-over into education of human capital theory in economics has been remarkably effective. It has taken two overlapping forms. The first, initially most observable and variously controversial, is in regard to mass skills generation for a higher-skilled workforce in knowledge-rich production.

The second is the expansion of universities' research functions in science and technology. The call for the university to supply advanced research knowledge to industry through direct collaborations and partnerships with business has followed the first, more publicly visible, demand for mass provision of higher skills. In regard to the first call, skill development requires investment. Business associations, as expressed through prominent organizations such as the European Round Table of Industrialists and various national Chambers of Commerce, repeatedly claimed that skill shortages were hindering productivity growth and employment as post-Fordist flexible systems were emerging (Bosworth 1992; European Round Table of Industrialists 1989; 1997). Skill shortages contributed to the sluggish growth and high unemployment levels in the 1990s. Business leaders successfully lobbied governments to increase the supply of education and skills developed through public education and training systems.

Business interests argued that European countries were exposed to competitive weaknesses and productivity decline in comparison to the US and Japanese economies (the serious rise of China and India did not have a notable impact until the 2000s). European political leaders were persuaded of the need to pursue a generalized policy of human capital development and high skills production. The pursuit of higher-skilled economies took various national paths, as Chapter 2 describes. Notwithstanding the variation in national policy models, their shared objective in response to the pressures of advanced technological production and uncertain dynamism of globalizing markets fuelled expansion and rationalization within education systems.

The pursuit of high skills economies in the 1980s and 1990s, soon to be prominently labelled by the OECD's definition in 1996 the "knowledge-based economy", attracted criticism irrespective of the national variation of the model pursued. Critics doubted that mass skills generation was the wise and viable response (Cantor 1986; Crouch *et al.* 1999). An important transnational study by Crouch and colleagues noted the considerable agreement on the value of high skills and highly productive workforces among business, education, academic and political leaders. The consensus on skills creation, the authors proposed, brought together public policy ambition and the market economy. But the researchers argued that while the political scope of that consensus was attractive to various parties, the extensive emphasis on education and training to resolve persistent employment and labour market disparities and diverse social problems was extremely ambitious and highly problematic. The extensive policy over-emphasis on a highly positive correlation between education and skills development and labour market participation and economic growth allows too much scope for employers' interests to dominate. Employment policy, the authors proposed, cannot depend on education policy; nor can education be expected to substitute for market-generated workers' insecurities.

However, the consensus view favouring a highly elevated role of education in the economy was further confirmed in the ambitious agenda set out in the Lisbon declaration of the European Union in 2000. That agenda, generally shared by other western welfare states, proposed a conceptualization of a knowledge-based economy that endeavoured to bring together various notions and models of high skills productivity, distribution and competitive advantage at transnational levels. The promotion of higher-level skills and better jobs needed further components and wider industry dispersion. The Lisbon Agenda consolidated and accelerated the policies of education reform and expansion already underway.

An earlier expansion of tertiary and higher education occurred in the post-war years. It had been widely welcomed, championed by many as advancing societal modernization and social equality through wider distribution of the goods of higher knowledge and cultural learning (Henkel and Little 1999). The expansion of education from the 1990s and 2000s, however, has both accelerated and taken a predominantly economic character in the service of both business interests and neo-liberal governments' interests in encouraging individual responsibility for employability and reduced dependency on the welfare state. The OECD, which adopted the term "massification" in its proposals for higher education expansion in the 1970s (OECD 1974), has intensified the demand for mass participation in the university sector in the current decades. The intensification of interest in pursuing the knowledge-based economy and high skills society has attracted more research attention to the economics of education. The humanistic approaches to education favoured by many educationists encountered quite a different set of approaches to education emanating from many economists and policy-makers. Education has frequently been the target of criticism from economists.[4] It was ripe for a concerted economic policy oriented reconfiguration.

For economists of education, education is viewed as comprising various sub-systems and processes of education and learning that have measurable outcomes (Foray 2004; Lorenz and Lundvall 2006; Kahin and Foray 2006). The economy's knowledge and innovation system is directly served by the education and training subsystem. Generally, for educationists, the economic view that reduces education to a subsystem of the knowledge and innovation system of the economy is distinctly objectionable. Yet the economists' view of education as a subsystem of the economy comprises the chief assumptions of the economic policy model put forward by the European Commission in its policy programme for education and training (Dolfsma and Soete 2006; Lundvall and Borrás 1999). Its fundamental basis is the proposition that a new economic environment of rapidly advancing technologies, dynamic and uncertain markets, and pursuit of competitive advantage through the development and dispersion of innovative production systems requires continuous learning capacities in production organizations. These learning capacities are enabled by society's education systems. Their reforms are required on the same basis and scale as that launched for institutions of employment relations. The modernization of education and training systems entails their alignment with and the efficient service of the requirements of competitive firms in knowledge-rich production.

For economic theorists, modernization is proposed to take the form of a synthesis of traditionally and currently opposed scientific and humanistic modes of conception and practice. At the EU level there is direct policy pressure on the education sector to move beyond improvement and expansion of the existing educational systems and toward large-scale change of the parameters of the knowledge base of the education sector itself. What that means, for the knowledge economists who conceive this proposition, is that education as a quasi-autonomous socio-cultural sphere, and with a mode of practice traditional to the classical humanities, requires intensive rationalization toward the epistemologies and courses of action favoured among scientific and economic arenas. As Dominique Foray, a prominent exemplar of this view (and advisor to the OECD) succinctly puts it:

> Most industrial sectors are shifting quite rapidly toward the scientific epistemic culture, which is rapidly displacing others. This is also the case of medicine which is now dominated by the epistemic culture of science, with a relatively smaller community that adheres to the culture of the humanities. It is not the case of education that is a divided community, not one dominated by the epistemic culture of science.
>
> (2004: 195–6)

Education, therefore, is in need of rationalization toward the scientific episteme.

Knowledge economists argue that the knowledge economy requires the proliferation of knowledge-intensive activities throughout all sectors, including education institutions. As leading theorist, Foray, puts it: "A key factor of rapid growth of knowledge and learning externalities is the extension of capacities to codify knowledge ... This makes it possible to multiply 'copies' of knowledge at a very low cost and to create new objects of knowledge" (ibid.: 36). Codification of knowledge enables it to be "detached from the individual, and the memory and communication capacity created is made independent of human beings" (ibid.: 74). Organization systems are thereby capable of increased and sustained learning. Foray contends that the education sector is traditionally characterized by slow development of knowledge. It is characterized by low innovation, low codification, "weak cumulativeness" and low dispersion of knowledge. The reliance on tacit, artful knowledge in education work and the weak role of science and competition in knowledge development and in the generation of knowledge "spillovers" hinder system development in the education sector. That lack of scientificity retards education's alignment with economic systems. Therefore, Foray argues, the "parameters of the knowledge base of education" require concerted policy intervention. That policy intervention, he maintains, must exert pressures on the education sector to shift toward the "scientific episteme".

These are immensely powerful propositions in regard to education. They pose notions that have been historically foreign to education's adherence to the mode of the classical humanist episteme. And they mark out the path for education's rational systems' subordination to economy and techno-science. The propositions and theorizations of knowledge economics influence policy development in European Union and OECD policy institutions. The programme of reform and expansion of education systems in the service of the knowledge-based economy takes up the rationale of necessary rationalization toward the scientific episteme. Under that rationale, business economic imperatives are at once obscured and normalized as an assumed public good. The reform, expansion and modernization of the education system seek intensified capacities for skills and knowledge generation for the knowledge-based economy. At the same time, that composite programme seeks an economic-scientific rationalization of education and the sweeping subordination of the non-economic, cultural rationale most especially for higher education and for lifelong learning. The learning society vision that challenged and competed with economic programmes for education has been repositioned. Policy-aligned with the pursuit of innovation, systems and organizational learning, the learning society shifts to a learning economy which ambitiously proposes to encompass the social, the community and the personal. People are imagined to be at once learners and workers whose civil citizenship appears conceived as dependent on performance as both. Education must reconfigure in the service of this delimited constellation.

THE KNOWLEDGE ECONOMY AND EDUCATION: CRITICAL EFFECTS

The neo-liberal economic agenda for education which demands the mass development of human capital for economic utility and epistemological reform of education systems toward that objective has won a sweeping incursion into the education sphere. Recent decades have seen intense debates on enduring concerns over core values and purposes of education. In the 2010s, virtually all aspects of education are targeted for rationalization reform and modernization. But undoubtedly the principal field of education targeted for policy implementation of this agenda is that of higher education, most especially the university.

The university is one of the oldest surviving institutions of Western culture. That long cultural heritage has bequeathed a tenacious idea of the university which, although often vaguely specified and contentiously practised, imagined the pursuit of higher knowledge and learning as being an irreducible good. The very pursuit of higher knowledge *eo ipso* serves a great socio-cultural good. This imaginary continues to animate contemporary concerns and debates over higher education. The targeting of universities by a sharply focussed economic programme of expansion and reform, predominantly in order for the education sphere to align more efficiently with economic imperatives, carries immense cultural and social effects including on the very idea of the university and its goods. The earlier decades of the post-war expansion of higher education were characterized by advocacy for an expansion that promoted a widening of democracy – of greater public access to higher education and its cultural riches as part of a vision of a learning society. The cultural ideal of the university and its forms of knowledge and education conceived and justified principally as ends in themselves, as in the Newman ([1852] 1976) and Humboldtian classical views, featured strongly in that vision of expansion. More people could experience the special place of the university and partake of its rich knowledge and culture. Universities, traditionally the preserve of elites and in the service of their socio-cultural reproduction and power, were rarely politically challenged and more or less left to their own sphere of governance, as Bourdieu (1988) demonstrated, even as they relied heavily on state funding. Many education and political reformers agreed on the necessity to widen and democratize participation in that elite cultural domain.

The European countries educated beyond compulsory schooling only a very small percentage of their populations. National systems of higher education remained steeped in national traditions and in reference to ancient elite practices of university education. It was still common up until the 1960s for a PhD dissertation, even in Economics, to be written in Latin (Borghans and Cörvers 2009). Germany, which is noted for its systems of wider distribution of higher skills and post-compulsory education qualifications achieved through its system of tertiary education, had nonetheless similarly retained a smaller and highly conservative university sector (Green 2002) just as had the United Kingdom (Ball 2008). France's higher education system is diverse and complex with only recent moves to integrate higher research into the wider university system (van Vught 2009a). The move toward expansion in the post-war decades largely occurred through an expansion of elite-model institutions. In addition, the policy drive for mass expansion required the establishment of new higher education institutions capable of handling vastly increased numbers of students.

The expansion of higher education to populations formerly excluded from participation has a generally popular appeal. There is no doubt that very many persons from the formerly excluded classes have richly benefited from the earlier phases of expansion in the post-war decades. But the character of the more recent, and prospective, expansions challenges much more than an elite cultural conception of university and exclusivity of higher knowledge. It effects a displacement of that conception, a dilution of its classical knowledge forms, and portends a paradigmatic shift in knowledge forms to technological science. Many educationists and policy-makers would wish to emphasize the intersections and continuity of value agendas between the democratic, learning society vision of higher education and that of the knowledge-based economy. Many educationists share with policy-makers aspirations for a greater dispersion of higher knowledge and skills across the population through wider access and improved opportunities to participate in tertiary education systems. But many educationists also seek to maintain classical notions of the cultural good of the university and champion the search for learning and knowledge that is irreducible to economic or principally employment objectives.

The expansion that has recently taken place no doubt includes some of the aspirations of the learning society and democratically widened participation. But the acceleration of the expansion with its distinct economic agenda has inevitably effected qualitative changes in the character of the university, and in the presumed cultural consensus on the role and purpose of the university. Two features are most salient across various national systems: that of massification of student enrolment (discussed below) and that of expanded techno-scientific knowledge generation. The mass production of skills and the scientific attention to the intricate needs of capitalism had a sweeping effect on the modern university. Still a third feature occurs in this course: that of the industrial transformation of the university and its ultimate assimilation into the corporate order.

The history of education in the European welfare state model countries, as elsewhere in the world, readily reveals national specificity in education traditions, practices, policies and forms of distribution and participation. These national specificities cannot be understated. The vast bulk of education research focuses on national contexts and national problems of education systems and education provision. Yet notwithstanding the particularities of national histories and systems of education, important general patterns across countries are observable (Dale and Robertson 2009; Rinne and Koivula 2009; Tight 2004). Many aspects of similarity are due to a substantive cultural heritage in European religious and Enlightenment thought, including normative agreements on the age of children for compulsory education and the establishment of core subjects of curriculum, and the historical role of the university. Within a general similarity of rationale and purpose, systems of higher education across the European countries have displayed considerable diversity. The structure and form of university degrees and their constituent courses of study, including the numbers of years students must, or may choose to, study for a degree; the pedagogical relationships and teaching and learning practices (Mazza *et al.* 2008) and what legitimately constitutes higher knowledge have varied historically and nationally. Still, these national systems of higher education have shared both an elite cultural domain and the relative inattention by both state, and European Union policy prior to the movement toward mass expansion in the late twentieth century. Virtually all national variations in the EU countries are now targeted for reform and rationalization under the EU's policies on *Making a European Area of Higher Education*. As universities are imagined to be the driver of Europe's economy of knowledge, their rationalization and inter-cooperation will enable knowledge generation, knowledge flow and knowledge agents' mobility (European Commission 2006).

The emphatic policy attention to innovation and techno-science forges a pivotal intersection between educational research, organizational research and applied economic research. That intersection yields new questions and inquiries into learning processes in production organizations themselves and to the development of new fields in the economics of knowledge. It also places much sharper policy attention on institutions of scientific research, typically universities and research centres, forming collaborations between industry partners and university-affiliated scientists. Institutions of higher education, as well as generating increased aggregate higher skills among the working population through teaching diverse degree programmes, also generate new knowledge through research. Governments and corporate interests, through the funding investments and direct participation on boards of governance, demand the economic utility of that research. As corporate industries seek to rationalize or outsource more of their research and development requirements, they exert pressure on universities to supply techno-scientific knowledge and to do so in cost-competitive forms. Research and education thus conducted shift toward the economic and scientific episteme and industrial application. The empirically observed dramatic expansion of university business schools over the past three decades devoted to the service of problem-solving for liberal capitalism, as well as the entrepreneurial imperative capturing the traditional sciences, is the current leitmotif of the generalized reform.

Policy statements through the late decades of the twentieth century at national and at EU level repeatedly endorse the expansion and crucial role of universities in economic development. That endorsement promoted a conceptual shift away from cultural ideas of the university as a quasi-separate sphere with forms of knowledge capable of reflecting and criticizing society and culture, and educating new generations with those capacities. In the United Kingdom, a prominent government inquiry into higher education, known as the Dearing Report (Dearing 1997), spoke decisively of a justification of expansion in serving the needs of a knowledge-based economy. The widening of university activities to include vocational and trade-oriented studies and expanded science and technical programmes directly served the demands of business interests for reform and greater productivity from the university sector. At the same time, those business interests withdrew investment in skills provision and workforce education.

Under the auspices of its policy programme, *Making a European Area of Higher Education*, the European Commission makes its programme objectives clear:

> Modernisation of Europe's universities involving their interlinked roles of education, research and innovation, has been acknowledged not only as a core condition for the success of the broader Lisbon Strategy, but as part of the wider move towards an increasingly global and knowledge-based economy.
>
> (European Commission 2005d)

Furthermore,

> [Universities] play a vital role in the Lisbon objective to equip Europe with the skills and competences necessary to succeed in a globalized

> knowledge-based economy ... University programmes should be structured to enhance directly the employability of graduates and to offer broad support to the workforce more generally.
>
> (European Commission 2006)

Moreover, the Commission recommends, universities must "go beyond the needs of the labour market and stimulate an entrepreneurial mindset amongst students and researchers" (ibid.).

The emphasis on the adoption of more entrepreneurial attitudes and behaviour as an accompanying part of expansion further accords with the objectives of the knowledge-based economy. The policy pressures to stimulate knowledge-intensive production and competitive innovation make fundamental changes to the university. Those pressures lead to a dramatic alteration of principal domains of university practices: of research and teaching, of professional and administrative systems, of student life and experience, of relationships with the general public, and of the university's historical socio-cultural roles.

HIGHER EDUCATION: EXPANSION, RATIONALIZATION, MARKETIZATION

Earlier reformers had sought expansion and democratization of university participation but without compromising the ideals of *Bildung*[5] of higher knowledge pursuit of the classical university. The ideal imagined was one in which the pursuit of higher knowledge forms, high standards and cultural enrichment would be retained alongside wider and greater population participation. A general upward levelling through democratization and cultural development was hoped for. However, the universalization of higher education, as imagined by the learning society visionaries, has occurred under a quite different imperative with quite different outcomes. Massification replaces the idealist democratic conception by a more earthy connotation with real-world effects.

The policy-demanded mass expansion of recent years has resulted in increased numbers on virtually all measures in higher education, especially in numbers of students, staff degree programmes and construction of new universities. From an early post-war percentage of the population of about 4 per cent or 5 per cent (Trow 2006), participation in higher education by the 2000s has increased to 30 per cent – or 40 per cent and is policy-targeted to reach 50 per cent in the 2020s. The number of tertiary institutions with degree granting status has accordingly multiplied. The European Commission's *Europe 2020* strategy further endorses mass expansion. It reports that European levels of participation at 30 per cent in the current decade lag behind the USA and Japan at 50 per cent participation in tertiary education. Massification has been accomplished by provision of a vast expansion of vocational programmes with direct economic utility (Delanty 2001; Mazza *et al.* 2008; Peters 2007; Tight

2004). New and old universities provide degree-level programmes in applied technical subjects, engineering, computer applications, hotel and tourism studies, media and communication studies, applied management fields such as sports and events management, operations management, education management and small business accounting and finance. These are undoubtedly all useful and worthy fields of study with clear objectives. However, their singular emphasis on utilitarian and economic applications of knowledge and learning illustrates the shifting character of the forms of knowledge and their acquisition that were historically privileged in universities. Even as the established pursuit of advanced scientific and cultural knowledge remains valued, it is itself under pressure to demonstrate some ultimate economic utility.

Mass expansion has been accompanied by extensive programmes of rationalization. For some commentators, rationalizing reforms are urgently necessary in order for European universities to close the quality gap with the US universities and for universities to appropriately serve the needs of economy and society (van Vught 2009b). Others regard rationalization as an ineluctable imperative of mass expansion and labour market demands that will enable European universities to successfully transition from elite to a mass and eventually universal system of higher education (Trow 2006). Massively increased numbers of students and the establishment of new universities and programmes exert immense pressures on extant university systems and their management. The programme of expansion has taken place, although at different paces, across many countries with reduced funds from the state for the costs of educating higher proportions of the population (Deem *et al.* 2007; Scott 2004). The often drastic reduction in funds further intensifies pressures on university systems to attenuate costly privileges and to rationalize the processing of students through their degree programmes. Mass expansion requires intensive rationalization of systems and processes which affect fundamental dimensions of academic professional life and student experience of university education. Structures and conventions of professional relationships and pedagogical practices modelled in the elite systems – although not without need of democratic and gender-sensitive reform – have been dramatically altered. A burgeoning literature in higher education and university criticism expresses the concerns and protestations of professional academics observing these transformation processes occurring in universities. Key aspects of these critical concerns are discussed in Chapter 6.

At this point, I wish to describe the general effects of the transformation pressures. These most saliently comprise the shift in the institutional and organizational forms of the university toward adoption of corporate firm models and behaviours. As part of the pressures from national and supranational policy-making bodies for reform and modernization, universities are urged to include in their governance institutions participation by business and industrial leaders. Even as firms and employers have retreated from participation in the costs of skills generation, business and industrial leaders now play an increasingly powerful role in institutions of governance in universities in Europe (Reed

2002; Shattock 2009). Their involvement intensifies pressures for universities to adopt the template of the corporate firm in the university's strategic business operations, organizational structure and market action. Universities, which once fiercely strove for their emancipation from religious and political authorities, now surrender to corporate authority with barely a whimper in the quad.

Universities and their personnel are urged to adapt to the purported superiority of the scientific episteme – as the rational face of ideological interests demanding corporate assimilation – in order to prosper in a pervasive liberal market order and retracted state funding. The business and market orientation of the reforming university transforms the collegial model of academy (including its particular internal antagonisms and dynamics) and professional administration and governance systems. The university's adaptation leads to its adoption of forms of organization, professional relationships, domain value and governance that were formally foreign to it.

Weber ([1922] 1978) had proposed an ideal type of professional expertise and behavioural ethics that promote the motivation for the pursuit of professional work as a good and duty in itself. Professional academic and scientific work pursues objective knowledge goods and a general public service. The organizational forms and governance principles of professional work in that ideal type of "functional collegiality" propose formal equality of members and consultative *primus inter pares* regulatory constraints on decision-making. That collegial structure is intended to facilitate professional institutional autonomy and superordination of an administrative bureaucracy. For Bourdieu (1988), institutional autonomy was achieved not by that rational-moral ideal type, but through the power struggles of the professional body. In his theorization, universities were characterized by internal academic power struggles for cultural capital rather than economic capital. That struggle was at the core of the self-preserving institution of the university. The university's autonomy and self-preserving internal struggles, within its *habitus* (sets of dispositions, norms and constraints) also served to maintain an antagonism between the academy and the economic sphere. The struggle for the power of cultural capital[6] (assuming the state provided economic support) and the university's cultural antagonism with the economy preserved the university and reinforced autonomies of spheres. Maintaining autonomies enabled forms of field regulation through their non-assimilation into each other. In other words, the cultural power of the university was maintained through the internal power of the academic *habitus* and kept at bay incursions of economic capital interests and their governing principles.

Both Weberian and Bourdieuian perspectives, within their evident differences, speak to the importance of a general proposition of the historical institutional autonomy of the academy. While that autonomy, for Bourdieu, reproduces cultural elites in society, it also enables a refusal of a reduction to economic capital. In resisting forms of power that were foreign to it, the university asserted an autonomy of its field from economy (as well as from religious and political fields). The economic incursion now underway, and its implementation of massification, rationalization and marketization, have launched a vast new apparatus in the governance of the university. It effects an alteration of the professional self-understanding of the university and a fracture of its institutional autonomy. The introduction of "new public management" models based on corporate business models of organization for strategic competitiveness over-ride former forms of professional administration and collegial practices (Deem *et al.* 2007; Reed 2002; Soguel and Jaccard 2008). There is no question that those former models were replete with class snobbery and gendered ignorance. But the potential democratic revision of the donnish model has been intercepted.

The decline of donnish dominion, as Halsey (1992) observed, and the transformation of the modern university into a corporate firm model demand altered forms of engagement among professional experts. The work of professionals engaged in the provision of higher learning and knowledge, newly imagined as market commodities, encounters a new calculus. The introduction of new calculation systems and performance targets in teaching and research productivity, in operational systems efficiencies and market responsiveness (Deem *et al.* 2007; Hussey and Smith 2009; Olssen and Peters 2005) brings dramatic alterations to the conduct of academic and student work and relationships.

The business model of performance, competitiveness and market orientation transforms a public, including students, into clients and customers presumed to be in demand of education construed as a positional commodity. The university has adopted mass production systems for its core and routine goods of qualifications and research outputs, all of which have massively increased in recent decades. At the same time, even as the university adopts neo-Fordist production systems, it also adopts in its advanced knowledge construction and innovation-generating role the corporation's post-Fordist strategies with comparable vigour. The privileged emphasis on management, accountability, performance and market orientation effect an elevation in the power of administrators in their relations with professional academics and scientists. It forges a powerful cultural shift in the ethos and daily life of the university. The new centres of expert knowledge and the power associated with that newly favoured expertise are located among the technocratic-managerial agents and their administrative apparatus. These centres of power, legitimated by their proximity to and service of economic capital, assume power of evaluation over the cultural goods of academic work and education "products". Among the consequences of the combined force of economic capital, scientific and market rationalities, universities struggle to maintain departments in the liberal arts including philosophy, history, languages and fine arts for which such monological rationalization and surrendering of cultural capital is a particular anathema. Their attachment to a humanistic episteme is now their Archilles' heel.

A further feature of the corporatization of the university accompanying its adoption of corporate management and governance behaviours is its pursuit of entrepreneurialism (Clark 1998; Slaughter and Leslie 1997). Universities pursue commercial relationships with business partners to raise funds from non-governmental sources, and to pursue new scientific knowledge products identified in commercial R&D sectors. Gaining funds from industry, charitable organizations, private benefactors and various public–private consortia has long featured in the North American model of higher education and research. But in the European model welfare states, private sources of substantial funds have been rare and predominately the preserve of the elite colleges.

The increased collaboration of higher education institutions with corporate and commercial institutions in order to simultaneously reduce the dependency of higher education on the state and to generate commercially useful techno-scientific knowledge encourages a sponsorship dependency with extensive implications (Amaral *et al.* 2002). Commercial collaboration demands an unprecedented adoption of market-style relationships. Researchers as market actors bid for funds from providers with vested political or economic interests in research outcomes. Those interests play an increased role in determining fields of research exploration and dissemination of research outcomes. University researchers in collaboration with commercial sponsors comply with sponsor demands for the generation of strategic knowledge (Bonaccorsi and Daraio 2007). The direct role of business and industry actors in the governance of universities ensures these measures are normatively pursued and accomplished. At the same time, as the university steps up its efforts to generate mass higher levels of employment-oriented skills, the corporate firm avoids contribution to the costs of generating skilled labour. It successfully externalizes significant production costs to the quasi-public sector of the university and fee-paying students.

The entrepreneurial mindset that has seen universities enter into new ventures with business partners and in diverse geographic locations has become widely adopted by universities within a remarkably short time (Deem *et al.* 2007; Shattock 2009). It is now an expected characteristic of their *modus operandi.* That adoption, along with that of the corporate business organizational form and subordination of academic professionals, occurs across even well-known conservative universities in European centres.[7] Rinne and Koivula (2009) report on a comparative European study that demonstrates the ways in which European countries, even with their different national histories of tertiary education institutions, have adopted market reforms and entrepreneurial behaviour. The study reports remarkable similarities in academics' experience of diminished professional roles in the management and governance of their universities and a general course of liberal marketization transforming their universities.

The European Union, as part of its objective of a European area of Higher Education, has embarked on a programme of comprehensive reform and rationalization of European universities. A key instrument in that is the Bologna Agreement, signed in 1999, which aims to establish a "harmonization" of

European universities in regard to degree structures, credit transfers, quality assurance and student mobility. The Bologna programme undoubtedly offers useful coordination, transferability and closer relationships among universities and enables many cultural and scholarly benefits to students. Certainly, elite and byzantine models are in much need of democratic reform. But there is equally little doubt that, notwithstanding the European Union's respect for national sovereignty over education, the harmonization process directly serves the Lisbon Agenda's knowledge-based economy imperatives (Fairclough and Wodak 2008; Reinalda and Kulesza 2006). The Bologna process, furthermore, portends a further considerable shift in the cultural ethos of the European university. Critics contend that the Bologna process of higher education reforms has been remarkably undemocratic. Academics have been subject to a top-down policy process of reform and the incursion of business interests in their universities' governance structures and valuation of higher knowledge pursuit. Some observe an "Americanization" and globalization of a neo-liberal, economic model of education (Dale and Robertson 2009). Reduced public funding of the universities stimulates the adoption of US-style relationships with benefactors to gain endowed funds and to increase their provision of services to the private sector.

The rationalization of higher education in the service of macroeconomic integration, of techno-scientific knowledge and labour market skills and competitiveness puts at great risk the socio-cultural benefits of university reform. It promotes a normalization of economic utility and market imperatives in the rationale and conduct of university life. The grand endeavour of the pursuit of higher learning and knowledge, its forms of provision and the participation experience of students are permeated with market economic rationalities. As the university spectacularly reforms in conformity with the neo-liberal policy-driven knowledge-based economy agenda, it transforms into a large corporate firm. In its displacement of cultural capital by economic capital value and pursuit, it adopts the institutional framework of the business firm in its organizational forms and management, its entrepreneurial behaviour and its governance. It acts to shape its markets, transnationally reach its operations and manoeuvre its clients to ensure its competitive advantage and institutional preservation. In this course, the university takes its place in the grand economic programme of the knowledge-based economy in which education systems are subordinated and vertically integrated into a meta system of liberal market economy.

LIFELONG LEARNING

There is little doubt that higher education is taking the lion's share of policy and budget attention in the education reforms. Other fields of education experience aspects of the effects of economic and utilitarian interests with analysts noting the directions of change in secondary education and also in primary schools (Kuhn and Sultana 2006). But more directly in regard to education's relationship to economic production systems and labour market employment, the field of lifelong learning has been powerfully influenced by the knowledge economy agenda and demands.

The economic model of a learning economy and learning society undoubtedly shares some aspects of the explicitly humanistic and egalitarian model of education and lifelong learning, outlined earlier in this chapter. The European Commission model favours an emphasis on expanded notions of education and learning. It shares with, and reinforces, the learning society advocates' promotion of a definitive shift away from historical attachments to schooling and formal education as exclusively privileged sites of education and learning. Educators welcome policy recognition of workplace and non-formal sites of learning. Moreover, an emphasis on an expansion of education across the life-course and to sectors of the population traditionally excluded from post-compulsory education, the pursuit of higher skill levels and the valuing of mass rather than elite intelligence, is shared by humanistic conceptions of education, social democratic politicians and the neo-liberal market economy proponents. This tense convergence formed the basis of the Lisbon Agenda's efforts to balance social democratic aspirations toward a socially cohesive society and wide participation in economic and social life with those of competitive market forces.

However, over the decade of the 2000s, it has become clear that the pressures of the policy pursuit of the knowledge-based economy have intensified demands on lifelong education and learning. That intensification has also carried a shift toward an emphatic skills-oriented conception of lifelong learning. For many educationists, the powerful political economic policy emanating from the European Commission and national governments casts a long shadow over the earlier accomplishments and progressive challenges of lifelong learning. Economic interests have been explicit in their demands. The formation of skilled workers is the task of national education and training systems, and of lifelong learning. As the World Bank succinctly expresses it: "lifelong learning is education for the knowledge economy" (World Bank 2003). The human capital model of lifelong learning promotes a continuing training system appropriate to the generation of learning human resources. The current policy conceptions of lifelong learning appropriate the innovative conceptualizations and the promise of the models of lifelong learning developed especially through the 1970s and 1980s. That appropriation includes that of the concept of learning. The earlier promotion of the concept of learning in the notion of lifelong learning was intended to differentiate the processes of formal education institutions from popular, informal sites of educational and learning activities. Learning is imagined as cognitive, social and emotional and as on-going through the life-course in diverse settings. It is a comprehensive and continuous capacity of persons and ought, according to the humanistic conception, be as far as possible under the direction and motivation of the individual learner.

The popular appeal of that wider recognition of learning occurring in diverse settings outside of formal schooling has been captured in subsequent policy discourse. Individuals are urged to continue learning and training in various settings, especially at work, to gain and maintain their employable skills. In addition, the concept of learning has dramatically shifted into a near-singular reference to cognitive and technical competences that is devoid of values and socio-cultural interests. In that shift, lifelong learning has become equated to learning for employment skills. Over the last two decades the flow of policy discourse on lifelong learning has intensified. It has culminated in the European Commission's initiative to place all of its educational programmes under an overarching conceptual framework of lifelong learning (European Commission 2006). The Presidency Conclusions of the 2008 Spring Council of Europe stated:

> Providing high-quality education and investing more and more effectively in human capital and creativity throughout people's lives are crucial conditions for Europe's success in a globalised world. This can bridge and facilitate the movement towards a "knowledge-based economy", create more and better jobs and contribute to sound fiscal positions.
>
> (European Council 2008)

To do this, more adults must be attracted into continuing education and training and their geographic and occupational mobility facilitated.

The EU's Lisbon successor, *Europe 2020*, strengthens this policy in its principal agenda objectives. The agenda for "new skills and jobs" requires lifelong learning to: "empower people by developing their … skills throughout the lifecycle with a view to increase labour participation and better match labour supply and demand, including through labour mobility" (European Commission 2010). The agenda also clearly notes that modernization of labour markets and greater participation in work across the life-course are necessary responses to demographic pressures on sustaining the EU's growth and prosperity aspirations: "Achieving longer working lives will also require the possibility to acquire and develop new skills throughout the lifetime". In what the European Commission call its "Flagship Initiative: An Agenda for New Skills and Jobs",

> [The] aim is to create conditions for modernising labour markets with a view to raising employment levels and ensuring the sustainability of our social models. This means empowering people through the acquisition of new skills to enable our current and future workforce to adapt to new conditions and potential career shifts, reduce unemployment and raise labour productivity.
>
> (European Commission 2008c)

Europe 2020 and the "new skills for new jobs" initiatives leave little doubt that lifelong learning is primarily aimed at skills development for labour market participation. Lifelong learning has manifestly become less an opportunity for personal development in a wide array of social and cultural domains than a command to maintain a person's employability. Furthermore, when other qualities of lifelong learning are referenced, it is in regard to their usefulness in stimulating citizenship identities and behaviour. But as Griffin (2006) points out, the notion of citizenship is a crude one and focused on economic activation in labour market work as though that were the principal duty of citizenship.

A sweeping economic policy agenda activated at European Union level has forcefully truncated the emancipatory vision and transformative agenda. Many lifelong learning educators conclude that lifelong learning is now virtually synonymous with human resource development in the human capital model (Field 2006; Griffin 2006; Jarvis 2007). Its earlier imaginary as a vital source for social and cultural human development in which economic interests would be subordinated and humanized by cultural learning and self-directed, self-motivated learners has been captured and re-branded. Critics argue that the European Union's human capital policy agenda now permeates all of education and training institutions across the European Union (Desjardins *et al.* 2004; Kotthoff and Moutsios 2007). An economic rationalization of lifelong learning has largely been accomplished.

However, the concept of lifelong learning continues to pose a considerable innovation to established practices of education and learning. Even as its practices have been co-opted into economic utility, the concept itself remains capable of assertion and alternative practice. The fortunes of the policy elaboration and implementation of the vision and agenda of lifelong learning continue to be very mixed. An underlying humanistic ethos of lifelong learning continues to draw much appeal among the population even as academic analysts observe the economic hegemony.

CONCLUSION

A general consensus continues to unreservedly emphasize the vital role of education in economy and society and to favour its expanded participation. It would, of course, be perverse in principle to be against more education for more people. A general policy option in favour of education would seem to be the best one in the general social and economic circumstances, in the face of technological expansion and globalizing market competitiveness. A high social and public good is accorded to a general upgrading of skills and competencies across the population. An aggregate increase in skilled workers and knowledge-intensive production generates greater opportunity for innovation and competitive advantage and may widen individuals' life chances and social and cultural development. On the other hand, however, the general policy aim of more education and improved labour market potentiality is being implemented in ways that stir up significant dilemmas for education and society more broadly. The substantial socio-cultural alterations to institutions of higher education are scarcely rendering a democratization of elite privileges to access to higher knowledge and cultural pursuits. Mass participation and poorer quality of education, a predominance of economic and instrumental imperatives, of managerial control and de-professionalization veer widely from a vision of higher education reform toward democratization and cultural enrichment for the many. The programme of changes underway, which is intent on altering education systems toward greater and subordinated alignment with business demands and economic epistemologies, poses severe distortions of education, most especially of university education, in its culturally valued conception.

Policy discourse, wittingly or not, disseminates particular corporate business interests asserted as being in the general interest of the public. Even as there is an apparent normalized acceptance of those assertions, the effects of corporate firm interests are far from being evenly socially distributed. The subjugation of education to those interests newly implicates education in the generation of worsened social risks of exclusion, wide inequalities and social injustice. Exploration of key dilemmas at a social level of the economic superordination and the social consequences of the knowledge economy of education is taken up in Chapter 6. Before that exploration, however, a close look at labour market utilization of the higher skills generated by the educational intensification is warranted.

The overarching programme of a knowledge economy for education is being conducted under crucial fundamental assumptions of the utility of economized and marketized education and indebted students. Yet, evidence of outcomes for education and skills development through the generalized policy pursuit of a liberalized, highly competitive knowledge-based economy is incontrovertibly mixed. In the midst of intensified education systems' reform and the university's unprecedented cultural adaptation to the demands of macroeconomic policy, some important realities of the world of work and labour markets are being widely, wilfully, overlooked. The massive economic and cultural reform of universities is taking place while the promised rewards for the many of that reform are distinctly limited. Yet these reforms undoubtedly benefit elite interests in private wealth creation reaped from techno-scientific research applications in marketable innovation. Close examination of labour market dynamics and organizational behaviours in regard to the availability of higher education and skill levels among more workers presents empirical disruptions to the economic model and pressing dilemmas for its social policy derivatives. Chapter 5 turns to address key discrepancies of the knowledge-based economy model in the utilization of the higher levels of skills that are coming onto the labour market.

5 Labour markets, organizations and the utility of education

INTRODUCTION

The prevailing policy models of the knowledge-based economy, and the learning society conceived as its corollary, promote normative notions of higher skill levels and lifelong learning across a wide population in society. It is assumed that the knowledge-based economy's demand for highly skilled workers is generalized and unidirectional. It is projected that high productivity sectors requiring high levels of skills will successfully displace low productivity sectors that require low levels of skills and accrue low wages. It is further assumed that the knowledge-based economy regime is "one of constant innovation" that constantly requires higher levels of education and higher skills development across the population in its pursuit (Foray 2004: 38). The increased capacities of higher skills further generate higher levels of production of increasingly knowledge-intensive products. This virtuous dialectic of skills and production is assumed as a core dynamic of innovation and growth. It is typically imagined that any gaps on this path of increasing proliferation of knowledge-intensive activities throughout all sectors of the economy are due to time lags, structural inertia and other behavioural hindrances to perfect dispersion.

The growth of knowledge-rich economic activities across many sectors of the economy and the development of many enterprising new fields including, for instance, in new branches of science in nanotechnology, xeno-transplant technology, bio-physics, and information and communications, as well as extensive new technological products in materials, pharmaceuticals, heavy industries and traditional industrial sectors is readily evident. There is no doubt that these developments are exciting and compelling. As well, activities in these fields assist the expansion of other technologically rich industries in marketing, communications, distribution and management systems. Moreover, the expansion of the financial services sector and its development of innovative new financial products and their markets is substantially a phenomenon of the application of advanced ICT characteristic of the knowledge-based economy and its liberalized institutions. All of these activities evidently require greater numbers of highly skilled workers. The expansion of jobs in the advanced technological fields has also, without doubt, achieved important objectives of the European Union's Lisbon Agenda of the pursuit of more jobs and (sometimes) better jobs across more industry sectors.

None of these accomplishments must be understated. Yet, as important as knowledge-rich production, innovation and successful market competition are to the contemporary economy, these activities do not disperse into a generalized trajectory of continual expansion and innovation prevailing across industries and labour markets. Amidst the general favourability of the knowledge economists' projections and the optimism of political leaders and policy-makers, there is also clear evidence of the persistence of contradictory tendencies and serious discrepancies in the knowledge-based economy path. These apparent contradictions raise many concerns about the real extent of the knowledge-based economy and the promised generalized improvement in jobs and prosperity for everyone. They challenge the wisdom of reforming and refocusing education systems in the service of this grandly imagined economy. Importantly, there is growing evidence from empirical economic and organizational research that adds heavy weight to critical social concerns and compels further questions.

Many economists propose that accelerated growth and technological advancement should, of themselves, facilitate greater absorption of knowledge-intensive activities throughout the economy. Other social analysts observe the uneven development of higher skilled economies and the persistence of low-skilled economic sectors and regions with their accompanying low-grade and poor quality jobs. That unevenness occurs not only at the global level, as Castells observed in the 1990s (Castells 1996) and as Brown *et al.* (2008) observe more recently in their extensive global study, but is evident within the advanced economies and regions. Moreover, as the evidence discussed below indicates, it occurs within knowledge-intensive organizations themselves. These uneven labour market dynamics – with a distinct tendency toward bifurcation and polarization – are not just the result of slow rates of absorption and dispersion of the knowledge-based economy. They are, rather, the consequence of three powerfully combined forces: (1) the liberalization of economic institutions; (2) an acceleration of competitiveness; and (3) the effects of rational corporate firm action at the organizational level. Liberalized reforms, the recalibration of capital and labour relations, and the free hand of the firm or business network to utilize advanced ICT applications and engage in market action in ways that favour the firm's interests in profitability maximization bring about, moreover, distinctly uneven outcomes of individuals' investment in education and training. The segmentation of labour markets and markedly uneven distribution of productivity gains in a knowledge-based economy portend a widening of social inequalities and a further weakening of social cohesion and participation in European model welfare states.

The question of whether or not it is a matter of time for the hoped-for expansion of the knowledge-based economy model to occur and for a more generalized higher skilled, higher productivity economy to emerge more evenly across nations and regions may be a crucial matter of scientific interpretation or political and economic opinion. Nonetheless, there appears in dominant economic and political discourses a distinct lack of attention to some factors which play a key role at everyday operational levels and in labour market dynamics. That lack of attention to, if not active ignorance of, those discordant and disconcerting factors encourages the current bias of interpretative opinion that is in unreasonable favour of a generalized march to the knowledge-based economy evenly benefitting all members of society.

This chapter looks closely at those key factors. First, it addresses general patterns in labour market dynamics that have become evident as the concerted economic policy interest in developing a knowledge-based economy ensues. Second, and this is the principal effort of this chapter, it draws sharply focused attention to the level of the firm and the firm's organizational behaviour. The role of liberalized corporate firm action in the generation of uneven outcomes frequently escapes attention. Yet the action of the firm produces outcomes which delineate real-world limitations to the knowledge-based economy. Close attention to organizational behaviour casts new light on economic models and policy programmes that propose a general trajectory of knowledge-rich production and overall high productivity and wage yields. Policy programmes that forge a political subjugation and contortion of education to the service of economic imperatives exact that very high price on education while in possession of partial data and little analysis of corporate firm, employer and organizational behaviour. The organizational level of the labour market and the intricacies and tensions of organizational change and inertia are seldom addressed in economic models of the knowledge economy. At the same time, the field of organizational analysis has in recent decades been over-focussed on problem-solving for business interests. A relative neglect in the latter decades of the twentieth century of sociological interest in organization and economic institutions has yielded a dearth of social analyses of organizational activity. There is therefore much scope for further research on the matters raised in this chapter.

Organized political-economic interests at the level of the firm play a decisive role in affecting labour market dynamics in knowledge-intensive economies. Firms, and the business networks in which they may be immersed, have no interests in broader economic and social models in regard to optimal skills development, dispersion and utilization across societal populations. The behaviour of the firm in everyday life can show little correspondence with the economic models favouring knowledge-based absorption in corporate organizational behaviour and dispersion of those knowledge-rich activities across economic sectors. These matters, which attract far less attention than the factors of competitive advantage and growth, are, nonetheless, constituent behaviours of knowledge-based economy developments. Their effects call into doubt assumptions that uneven dispersion of knowledge-based economic activity may simply be understood as temporal maladjustments or inefficiencies of application.

Principally, the concern at stake is that the knowledge-based economy's assumption that labour market demand for educated, skilled and lifelong learning workers will continue to substantively expand as the markets for information-rich products and continuously innovating production and organization systems predominate and globalize, may be irreconcilably flawed. While a number of education critics certainly think that is the case (Brown and Hesketh 2004) economists and policy-makers show little alteration in the assumption of expansion, as the EU's *Europe 2020* policy proposals indicate. However, closer examination of labour market dynamics and the requirements of the firm for, and utilization of, high skills and general education indicates that the knowledge-based economy is far from universal and, moreover, has no economic necessity to become so. Indeed, it may even require conditions of structural disparity and segmentation to compete on liberal economic terms.

In the first instance are factors pointing to the limits of the knowledge-based economy which are more readily observable. These factors arise out of everyday forms of work and jobs in the contemporary economy that ineluctably include activities in which productivity, as conventionally measured by growth and profit, remains low. The continuing social necessity for the provision of everyday urban services including, *inter alia*, transportation, delivery, public health and hygiene, security, food and catering, requires sustained numbers of moderately skilled jobs with little need for lifelong learning of a job-skills nature. The socially necessary work of bus drivers, couriers, nurse-aides, waiters and many others, which requires performance in physical locations and in real time, shows no signs of being technologically displaced or requiring substantively higher skills in its performance. A bus driver, for instance, requires a good level of skill as demonstrated in the qualification and licence to drive an omnibus vehicle, in the mastery of route maps, of on-board technologies, and coping with traffic congestion, security and passenger behaviour. These skills are crafted in daily practice. Formal lifelong learning interventions and further practical qualifications beyond training up-dating occasions propose little added value. A competent bus driver does not require extended periods of post-compulsory education to perform his or her job to a satisfactory standard.

Second, however, in addition to these moderately skilled, lower-paid services, is the retention and expansion of lower-skilled and skills-restricted jobs *within core* industries and organizations of the paradigmatic knowledge-based economy sector itself. There appear, even within the high-tech, knowledge-rich sectors, distinct and *rational* limits in the capacity of individual firms to utilize highly skilled workers, or to provide opportunities for further education and training of their broader workforce. Taylorist-Fordist production systems and knowledge-rich, learning organizational sectors share not only the same post-code but can occupy the same building. Importantly, key factors of those limits, and of corporate firm action, appear to be the consequence of practices that are constituent of the knowledge-based economy's expansion and its imperatives for rationalization and efficiency alongside competitive innovation. These factors are less readily visible and seldom recognized. Alongside the excitement of globalization and off-shore relocation of ICT-enabled functions, the occurrence, within the high-tech, knowledge-rich sectors, of sub-knowledge-based economies is ignored. The discussion below draws into focus core aspects of the knowledge-based economy that both produce uneven and polarizing outcomes and that define its limits.

LABOUR MARKETS: DISCREPANCIES AND DISPARITIES

Liberalized economic reforms and the pursuit of a high-skill, knowledge-based economy are described in Chapter 3. Analysts report the figures which indicate that liberalized market expansion and higher skill levels stimulated the generation of more jobs across most of the European countries in the 1990s and 2000s (Felstead *et al.* 2002; Gallie *et al.* 1998; Green 2006; Warhurst *et al.* 2004). The especially rapid increase in the 1990s prompted many observers to assume a continuation of that trend. As the OECD (2001) reports, in the developed economies, employment growth in the 1990s was greatest in the highest paid sectors of the labour market. That development corresponded with economic models of expanding knowledge-based, high technological activity and the decline or off-shoring of traditional heavy industry and manufacturing. Higher paid workers typically (but not always) possess higher levels of education and skills, and typically manage the work of others with fewer qualifications and performing lower-skilled jobs.

The pursuit of new products and new markets places considerable emphasis on the requirement for continuous innovation. The demand for innovation requires not only product development but deliberate strategies for organizational and worker learning, and for smart business responses to market dynamics. For many commentators, the promise of the expansion and diffusion of knowledge-rich activities proposes, along with higher productivity and profitability yields, continuing changes to the organization of work. In the 1980s and 1990s, it was often excitedly argued that the changes underway in the world of work would permanently do away with Fordist industrial organization and employment practices just as the Fordist accumulation model had been surpassed. The prevailing theories of organization and philosophies of management argued that organization structures are becoming, or ought to be made, flatter, i.e. comprised of less hierarchy, fewer rules and more diffuse and flexible processes and roles. Furthermore, many assumed that post-Fordist, post-Taylorist organizational structures would launch favourable new forms of collaborative employment practices, the invention of the post-bureaucratic organizational form, and the continual learning of knowledge-seeking employees and innovation-producing companies. These popular views among organization and business analysts were encouraged by many economists, especially those advocating the knowledge-based economy paradigm. As the prominent economist, Joseph Stiglitz saw it in the 1990s:

> In industry the shift towards a knowledge-based economy involves a shift in organization away from top-down hierarchical structures to flatter structures such as networks of semi-autonomous teams. Tayloristic vertical structures were designed to enforce and coordinate certain physical behaviors while knowledge-based work organization involves greater recognition of the autonomy and self-direction of the mind.
>
> (Stiglitz 1999: 6)

Stiglitz's view illustrates a popular favourable view that the knowledge-based economy and its accompanying forms of work organization, and its new emphasis on workers' knowledge and skill, have left Taylorist and Fordist work organization behind. Contemporary organizations are structured to facilitate knowledge-sharing and highly cooperative teams pursuing innovative production and process. These organizations will require knowledge workers with the skills and competencies to perform their high-level roles, and these workers will become the significant new and continually growing sector of the advanced economies. Robert Reich's (1991) well-known study at the beginning of the 1990s widely popularized this view. For Reich, the "burgeoning demand" for "symbolic analysts", the knowledge workers of the new economy, "will continue to surge" (ibid.: 225), and their cooperative, collaborative, team style of working will be essential to innovative production and market competitiveness.

In contrast to this view, other researchers report evidence that contradicts expectations of a dramatic and widespread decline of hierarchy and deep change in the internal logic of the organization. They point to evidence of the persistence of economic sectors of conventionally Taylorist and neo-Fordist forms of work organization that not only remain viable and competitive, but that may be found in the heart of knowledge intensives' organizational activities themselves. Furthermore, as discussed below, the economic returns to maintaining hierarchies are favourable. Nonetheless, the popular analytical and policy depiction of the globalizing knowledge economy typically ignores or glosses over the persistence of rigidly controlled systems of work organization and low-skilled jobs observed in current practices of work in the advanced economies, and in the normative continuity of competitive systems for positions deliberately made scarce in everyday operations of the firm.

Many of the new jobs that have appeared in the highly competitive, information and knowledge-intensive economy and deregulated labour markets are found in an expanded lower-skilled, poorly paid and poorly protected service sector. Some economists do recognize the persistence of low-skilled and neo-Taylorized jobs and workers. Lundvall and Archibugi (2001: 5) report that "a growing proportion of the labour force is excluded from the learning economy". Warhurst *et al.* (2004: 14) find that during the 1990s, while skilled work was growing, job growth was most evident in part-time jobs in services such as "hair-dressing, waitering, guarding, cooking and cleaning". Warhurst *et al.* conclude that skills are "by no means a first factor" in regard to measuring both the expansion and quality of employment in the new economy. Goos and Manning (2007) report in regard to the United Kingdom that lowest wage jobs have grown faster than middle-ranking jobs at the same time as growth in the highest-paid, higher skills sectors is also evident. They argue that there is a rising polarization of work in Britain and that polarization distinctly affects not only income disparities but the quality of people's jobs.

Francis Green's (2006: 36) extensive study on contemporary work and labour market patterns reports "elements of polarization" where the next highest growth rate to that of higher-skilled sectors was to be found in the low-paid sector. This occurrence was evident across many European countries, with the notable exception of France (likely to be attributable to France's retention of high minimum wage levels and job protection measures). Other recent European studies on low-wage work including that in Germany (Bosch and Weinkopf 2008), Denmark (Westergaard-Nielson 2008), the Netherlands (Salverda *et al.* 2008) and the United Kingdom (Lloyd *et al.* 2008) each report that there has occurred an increase in the growth in low-waged jobs. The persistence of low-skilled, low-paid jobs cannot be dismissed as either exceptional to a general upgrading trend or to temporary inefficiencies in the labour market's adaptation to the policy drive toward a generalized knowledge-based economy.

SEGMENTATION AND DELIMITATION OF KNOWLEDGE-INTENSIVE PRODUCTION

The above traverse sketches a picture of unevenness, segmentation, disparity and limitation in the expansion and reach of the knowledge-based paradigm. Analysts have observed patterns of labour market segmentation in various forms for many decades. In addition to classical class analyses of labour segregation, segregation on both vertical and horizontal axes on the basis of gender has long been noted. The structural position of very low-paid workers is frequently regarded as a form of segmentation even if class analyses of labour relations and markets have declined in popularity. But research debates in the 1990s and 2000s proposed that new or intensified forms of segmentation had emerged as a distinct characteristic of contemporary, liberalized labour markets and as a consequence of the flexible firm. Many debates have focused on segmentation and fragmentation brought about by the flexibility of labour markets to effect divisions of workers by security or insecurity of tenure, and the rise in the numbers of workers employed involuntarily in part-time and discontinuous jobs with different employers (Burchell *et al.* 2002; Heery and Salmon 2000; Marginson and Sisson 2004). But, as the discussion below emphasizes, flexibility of employment contract may be considerably less significant than segmentation of learning and skill utilization and quality of jobs.

Current patterns of labour market segregation are observed in sectors that retain lower-skilled work in primary production (agriculture and horticulture), in the extractive industries (mining, fishing, forestry), in heavy construction and transportation industries (roading, building, shipping) and in labour-intensive production, in services such as cleaning, custodial and maintenance, goods distribution and delivery, warehousing and in many retail jobs. Each of these sectors also contains sophisticated high-tech applications alongside traditional skills and physical exertion. In addition, there continue to exist market sectors and firms that, in reference to the knowledge-based economy paradigm, are described as traditional or "old economy" practices. A range of goods continue to be produced in typical industrial methods of manufacture and organization and under the retention of Fordist-Taylorist organizational systems even within advanced knowledge economies.

The retention of typical industrial production systems appears in the production of goods that tend to favour low cost and low value-added production. Their operations continue to require only moderately or low-skilled workers. There remains good profitability in competition on price rather than on quality or innovative variation in the production of a vast range of non-durable goods or basic services – from the manufacture of tee-shirts to the provision of street cleaning. Value-added qualities and higher-level skills in the production of these product ranges, especially when profitability is sought in low-price competitiveness, and not on international markets, are not required. Firms in these industry sectors typically, but not necessarily, strategically utilize ICT applications in the management of their business operations and employment relationships. Selective, strategic adoption and dispersion of ICT applications, and the employment of appropriately skilled workers, occur in consort with the maintenance of established routine and low-skilled operations. These strategies for technological utilization and organizational arrangements favour the pursuit of efficiencies and low-cost competitiveness in which innovation is not required or pursued. Skill levels and further, or lifelong, learning and development for workers are restricted and low wages maintained.

In the 1980s and 1990s, the prevailing analytical view was that operations such as these, and the jobs and workers they required, would dramatically diminish to the point of insignificance.[1] The advance of both new production technologies and the knowledge-based economy paradigm would render them either obsolete or virtually entirely automated. Empirical evidence in the 2000s shows that these practices have endured and remain economically viable (Bosch and Weinkopf 2008; Laursen 2004; Tolsby and Kirkebak 2006). Classical industrial forms of production occur within the advanced economies and not only in the new industrializing countries (Kuhndt *et al.* 2003; Lomba 2005). The retention of "old economy" production is not an historical anomaly, but an occurrence that exhibits economic and market viability.

The second dimension of unevenness and limitation in the dispersion of the knowledge-based economy occurs in the expansion of low productivity, low wage, non-internationally tradeable service sectors alongside sectors that are engaged in knowledge-rich production and globalizing trade. The considerable expansion of newer services (or newly restored servant work) that includes personal and domestic services, food preparation and catering, leisure and entertainment, and child and elder care jobs. In this sector neither high skills nor substantial productivity gains are expected. The economic aims in the production of these services, which may be privately or publicly provided, are to minimize labour costs, sustain production and operation efficiencies and to compete on price. Even as the organization of the production and distribution of these services frequently involves applications of advanced technological and management systems, the frontline of their provision to consumers requires little or negligible advanced technical application. The in-person provision of these forms of services takes the form of jobs that are structured to contain minimally skilled tasks and to be performed by predominantly low-skilled workers.

The nature of these services requires that they be produced and consumed in real time and in fixed locations in geographic space, usually cities and urban areas. Both worker and consumer live and trade within practicable distance of each other. These services cannot be performed remotely, they cannot be stored up for future sale at a different price, and they cannot be relocated off-shore or traded on international markets (Crouch 2005b). The labour market in these sectors requires workers who possess types of skills that are formally considered to be of low and general levels and which are expected to be widely held across the adult population. Not all of the work in these sectors is objectively low skilled but the labour market predominantly trades on factors other than skills. Workers often need to possess and utilize tacit skills, such as good judgement in interactions with clients, and to perform emotional labour – which may be both taxing and rewarding – in many jobs in the new service sectors (Webster 2007). But these skills, which are generally not those formally taught in education and training systems or assessed in qualifications systems, tend to remain officially unrecognized and unremunerated.

The continuing presence of sectors of formal economic activity that are peripheral to the knowledge-economy model of expanding innovation and increasing demand for and utilization of higher skills draws varying response. For some economists, the uneven expansion of the knowledge-based economy and an apparent limitation in its capacity are regarded as a consequence of its imperfect dispersion. These inefficiencies are projected to diminish as innovation capacities expand as a consequence of greater development and dispersion of innovation systems developments, including expanded education and training systems. These forces stimulate the generation of new, as yet unknown, goods and production systems and "spillover" into the broader economy (Foray 2004; Lundvall and Archibugi 2001; Soete 2006). Educationists find some agreement with that view. Brown and Lauder (2006), for instance, suggest that the problem may lie with employers. They observe "the failure of employers to exploit the potential for higher productivity and growth that mass education now offers" (ibid.: 49) and suggest that greater uptake of higher-skilled workers will help the dispersion of a high skills economy and society. Mayhew and colleagues (Mayhew *et al.* 2004) point to empirical evidence of the variability of employers' use of skilled workers. They note that while the education and training system is producing more highly skilled people for potential employment in high-skilled work, employers are using graduates to perform jobs formerly performed by non-graduates. Mayhew and colleagues conclude, as a result of this employer behaviour, that: "The knowledge-intensive sectors are not growing fast enough to absorb more than a proportion of new graduates" (ibid.: 78). Brown and colleagues point out, however, that employers' utilization of higher qualified workers frequently retains the wage structures used for non-graduate employees that may result in a "high-skilled, low-waged workforce" (Brown *et al.* 2008: 1).

The factors of employer tardiness, and employer sophistication, in the utilization of higher qualified workers are both evident. Employer and organizational behaviour, while typically assumed in economic models to be rationally aligned, is subject in practice to various institutional pressures and imperfect knowledge. In addition to economically expected rational organizational action, firms take political action in pursuing their strategies in their market environments. As many analysts of organization observe, following Weber's ([1922] 1978) classical analysis, organizational rationality is itself a source and conduit of power. It is to this force of rational and interested power that a third dimension of limitation in the configuration and dispersion of the knowledge-based economy may be attributed. The two dimensions described above, those of the expansion of a low-skilled and low productivity service sector and the retention of industry sectors of economically viable Fordist-Taylorist production systems, do attract much critical attention. The occurrence of a third dimension of the knowledge economy's unevenness and limitation is more often overlooked. Yet this aspect exerts a further powerful effect on labour market structure and dynamics in the knowledge-based economy, and on the fortunes of skilled workers in the new economy. That dimension is the role of firm action and organizational behaviour in its internal division of labour and in the rational and strategic utilization of employees' skills.

The bifurcation of labour markets, which economists identify as occurring at macroeconomic levels of region and industry, also occurs at the organizational level. Rational organizational practice, famously since Taylor and Ford, divides work into sectors. The principal division is based on sectors of routine and systemically controlled operations, and sectors that utilize higher order knowledge and skill in addressing more complex problems and generating competitive innovation. Organizational regulation by principles of hierarchy and command that may be incorporated into technological control systems endeavours to ensure the efficient and cost-effective utilization of skills and knowledge applications. This is a vitally beneficial capacity for the firm, and it is no less rationally applied in contemporary high-tech, knowledge-rich organizations employing greater numbers of formally qualified workers than it was a generation ago when Fordist organizational and operational systems were at their zenith. The pursuit of both rational and political organizational behaviour and structure *intensifies* under liberal regulatory regimes. It is a highly significant factor in current economic action and in labour market dynamics in the knowledge-based economy.

In the 1990s, analysts began to observe the effects of outsourcing and re-contracting of workers in new corporte firm subsidiaries. These practices resulted in a lowering of labour costs for the firm and lower wages for workers. Firms employing flexible organizational structures in consort with heightened managerial control systems are able to displace labour costs incurred in the continuous employment of workers by utilizing flexible and temporary labour contracts in which labour and skill utilization and cost are intermittently demanded. These "just-in-time", tight flow arrangements (as described in Chapter 3) have intensified in the 2000s. Workers in sectors of the firm's operation considered to be part of the core business are more likely to be retained on secure contracts and with better conditions than those whose labour costs can be more readily controlled. Workers in sectors in which routine production of goods and delivery of services can be provided through competition on lowest price are more likely to experience insecurity of tenure, lower wages and poorer conditions (Boltanski and Chiapello 2007; Lloyd *et al.* 2008; Marchington *et al.* 2005, Supiot 2001).

The existence of sectors of insecure wage-workers who bear the brunt of the continuous labour costs due to the displacement of the firm is a well-known consequence of liberalized economies and strategic organizational management. In addition to the conventional managerial objective of constraining labour costs, firms are now able to constrain the cost of and command the deployment of higher-skilled workers while at the same time pursuing innovation in strategic arenas. Firms now operate scarcely visible forms of segmentation in their practice of wide diversity in the conditions and pay of workers employed on the same enterprise site. At the heart of high-tech, knowledge-based, innovation-seeking firms, a strategic intra-organizational bifurcation of skill utilization fuels a wider labour market structuring of lower-skilled sectors that are immediately proximate to higher-skilled, knowledge-rich jobs.

Substantive numbers of low-skilled, and skill-restricted, jobs are retained. Firms operating in knowledge-intensive industries, including banking and financial services, medical and health care, airlines and telecommunications, electronics, marketing, retail chains and utilities, configure their organizations and deploy their workforces in ways that segment and polarize the utilization of skills. From the point of view of rational action by the firm, there are perfectly good reasons to structure jobs and skill requirements in various organizational production levels in ways that strategically utilize high-level skills, which, as demonstrated below, includes the recruitment and under-employment of qualified personnel. The uneven, segmented and delimited dispersion of the knowledge-economy paradigm and the variable utilization of higher levels of skills in contemporary organizations are not a mistaken application of corporate firm management or a residual organizational inefficiency due to rapid system change and institutional lag. It is, on the contrary, a consequence of rational and strategic action by the firm in organizational design and behaviour in the pursuit of the firm's interests. The organization's management of knowledge combined with mundane efficiencies of labour and functional operations costs and maximized utility of resources are the core of the matter. The following discussion attends to these internal logics of the organization.

FIRMS, ORGANIZATIONS AND PRACTICES OF KNOWLEDGE

The firm in capitalist economies, as has long has been observed, has a rational interest in the intensification of the search for maximizing gain. The politically increased role of shareholders in the current neo-liberal climate has intensified that rationalistic search. Firms endeavour to structure their organizations toward efficiency gains, costs control, and labour rationalization. An extensive literature in organization theory and analysis[2] analyzes the variables and dynamics of rational organizational structure. In firms which are actively pursuing knowledge-based economy objectives of continuous innovation, which as knowledge economists know, is inefficient, risky and costly, further measures must be taken to minimize efficiency loss. The incompatible demands of innovation and risk and of efficiency and system maintenance require a heightened and strategic management of organizational action. Strategic management, theorized as both intensively rational and politically conscious (Casey 2002), has risen prominently in recent decades as the business-favoured optimal management model in the liberal knowledge-based economy. The factors of knowledge and information have been discussed since classical economists. Friedrich von Hayek (1945) observed that a key economic problem was the optimal use of available knowledge to economic agents including firms. The recent accelerated growth of fields of inquiry and practice in regard to knowledge management readily demonstrates the intense focus accorded to the dynamic role of knowledge in contemporary production in which innovation is privileged.

"Knowledge management, which is not to be equated with information management, refers to any intentional and systematic process of acquiring, capturing, sharing, and using productive knowledge … to enhance learning and performance in organizations" (Foray 2004: 207). The new field of knowledge management studies includes prominently attention to communities of practice, the dynamics of knowledge sharing and knowledge "spillovers" and means of extraction and codification of tacit knowledge (Davenport and Prusak 1998; Wenger 1998). The optimal management of knowledge, it is proposed, increases the capacity for innovation.

The expectation that the successful post-Fordist firm is nimble, flexible and dynamically innovative further assumes that organizations are restructuring toward post-bureaucratic forms. The post-bureaucratic form includes multi-dimensional flexibilities and, it is widely assumed, flatter hierarchies, shorter chains and wider span of control, increased team work, greater knowledge-sharing and dispersed problem-solving channels. Certainly, flatter hierarchies have been enabled by ICT applications which have extended the capacities of managers to control larger numbers of workers and operations across a wider span. In addition, more horizontally linked and flexibly comprised teams with greater degrees of operational autonomy, while still managed by strong vertical integration, feature prominently in contemporary industries (Green 2006; Rajan and Wulf 2006). That evidence, and the excitement over the capacities of ICT and the new organizational forms and management structures it assisted, may have led many analysts to over-emphasize the potential for less rule-bound management and reduced hierarchies. Flattened hierarchies and collaborative team cultures in enterprise suggest generally more favourable conditions than conventional hierarchies, command and control and contestational workplaces. A general expectation that bureaucratic forms were dying out may have inspired an over-statement of their potential, or an overlooking of other evidence in regard to the patterns of organizational change.

The effectiveness of Human Resource Management (HRM) and of knowledge management systems has had some results that were seldom expected in the 1990s. The firm that is culturally integrated through HRM systems, functionally integrated and flexibly structured is able to strategically utilize employees' knowledge and skill as company-owned human capital. Functional and flexible integration and collaborative team work intended to both efficiently integrate production activities and to stimulate innovation and competitiveness appear to invite lower hierarchies, less supervision and more laterally integrated employees. The extraction and utilization of human capital can be achieved through active demands for appropriately skilled and knowledgeable workers who are willing, or compliant with the requirement, to share their knowledge in team networks. A combination of team collaboration, wider spans of control, and tighter vertical integration alongside institutional liberalization accords new powers to the firm in its organizational designs and management of knowledge. Institutional liberalization has enabled firms to split sectors of activities into subsidiaries or quasi-separate profit centres, and to reconfigure their employment relations. These developments unilaterally serve the interests of the firm and obscure the occurrence of new sets of structural divisions of employees.

The following discussion of illustrative empirical research of organizational practices reveals the contemporary practices of hierarchy, segmentation of skill and knowledge and structural polarity as efficiencies of the firm. We are witnessing in the midst of new complexity in organizational forms the strategic retention of core organizational powers. Rather than widely decreasing, hierarchies of command, control and structural differentiation persist and reconfigure under conditions of flexible and networked organizational forms. Their persistence is not due to institutional obstructions, poor knowledge management or organizational irrationalities. Rather, the persistence of hierarchies occurs precisely because hierarchies return economic as well as political benefits to the firm. The firm retains in its contemporary organizational forms, just as in the past, the utilization of structures that seek to channel and curb knowledge, skill and task differentiation, and wage costs. Moreover, the retention of hierarchies in a somewhat flatter form – that is, fewer layers and stronger vertical integration – as well as through the newer form of subsidiaries and dependent profit centres, enables an effective division of knowledge-rich work and less complex work. At the heart of knowledge-intensive enterprises there are evident structures that retain and intensify high routinization, command and control management, rigid structures and procedures, and constrained employee involvement. These highly rationalized actions are all practised in the interests of gaining efficiencies in knowledge and skill application, in managing labour costs, and in strategic flexibilities for the firm. A key point to stress in this configuration is that it is not only traditionally lower-skilled jobs that are clustered in the lower levels of the hierarchy. A considerable range of jobs that require skilled workers are similarly clustered in lower levels. A bifurcation occurs between the highest-skilled, knowledge-intensive producers and the rest.

A further point must be noted on the firm's strategic retention and utilization of hierarchies, and on the importance of internal labour markets. These remain both possible and effective because large firm organizations – even when they are fragmented into multiple subsidiaries and distinct legal employers – remain highly effective in contemporary competitive economic environments. The proposed "disintegration" of the firm through subsidiaries and flatter, more flexible structures and permeable boundaries is at once a tighter vertical hierarchy dominated by shareholder imperatives. The classical liberal economic maxim that "markets motivate and hierarchies coordinate" is reinvigorated in today's innovation-seeking, highly competitive knowledge-based economies.

Hierarchies, sorting systems and skills use

Firms use hierarchies for strategic reasons. The firm can maintain or increase its organizational hierarchy and coordination through the polarization of its internal labour market, and through breaking into smaller business units. That strategy can reduce external labour market dependency for appropriately skilled workers through providing more steps up salary grades on a wider range. And it can delimit internal labour mobility by constraining the skills applications of other sectors of workers. The increased wage costs of internal labour mobility are expected to be offset by increased productivity from promoted employees. For low-skilled and skills-restricted workers, who are typically employed on flexible contracts, higher turnover is expected. The transaction costs incurred in higher turnover of skills-restricted workers is offset by lower wage costs. Another strategy for the firm is the reduction of hierarchy. The firm can reduce organizational hierarchy and introduce a wider rank and a lower range (delayering). That arrangement involves a wider span of control among fewer senior managers and a lower range of movement and motivation. The latter strategy enables lower wage levels but risks lower worker effort. When labour market competition increases, the firm has to pay more for skilled labour. However, a reduction in labour market competition can be gained (for the firm) through the encouragement of higher aggregate skill levels in the wider societal population. The firm then does not have to pay a skills premium formerly typically expected by higher-skilled workers. It further gains by having a larger pool of skills for potential later utilization or stockpiling. The mass expansion of higher education skill systems directly serves the interests of the firm in providing more and cheaper skills.

In the first instance, hierarchies as sorting systems and ranking systems are premised on a primary efficiency and division of labour. The organization has a rational interest in increasing the number of problems that can be solved routinely. Routinization, as we have known since Taylorist-Fordism, is a principal factor in gaining production efficiencies and in keeping labour costs as low as practicable. At the same time, firms pursuing knowledge-rich and innovative production require and encourage non-routine, problem-rich activities and skilled workers capable of undertaking them. The firm, therefore, has a rational interest in establishing knowledge hierarchies *and* routinization. Both strategies sort, utilize and cost-manage employees while pursuing knowledge-intensive production and possibilities for innovation. The rationale in this action is to identify the knowledge-rich sector, generate the teams or devices useful to maximizing knowledge flows and innovation capacities, and to tightly control, or split off into a dependent business unit, the production components that can be routinely performed and managed.

Economists Garicano and Rossi-Hansberg (2006) empirically investigated the optimal use of knowledge and knowledge flow efficiencies in knowledge-intensive organizations. They found that the firm's pursuit of innovation and efficiency establishes a series of internal polarizations, or knowledge sorting systems within the organization. Garicano and Rossi-Hansberg found that the organization, acquisition and communication of knowledge are achieved via "knowledge hierarchies". Knowledge management systems target knowledge flows, processes and agents in the organization in order to optimally utilize knowledge and manage costs. Knowledge hierarchies are prevalent in upper management just as they are among low-graded jobs in the same organization. The researchers found that the organization displays "positive sorting" in its channelling knowledge flow through the organization. "Positive sorting" means that:

> the higher ability agents share their knowledge with higher ability subordinates (production workers or lower level managers). Efficiency requires that the expertise of more skilled problem solvers be shielded from easy questions, and hence those posing questions to them must be among the most skilled in their rank or layer.
>
> (ibid.: 1384)

They conclude that, "The efficient allocation of tasks must be that the time of more knowledgeable individuals is only used when it cannot be substituted for the time of less knowledgeable agents" (ibid.: 1386). Hierarchies conserve the time of more able agents by less able agents solving routine problems. Hierarchies also channel the knowledge flow, and where they are flatter, allow for lateral dispersion of knowledge and the greater use of ICT. "Production workers draw problems and learn how to solve the routine ones, while problem solvers learn to solve the more difficult ones and contribute their knowledge to production workers as needed" (ibid.: 1384).

Reductions in the cost of utilizing ICT enables more dispersion of knowledge among agents and increases the number of problems that can be solved by agents at all organizational layers. This technological change "results in an increase in the knowledge content of production work ... as well as an increase in wage inequality in the economy [of the firm] as a whole". As a result of the efficient use of hierarchies of knowledge, " wage inequality among workers decreases, but wage inequality among top managers, and between them and workers, increases" (Garicano and Rossi-Hansberg 2006: 1385).

Knowledge-sorting systems of the type described by Garicano and Rossi-Hansberg have been theorized within knowledge-generating and innovation models, as Foray (2004) indicates. But for Foray, and the predominant policy model of the knowledge-rich enterprise, the unequal outcomes of knowledge-sorting into skill hierarchies are ignored. The organizational structural retention of strategic hierarchies and the application of HRM are effective organizational methods that enable, *inter alia*, the establishment and maintenance of new sorting systems of workers under the guise of both flexibility and efficiency. The knowledge-rich management sector within the firm regulates the demand for skill use which in turn regulates employee opportunity for skills upgrading and higher skills application within the firm. Garicano and Rossi-Hansberg report in concluding their study that, "economic organization provides incentives for the acquisition and communication of knowledge". This is achieved through "a universe of knowledge hierarchies competing for workers and managers that exhibits positive sorting, the stratification of agent skills into ranks, and the accentuation by organization of innate ability differences the best and the worst agents" (ibid.: 1413).

Another illustrative study provides further data on the retention and profitability of hierarchy and structural inequality. In an extensive empirical study, Smeets and Warzynski (2008) investigate the hypothesized economic returns to hierarchies in knowledge organizations. The researchers note the recent turn of interest in hierarchy and theoretical propositions on its role and benefits. But they argue that there is little empirical data on the returns to hierarchies because of the methodological difficulties in assessing and measuring hierarchies. Their particular and extensive data set enabled the researchers to identify returns through the chain of command and the span of control, and the remuneration levels of workers in that chain. The study utilizes empirical data spanning the period 1997–2004 in "a large European firm" which "operates in a high tech manufacturing industry, has grown significantly over the last decade, has been very innovative and has remained one of the world leaders in its product line" (ibid.: 688). The researchers report that the company had introduced new and improved communication technologies at the time the research data were gathered. Consistent with many theoretical models, the researchers find that the hierarchy has become flatter over time and the span of control of managers at each level has become wider. The also find that wage gaps between levels in the hierarchy have become wider over time. They found larger differences in the knowledge acquired by workers between the levels which effect higher wage inequalities between the levels. The researchers found that "knowledge can be partitioned more precisely" (ibid.: 691) even as communication costs are reduced due to improved systems and easier dispersion across workers. At the same time they observed the introduction of a new hierarchical level in the partitioning of knowledge. Their findings, similar to those of Garicano and Rossi-Hansberg (2006), describe a knowledge-based hierarchy and positive sorting system yielding positive returns to the firm.

The retention of strategic hierarchies is an action of highly rationalized organizational and management systems. Strategic hierarchies entail specific requirements of workers. Collaborative, knowledge-sharing teams, networks, flexibility and degrees of semi-autonomy are organizational forms useful for sectors of workers employed to produce knowledge, product innovations and systems operations. Routine, rigidity, adaptation to system requirements and contingent employment relations are required of workers employed to carry out production designs. Importantly, it must be emphasized, these different organizational forms occur within the same firm. They simultaneously allow for necessary vertical integration and the loosely boundaried, flexible networking and inter-organizational communications found fruitful for innovation development. A consequence is the *strategic*, structural segmentation of highly skilled workers, on the one hand, and medium and lower-skilled workers on the other. These segmented groups work alongside each other and are subject to differential management strategies and opportunities for continuing education and training and skill development. The firm, through its flexible organizational structures, effectively segregates its utilization of knowledge and skill into knowledge-rich sectors and knowledge-poor sectors.

Earlier studies have shown the prevalence of knowledge hierarchies in manufacturing organizations (Burawoy 1979; Schonberger 1986). Castells' studies in the 1990s demonstrated a pattern of industrial configuration into bifurcated segmentation of core and periphery workers as post-industrial technologies and organizational forms accelerated in the 1980s and 1990s. But the policy models of the knowledge-based economy have assumed that the spread of knowledge-intensive production would demand and productively utilize more skilled and collaborative employees. That in turn would stimulate greater dispersion of higher-skilled, higher-waged work and better quality jobs. However, the use of knowledge hierarchies as "positive sorting systems", in Garicano and Rossi-Hansberg's term, is prevalent across diverse industries utilizing knowledge-rich and ICT-rich capabilities.

De Fraja's (2004) study in labour economics offers a further perspective on the firm's composition and use of organizational hierarchy. De Fraja argues that most economic approaches to hierarchy assume that hierarchies are exogenously determined by external factors such as technological change and economies of scale. His study proposes that the current trend toward delayering may also be determined by endogenous factors. Key among those factors are the skills and abilities of a firm's employees. De Fraja argues that firms have an "informational advantage" over their employees. Firms, through their HRM systems, know the ability of workers but workers do not know their own ability. In the case of skilled workers, outside firms can observe the position of a worker in the firm's hierarchy. The more ranks in a firm's hierarchy, the more it signals to the market the skills and abilities of its workers. Competing employers may attract skilled workers with an increased wage offer. The worker's wage must therefore be increased to prevent her/him from leaving. De Fraja argues: "The degree of substitutability between outside workers in different firms is a measure of the firm's specific human capital, and therefore of the strength of labour market competition" (ibid.: 670).

When labour market competition increases, skilled workers become more valuable to other employers. In order to stop workers being poached, or to prevent having to pay them higher wages, the firm can strategically reduce its hierarchy. "The wider the rank, the lower the wage needed to stop workers being poached." It is cost effective for an employer to both create ranks and to bunch workers. The positioning of workers in this structure determines their fate on wage levels and marketability, even as the breadth and quality of skills within bunched workers may be diverse. Some highly skilled workers may be bunched with lower-skilled workers which increases, without reward, their usefulness to the firm and obscures their marketability to outside competitor firms. The shape of the hierarchy: longer or shorter, polarized, or segmented, is the strategic choice of the firm. De Fraja further notes that "bunching contracts" in which mixed ability workers are knowingly (to the firm) bunched together and paid the same rates are "pervasive in dynamic environments" (ibid.: 675). (Dynamic environments, it must be noted, are precisely those sought and generated by highly liberalized institutional regimes.) Hierarchies and dual labour structures are efficient for the firm. Firms incur the efficiency costs of creating hierarchies in order to hide their employees' ability to outside firms and to effectively utilize skills that are relevant to the firm without incurring higher wage costs. A hierarchical and dualized structure enables lower-ranked workers to be employed on more flexible and often casual contracts in which high turnover and low commitment are expected. The everyday functions of these workers may also be out-sourced to the firm's subsidiaries of dependent sub-contractors with weaker bargaining power and protection.

ICT, functional integration and flexibility of organization enable an intensification of management action by the firm across the organization. This occurs not only in more routine process work but through knowledge-intensive operations as well. Only an elite sector of workers accrues the advantages of the rents gained from higher skills and hierarchical position. The competitive drive for knowledge-rich, innovative production and profit maximization is operationalized through intensified management practices. The normalization of HRM has facilitated the hierarchy and sorting systems and skills bunching described above that integrate employees into the firm's prerogatives and obscure the reach of its advantages.

Durand's (2007) extensive empirical study adds further evidence, and critical concern, in regard to the dispersion and utilization of skilled work. Taking up the point made by Garicano and Rossi-Hansberg's study discussed above in regard to the increased competitiveness that knowledge hierarchies stimulate among workers, Durand analyzes the contradictions of the new, knowledge-sharing collaborative teams promoted in knowledge-intensive organizations. The organization of intellectual work into teams, which he calls "groupware" (*collecticiel* in French) (ibid.: 77) simultaneously integrates input from diverse sources, which may include workers separated by geography and time zone. Under this arrangement "the group or collectivity takes precedence over the individual" (ibid.: 77). Every individual is required to contribute knowledge and expertise to the collective project and in a timely manner that enables other individuals to exchange and produce the collective product of the project. The experience, knowledge and know-how of everyone are integrated into a collective pool of knowledge. (Foray (2004), as noted in Chapter 2, proposes and models precisely this pattern in his theory of knowledge flows.) In this manner, Durand argues, intellectual work is streamlined. The codification of interactions between different actors renders behaviour more predictable and reduces uncertainties. It speeds up and renders more efficient knowledge generation and flow. Codification of behavioural expectations enables the control of subjective behaviour.

In this way, the collective domination of the individual brings about an instrumentalization of the individual's intellectual activity for the attainment of the collective result. That collective result may be gained without the individual participating in the setting of the project's objectives. Moreover, while the individual is dominated by the group organization and its "tight flow" of exchange and deliverability, she or he is employed on individual contractual conditions of pay and tenure. For Durand, the organization of white-collar work, of "knowledge workers" in Reich's (1991) term, has achieved a new system of coordination. The new system "simultaneously combined hierarchy and contract, rule and negotiation". It has fundamentally changed the hierarchy established under Taylorist-Fordist systems which was based on command and obedience into one based on employee internalization of the demands and pressures of managerial work objectives as "natural". Intellectual workers voluntarily "behave themselves".

The evidence from these studies, which focussed particular attention on the organizational level in the practical uses of knowledge flows and rational efficiency of time and cost, shows that the use of hierarchies of knowledge enables the simultaneous pursuit of both knowledge-rich innovation and cost efficiency. The use of knowledge sorting systems and of curbed and delimited utilization of wage-able skills empirically contradicts the ideal models of the knowledge-based economy and its assumed generalization of a higher-skilled, high productivity and higher-waged economy.

A further illustration of skill delimitation emerges from the findings of an extensive pan-European sociological study by Webster and colleagues (Webster *et al.* 2003). The researchers investigated the use and provision of training and skills among women workers and opportunities for advancement for women into better jobs. The research conducted in eight countries (Denmark, France, Germany, Ireland, Sweden, Italy, Spain, the United Kingdom) during 1999–2001 focussed on financial and retail sectors. The researchers' primary concerns focussed on the situation for women workers in these knowledge-intensive sectors and on opportunities available to women workers to progress into better jobs. Their investigation was not focussed on knowledge flows or cost effectiveness or on the utility of knowledge hierarchies that the economists discussed above had been interested in. Yet their findings, from the vantage point of skills use and opportunity for women, provide additional detail to the picture on the utility of knowledge-sorting systems. The researchers found that individual firms in each of the financial and retail sectors provide restricted education and training for employees performing lower-skilled and routine work. They found overall in both sectors distinctly limited opportunities for women to gain further skills and to advance into more senior positions.

Respondents in the financial sector firms reported that jobs involving skills beyond routine tasks such as face-to-face client interactions were kept to a minimum. Potentially complex functions are "pulled into back offices where routines are established" (ibid.: 72). The routinization of functions requires less quantity and quickly administered training. Once established as lower skilled, the jobs are remunerated at low wage levels. Women employees in the financial sector are more frequently bunched in high routine functions with little opportunity for mobility into more skilled and better remunerated positions. In regard to the retail sector, the researchers summarily report: "with the exception of companies which operated retail apprenticeships, the majority of retail companies in the study provided only very basic and very brief training for their junior (female) staff" (ibid.: xv). Retail workers are generally required to know *less* than former sales workers in retail firms. Retail workers know little about the product, the pricing system, or the operations of their employing organization. Their job skills and learning are restricted instead to company-preferred styles of self-presentation, sales transactions processes (EFTPOS), and customer interaction. In both sectors, the researcher findings revealed that the training that the firms provided was specific to that organization's particular requirements. "On the job", company-based training makes workers more immediately useful to the employers but it does not develop the workers' skill sets or add greater labour market value to their skills.

The researchers in this pan-European study were primarily concerned with evidence of limited opportunity for women workers to gain skills and advance into better jobs. Yet in the course of their discovery of restricted opportunity and gender discrimination, they observed the application of a highly rational strategic management practice. That rational management practice, just as the economic studies illustrated above found, sorted the organization into sectors that required higher and low skills and structurally constrained workers' opportunities for skill upgrading or job improvements. This occurrence and that experienced by the women workers in their study were not attributable solely to that of the socio-cultural behaviour of gender discrimination. Rather, the occurrence is implicated in the rational economic action of firms pursuing knowledge-based economy policies effective at the intra-organizational level. (The gender effects of these rationalities and policies beg much more investigation.) Importantly, the research reported disparities between training and learning opportunities actually provided for employees and the discourses on the learning organization that advocates such opportunities.

Skill demands and contradictions

At the same time as the firm practises mixed organizational forms, strategic use of hierarchies, sorting systems, skills deployment,and opportunities for workers to gain and use higher skills in their work, the firm also exerts pressures on public education and training policies and institutions. Those pressures, which in turn fall on workers, demand overall increased levels of skills available on the labour market. Yet the firm offers no guarantee that specific educational products and workers' skills will be utilized. The retention of lower-skilled and tightly regulated jobs within the innovating, knowledge-rich economic sector is highly rational strategic action on the part of the firm. In addition, the recruitment and retention of more educated workers add to the firm's potential knowledge base. Research findings show that firms take on workers with higher levels of skills and qualifications than are required for the particular jobs available in the firm. They engage in a stocking of surplus skill (Borghans and de Grip 2000; Brynin 2002a, 200b; Jenkins 2000; Méhault 2006) even as they hide higher-skill levels through bunching workers of mixed skill levels.

Employers may demand relatively higher levels of skills and qualifications even for jobs which they know remain of low productivity or for which there are strategic organizational limitations in opportunity for employees' skill application or development. They do this for two reasons. One reason is the existence of a larger pool of qualified people on the labour market that has occurred as more individuals have participated in longer periods of schooling and training and thus generate an overall higher aggregate of labour marketable skills. Employers take more qualified workers for existing jobs simply because such workers are available. Another reason is that employers endeavouring to take strategic actions toward the expansion of knowledge-based economy activities, rapidly changing environments and uncertain production innovations take on more highly skilled workers for jobs in which those skills are not currently required as a contingency, just in case the firm may at some point need to utilize those higher skills (Battu and Sloane 2000; Borghans and de Grip 2000). Educated and qualified workers are treated like good quality parts rather than as participants in generalized innovation imperatives. The employment of over-qualified workers for lower-productivity jobs generates further labour market effects. As Borghans and de Grip (2000) show, these effects can include a lowering of wages for skilled workers who are over-qualified for their jobs and a bumping down the labour market of lesser qualified workers competing for the same jobs. Analysts debate the percentage of graduate workers being employed in jobs that under-utilize their skills. Brown *et al.* (2008) find that in the United Kingdom around a third of graduates report being over-qualified for the jobs they are doing. Elias and Purcell (2004) find that skills mismatching declines over time and a wage premium for graduate skills, though lower than for previous cohorts, may still be expected.

Buchel *et al.* (2003) propose, following their comparative European study, that an "over-educated European" competes on flexible labour markets that are unable to absorb their higher skills. Over-education (which may be better termed skill mismatching) benefits employers and at aggregate levels may be said to benefit the economy. Skill mismatching accrues gains to employers and costs to workers. When mismatching is a frequent factor, it stimulates further pressure on individuals to gain higher skills for competition for the genuinely higher-skilled jobs which actually utilize their higher skills. An overall higher level of skills and qualifications is evident in the labour market population. But that does not represent an equal accompanying trend of higher-skilled work.

Brown and Hesketh (2004) add further data on what they call the "mismanagement of talent". In their empirical study of employer recruitment behaviour they found that employers use formal qualifications as a sorting device in the selection of candidates prior to the interview stage. Employers evaluate candidates' educational qualifications and formal achievements as "hard currency of employability" (ibid.: 162). These achievements are basic criteria. But it is the "soft currencies of employability" that play the decisive role in the appointment decision. These criteria include the recruiters' assessment of the candidates' communication skills, team working skills, personality features, likeability, durability, creativity, conformity, and so forth. As Brown and Hesketh show in fine detail (ibid.: 104–8), the subjective assessment of these criteria is nonetheless couched in the language of objective scientific testing. Candidates may be assessed on the basis of psychometric tests alone or in conjunction with an interview informed by the candidate's psychometric test results. Both recruiters and candidates, the researchers observe, accept the legitimacy and accuracy of these recruitment devices and expect their results to add substantive data to selection beyond the candidate's possession of advanced educational qualifications. The researchers conclude that the formally and highly educated candidates were like "peas in a pod" with little to choose between them. Therefore, employers and recruiters behave in ways which, despite their sophisticated recruitment procedures, rely on the old adage that winning depends on your face fitting the desired profile. "And this usually depends on the same cultural props of class and ethnic privilege that characterized social elites in the past" (ibid.: 187). The highly desirable jobs of the knowledge-based economy remain the prerogative of only a minority, notwithstanding the increased supply of high levels of skills. For Brown and Hesketh, this market congestion counters the promise of greater organizational diversity and the utilization of the skills and talents of employees. It amounts to a mismanagement of talent.

Once again, the evidence poses a disruption to prevailing assumptions in the knowledge-based economy discourse. Particularly, the assumption of labour market capacities to absorb, sooner or later, an increasing pool of higher-skilled workers and to reward them with the higher wages expected to result from individual investments in longer periods of education and training is called into serious question. Brown *et al.*'s (2008) extensive comparative international study proposes that a "high-skilled, low-wage workforce" is emerging in the European and broader international labour market. The researchers argue that there is a clear distinction between high-skilled jobs and high-skilled workers, and that the numbers of each are widely disparate. The disproportionate numbers of qualified workers enables a downward pressure on wages. Human capital is subject to the law of diminishing returns. "The knowledge economy is not characterized by the rising value of knowledge as companies are not only attempting to do more with less but also to know more for less" (ibid.: 49).

Much policy discussion emphasizes the rate of return on investment in education and training. Economists model the rate of return by assuming that extra earnings reflect the extra productivity of the individual. There is much variation and unreliability of figures estimating and projecting the earnings premium on gaining higher education qualifications. Analysts seeking to measure the rates of return on investment in education question the extent of the economic and social returns from higher education (Hartley 2003; Mayhew *et al.* 2004; Wolf 2002). Hartley (2003) argues that the drive toward performance, standards, measurements and general aggregations of improved efficiencies that are economically modelled and driven do not necessarily deliver the economically desired results. Estimates of the rates of social return – defined as the social value of the extra output produced – are even more disparate. Nonetheless, high social rate of returns are used to justify further expansion of the higher education sector. Employers' rational and efficient utilization of skill at the organizational level contributes to the production of structural differentiation of skill-rich jobs and skill-poor or skill-restricted jobs, and restricts in-firm labour mobility and human resource development. The rates of return to education, therefore, will trend toward increased unevenness and diminishment (Brown *et al.* 2008). Even as the overall number of skilled jobs on the labour market increases, the economic returns to individually skilled workers is not commensurate with their expected returns of a generation ago (Borghans and de Grip 2000; Brown *et al.* 2008; Brynin 2002a). The structurally uneven intra-organizational use of skill, which as studies show is not a new phenomenon (Doeringer and Piore 1971), intensifies. Its intensification, even as that is obscured by the policy demand for knowledge-intensive economies, is the result of highly rationalized and politicized managerial practices.

CONCLUSION

The tensions and contradictions arising from discrepancies in the labour market's capacity to utilize and reward skill-upgraded workers give rise to a number of questions. The continuing policy emphasis on high-skills economies, heightened investment in higher education systems and increased public participation in education and training obscures attention to – indeed, denies – the practical realities of business organizational behaviour. Practices of skill sorting and retention of low-skilled jobs are commonplace in contemporary organizations. That many of those low-skilled jobs are performed by workers with higher levels of formal qualifications than those widely held a generation ago does not alter the objective low-skill content of routine jobs.

Constituent of heightening rationalization, as it was in classical industrial conditions, is the reduction to a minimum of skilled jobs that accrue more labour costs. Despite the rhetoric of human capital theory and HRM promises of valuing workers, the contribution and accounting of workers' exertion remain measured as cost-effectiveness. As well established as these rationalizing measures are, in the new economy's discourse, they are depicted under two contradictory forms. These hyper-efficiencies and sophisticated forms of worker control under normalized HRM are either exhorted as constituting innovations and restructurings or they are ignored or denied under the policy imperative toward knowledge-rich, higher-skilled, higher-waged, continually-innovating and competitive economy.

Current trends in the strategic structures and behaviour of organizations, in work arrangements and employment relations, pose a disjuncture of the correlation between education and employment opportunity. The implications of large numbers of learning-restricted workers in non-learning, intensively routinized and efficient economic sectors and of hyper-managed workplaces pose considerable challenges to ideological assertions of an economic correspondence of the learning economy and the learning society. They pose direct implications and challenges to education and training systems' expansion. A normative discourse advocates the provision of opportunities for workers, young people and families to advance from low-skilled jobs into "better" and more skilled jobs. Such recommendations, at face value, are hardly to be criticized. Yet, as the evidence readily demonstrates, from the point of view of the firm's rational organizational configuration, there is no need to generally increase opportunities for employees to gain further training. The jobs which lower-graded workers perform remain skills-limited yet efficiently productive for individual organizations. Low-skilled jobs are structurally retained in the advanced economies and some people, therefore, will be required to perform them. As the current organizational positioning of lower-skilled workers into clusters and strata in which low wages, scant opportunities and low commitment are expected, the negative externalities of those actions are borne by workers.

At the same time, the policy drive to expand post-compulsory education and training and to urge young people to aspire to higher-skilled jobs fuels popular belief that such higher-skilled jobs will be widely available. For workers, the stimulation of heightened aspirations with respect to learning and training for improved jobs and upward mobility within firms or labour markets is a direct consequence of the knowledge economy/learning society model that promotes an overall aggregation of higher-level skills available on the labour market. Notwithstanding the normative attractiveness of these aims for knowledge-intensive production and high-waged workers, the retention of assumptions of upward mobility for individuals or groups subsequent to education and training is manifestly problematic. As more companies pursue a highly rational, knowledge-rich organization strategy with the aim of achieving strategic process and product innovation, the learning and skill requirements of workers are accordingly brought under the rubric of strategic managerial design and control. Learning and skill development in the real workplace setting – although workers always seek and experience diverse learnings that are beyond a managerial reach – are effectively structured to meet the specificities of the firm's objectives and requirements. This learning, styled and specified by the firm, and the containment of learning and skills development opportunity are a rational organizational strategy of firms oriented toward maximizing their own self-interest and profitability.

Firms have no rational interest, as Crouch (2005b) points out, in maximizing collective interests. Firms strategically utilize the available skills and make general demands on society for their availability but they will not act to maximize the level of education and skills for society as a whole. The demand and burden of skill formation fall to governments and individuals. The situation of intensified economic pressures under a policy programme of the knowledge-based economy of educational reform and expansion, and discrepancies in the real world of work and organizations raises serious dilemmas and questions. Chapter 6 turns to explore more closely significant critical concerns.

6 Critical dilemmas for work, education and workers

INTRODUCTION

The discussions in the preceding chapters have brought into focus current trends in the spheres of work and education. The sweeping influence of a neo-liberal economic world-view and approach to social practices has made a particular set of assumptions about work and education appear commonplace and taken-for-granted in much of society. That normative acceptance, though, does not diminish the seriousness of concerns and dilemmas that have arisen through the course of the neo-liberal knowledge-intensive economy. In the 2010s, the powerful hold of an idealized knowledge-based economy may be showing signs of weakening. The public may be guessing that the promise of good jobs for all is turning out to be false, if indeed it ever were a viable prospect in a radically marketized and intensively competitive economy.

Yet there appear few signs of a weakening in adherence to the dominant policy model and assumed advance of the knowledge-based economy. On the contrary, a strengthening of policy demands in its pursuit and intensified pressures on education, on workers and on social institutions to comply with its demands is apparent. Current policy directives in the European Union, with the launch of *Europe 2020*, persist in emphasizing an imagined "skills deficit" and urge increased participation of young people in higher education and skills training. Education systems are pressured to further expand and rationalize in correspondence with the overarching policy framework for a knowledge-based economy and assumed labour market demand. That policy pressure in the midst of persistently disparate labour market utility of higher-level skills and structurally obstructed dispersion of their benefits presents many contradictions and dilemmas. These discrepancies and dilemmas are scarcely acknowledged and, when they are, frequently dismissed as necessarily tolerable irregularities and social inequalities.

This chapter examines critical concerns and dilemmas that arise in the pursuit of the liberalized knowledge-based economy and learning society in regard to work and education. These concerns affect the world of work and education in both similar and particular ways, all of which warrant specific attention. My discussion draws attention to general, overarching concerns that critically connect education and work. Orienting the discussion is a paramount concern for the dilemmas that arise for working people, for the majority of people who participate in education and training systems and who work in jobs traded in liberalized and dynamic labour markets. Workers, rendered employees in subordinated labour or, more commonly, as "human resources", are the living, personal subjects of the generalized policy pursuits and business firm demands. They bear, in their everyday working and learning lives, the brunt of the knowledge-based hyper-productivity and competitiveness drives. The dilemmas that arise for institutions arise, more personally, for them.

PARADOXES OF HIGHER-SKILLED ECONOMIES

There is no doubt that the education expansion, the technological acceleration and the liberalization of markets have brought considerable economic development and benefits. But that knowledge-based economy is far from universal and its distribution of benefits far from socially wide and inclusive. Policy drives toward a knowledge-based, continuously innovating and highly competitive economy produce increasingly discrepant outcomes. In the midst of conditions of increased levels of skills and qualifications among more adults in society, of rapid technological innovation, of new products and unprecedented expanse of markets and consumption behaviour, we witness disturbing paradoxes. The resurgence of the power of the firm in demanding and shaping the neo-liberal economy has won a substantive weakening, if not neutralization, of workers' power and rights. With weak trade unions and worker collectivities, workers experience greater exposure to the power of the firm and capricious markets and are confronted with simultaneous and contradictory demands. Workers are subjected to intensified managerial control over the organization of work and the determination of labour contracts and conditions. They are expected to be integrated into the firm's organization as human resources of knowledge and skill, to intensify their productivity and to accept managerially determined goals. At the same time they are expected to be flexible, mobile and agreeably compliant to employer-induced insecurities and the vagaries of human capital utility and accumulation. In consequence, we observe a loss of workers' participation in the organization and regulation of their work. We observe increased individualistic, competitive action, loss of intra-organizational trust and cooperation and diminished organizational cohesion. We witness, moreover, a condition of organized insecurity for wide sectors of workers and increased social inequalities in society more broadly.

In the sphere of education, we observe a policy drive toward an emphatic economic role of education and a severe reduction in its socio-cultural *raison d'être* and non-economic value. A policy programme of rationalization of education systems toward the logic of the corporate business firm under the guise of the "scientific episteme" advocated by knowledge economists is powerfully under way. The pursuit of models of education and training that are directed toward the needs of knowledge-intensive production and the satisfaction of employer and shareholder priorities and the competitive advantage of the firm pose considerable social risks, as well as individualized risks. As education institutions, especially the university, are brought into direct correspondence with economic imperatives, the state and employers retreat from funding the provision of higher-level skills. The means to participate in tertiary education and training is left in the hands of increasingly indebted individuals and families at the same time as qualifications acquisition is demanded by government policies and business interests for strategic and uncertain utilization. Moreover, and of another quality of import, the valorization of the scientific episteme and discrediting of other forms of knowledge narrow the social and cultural imaginary.

The expansion of knowledge- and skill-generating institutions has not, paradoxically, generated a democratization of distribution of higher knowledge forms and a general population-wide pursuit of cultural enrichment. At the same time as more people participate in post-compulsory education and training systems, we observe an attenuation of participatory democracy and increased social inequalities (OECD 2008b; 2009). Young people are entering labour markets with higher levels of qualifications and skills without the accompanying cultural development once expected of participation in higher education institutions. All of these developments raise pressing questions in regard to the social goods of work and education drafted into the service of corporate firm interests in a neo-liberalized knowledge-based economy. They raise substantive questions over wider purposes and practices of education for persons and society. And they raise questions in regard to the degree to which Western social democratic societies can, or ought to, tolerate the current conditions of work and workers, and the grossly distorted power of the firm. My approach to the discussion of these considerable questions – which the literature reveals to be extensively shared – focuses on clusters of thematic concerns. The first section focuses on work and workers and the second section on education.

CRITICAL CONCERNS FOR WORK AND WORKERS

Contingency, individualization and widened inequalities

The firm's adoption of flexible and contingent organizational structures extends to contingency and flexibility of employment relations. The firm's interest in flexible employment relationships lies in the increased capacities for control and strategic action in regard to organizational and market action. Flexible employment relations are characterized by individualization and weak contractual obligations. Weak contractual obligations typically include limited tenure (casualized, short-term, fixed or zero-hours contracts), attenuated conditions in regard to training or participatory avenues, and of employer contribution to pension schemes. Firms strive to employ on permanent contracts only the minimum number of workers. Employers, through strategic HRM practices, increase investment in sectors of workers at the centre of production activity. Other sectors of workers may be employed on contingent or fixed term contracts or "leased" through sub-contracting firms and subsidiaries. The more elite sectors of workers gain advantages and remuneration that widen conditions and wage gaps with other workers. Temporary contracts enable firms to externalize risk associated with retained labour.

A further feature of flexible employment relations, utilized as part of organizational structural contingency strategies, is the ability to re-structure jobs into modulated forms while maintaining continuous functional operation. Job modulation (often called fragmentation) breaks down conventional job structures into skill sets that can be deployed across similar tasks as contingently required. Differing from Fordist routinization of set tasks, modulation of jobs and skills enables employers to deploy workers to various functions or locations in ways that allow maximization of labour utility in regard to operational demand. It can enable employers to break work into shorter shifts and avoid payment for non-productive time (such as lunch breaks) or avoid retaining workers during less busy times of trading hours. For instance, the utilization of 4-hour shifts enables employers to deploy workers at busier times of the day, and maximize a worker's energy expenditure ("freshness") in a shorter shift and gain wage cost efficiencies.[1] Modulation impedes workers' efforts to construct coherence and intrinsic satisfactions in work and its potential sociality beyond the rudimentary and instrumental, as well as earning sustainable wages. Modulation normalizes casualization and worsens conditions for workers holding lower-skilled jobs – even as these lower skill levels are sufficient to operational demand. Researchers have observed a general trend toward an increase in flexible employment and fragmented jobs over recent decades. A growth in semi-formal and contingent work occurs alongside formal employment and regular jobs (Barbier and Lindley 2002; Bollier and Durand 1999; Felstead *et al.* 2002; Pfau-Effinger 2009).

For the firm, flexibility and freedom from conventional commitments to workers offer a distinct advantage. It enables strategic rationalizations, cost savings and risk management. Flexibility and contingency enable, in the midst of horizontal networking forms of business firms, intensified vertical integration of the organization and dispersion of risks. Flexible employment practices can benefit some sectors of workers, often women, for whom flexible or part-time work can enable more participation in the labour market and accommodation of other life commitments and values (Casey and Alach 2004). It can also benefit sectors of elite, highly skilled technical workers with enhanced capacities to negotiate fixed term contracts. But more generally, employer power in the application of flexible employment relations directly positions many sectors of workers in an involuntarily insecure relationship with their employers. As employers displace risk onto workers, workers are pressured to bear a much greater burden of actual or threatened insecurity.

Contingent and precarious jobs typically incur for workers reduced or negligible protection from exploitation. Contingent workers typically fall outside union capacities to collectivize and organize them, and they typically lack capacity to engage in direct negotiation with employers. The utilization of new organizational forms, subcontracting and subsidiaries, and fragmented employment relations enable both demand for intensification of workers' effort and fewer avenues for workers to participate in regulating workplace life, the organization of their work and negotiating their wages. Workers are pressured into risk-taking actions and toleration of deliberately birfurcated labour markets. The sectors of insecure and low-paid employment in the European Union are substantial. They show no signs of diminishing in size or significance (Barbier 2008; Gallie 2004; Streeck 2009).

Flexible individualization effects a powerful organized insecurity on workers. Contingent and precarious jobs lead to a more generalized precariousness for sectors of the population. Conditions of sustained low pay and precarious employment affect significant dimensions of a person's life, in addition to income. People holding temporary and intermittent jobs are at greater risk of poverty and social exclusion than those on continuous employment contracts (Debels 2008; Gallie 2004; Gray 2004). They are at greater risk of insecurity in regard to housing, family and relationship stability, and inclusion in basic social networks. Kalleberg (2009) reports on the manifold increase in mortgage foreclosure to which insecure workers are especially vulnerable. That social precariousness extends to poorer health, shorter life expectancies and risk of divorce (Esping-Andersen 2009). Moreover, the rise in flexible and temporary jobs and the individualization of employment contracts informs a general discourse in society that stimulates a climate of fear of uncertainty among workers. The concrete existence of temporary, contingent jobs as well as the fear among sectors of workers of employment precariousness and the social precariousness typically associated with transient work fuel an effect of lowering tolerable levels of wages and conditions even for those in permanent (or continuous) employment contracts (Barbier 2008). As Esping-Andersen (2009: 55–6) reports: "We are witnessing a tidal wave of rising income inequality ... With only one or two exceptions, all the OECD countries have experienced widening income differentials over the past decades; in some cases, like the UK and the US, dramatically so."

The insecure workforce that results is subject to further vulnerabilities and simultaneously to policy demands for their activation, skills acquisition and social inclusion. Policy response (European Commission 2007a, 2008a) to these concerns of social exclusion and poverty resulting from flexible labour markets and transitional workers proposes the notion of "flexicurity" – a notion intended to contain the negative externality of liberal corporate firm behaviour and workers' risks. The term "flexicurity" endeavours to link work and employment flexibility with workers' security of income and stability of life conditions. Developed primarily in Dutch and Danish employment regime contexts (Wilthagen and Tros 2004), flexicurity assumes that labour market and employer requirements for flexible, contingent jobs in dynamic and highly competitive markets will continue to expand. The thesis proposes a necessary trade-off of the secure employment relationship with one employer for serial employment on the flexible labour market more generally. However, while the Dutch and Danish best practice models emphasize a mutually reinforcing relationship between flexibility and security, the ways in which different countries and labour market institutions adopt flexicurity measures is highly variable (Muffels 2008).[2] Flexicurity is a neo-liberal response. At best, it might mitigate the worst of precariousness but it makes negligible demands of employers while maintaining their advantages secured under neo-liberal conditions. It retains inherent and grossly unequal risks for workers.

For workers, involuntarily rendered insecure as firms adopt contingency measures across many dimensions of organizational operations, the concomitant demand placed upon them in order to gain flexicurity is the requirement to achieve "employability". The premise of dispersed security – that is, security maintained not by stable employment at a living wage with one employer but through multiple, often simultaneous, employment relationships – is that workers will transition between jobs on a frequent basis. The ease of that, allegedly necessary, frequent transition depends on the worker's ability to acquire and maintain sufficient and appropriate skills. A worker must market her or his skills in a dynamic and highly uncertain labour market in order to achieve individual security. Insecure workers, whose jobs themselves are contingent because the firm cannot predict, or has no interest in assessing, their future requirement, are expected to possess knowledge that the firm does not have. The hypothesis of flexible security implicitly expects workers to predict which skills they ought to invest in, in order to compete with other contingent workers on the labour market. The notion of employability as a worker's responsibility to predict and invest accurately places an inordinate, manifestly unreasonable, burden on workers. At the same time it enables the firm to increase its rational contingency and avoid reasonable future projections and responsibilities. The risks incurred in opting for stability are freely displaced onto chance-taking workers. That burden increases pressures on young people to invest in higher education which in turn mass-produces degrees for their potential utility in winning jobs in a capricious labour market. This wildly unfair burden placed on workers is, or ought to be, an intolerable inequality in social democratic societies.

Problems of flexibility and the insecurity typically attendant on it are significant and pressing concerns. Their importance can tend to overshadow still other crucial concerns which are widely neglected in policy discourse and corporate firm behaviour. Salient among them is the problem of quality and its degradation.

Quality, intensification, voice

The immense influence of the rhetoric and projections of the demand for and advance of higher-skilled jobs across an imagined universalizing knowledge-based economy has brought about a normative belief and expectation that higher-skilled jobs will employ most people and be of higher quality. It is routinely expected that the knowledge-based economy brings a spread of "new standards for employment, based on responsibility, initiative, autonomy, and relational skills" (Salais 2003). In the midst of the successful uptake of this imaginary, the persistence of poor quality, and the deterioration of former qualities, are an ideologically hidden problem. The problem of poor quality jobs persists despite the rise in skill levels and assumptions of better quality, as heavy and dirty labour occupies a smaller sector of workers. Researchers report a decline in the quality of jobs across a wide spectrum of the labour market. Poor quality is evident even among securely employed workers. The concept of quality is measured on a range of variables that enables comparison with job quality in earlier post-war decades.

Francis Green's (2006) comprehensive study documents evidence and concerns in regard to a reduction of quality in the affluent economy. For Green, the problem of intensification of work under conditions of technological acceleration and increased managerial control looms large. Intensification means pressures to work harder and yield higher productivity.

> The intensification of work effort in many countries during the 1990s … has been a considerable blow to hopes of increasing the quality of work life in the current era of affluence in the Western industrialized world … Work intensification may be a source of economic growth for firms and nations, as well as a negative influence on the quality of work life.
>
> (ibid.: 84–5)

As well as the degradation of quality generated by intensification, researchers demonstrate a decline in the quality of contemporary work in terms of basic securities, protection and rights (Burchell *et al.* 2002; Edwards and Wajcman 2005; Kersley *et al.* 2006). Intensified managerial power alongside reduced trade union activity affects the effectiveness, or existence, of forms of worker participation in running the affairs of everyday life in workplaces. The weakening of workers' voice and avenues for participation enables organizational conditions which facilitate and normalize trends of a worsening of former qualities of workplace life. Prominently, trends toward longer working hours and expectations of workers' availability to attend to work demands (email, mobile messaging, etc.) even outside their contracted hours are increasingly normalized. Popularly expressed as the "time squeeze" or the "long work hours culture" (Burke and Cooper 2008), the experience of greater demands of working life and reduced participation in its regulation affect more sectors of workers than under Fordist regulatory regimes. Workers' reduced protection from organizational demands, production rationalizations and systems imperatives occurs as strategic managerial efforts bring more aspects of workers' "resources" under managerial control. Business literature reports ways in which "extra-role behaviour" can be elicited from workers, even those employed on temporary contracts with low employer commitment (Organ *et al.* 2006). Workers are pressured to be good "organizational citizens" and display commitment considerably beyond that which their employers accord to them.

Managerially determined strategic learning and knowledge legitimation selects and represses specific types of knowledge. While some types of advanced knowledge and skill are highly valuable and sought after by employers in the pursuit of innovative production and competitive advantage, other types of knowledge and skill are less desired and their expression curtailed or disciplined in the workplace. The knowledge and skills needed for workers to raise and negotiate worker interests, to participate in decision-making, to organize jobs and set goals are repressed in preference for managerial systems' control and command in flexibly bureaucratized work. Gallie's extensive research on quality of work reports a loss of workers' voice and discretion over their work and fewer opportunities for workers to participate in decision-making in their workplaces (Gallie *et al.* 1998; Gallie 2007). This diminished opportunity to effectively participate occurs across diverse industry sectors. Professional and university-educated workers who may gain greater quality of work tasks and application of higher-level skills are nonetheless subject to managerial conditions that diminish their professional expression. Their "quality of voice is weaker" (Gallie *et al.* 1998: 116). The extensive research respectively of Gallie, Boltanski and Chiapello (2007) and (Durand 2007), among others, indicates that the relationship between improved education and skill levels and greater professional control over organization and work is limited. Highly educated professionals and technical knowledge workers possessing crucial and highly tradable skills for application to innovation generation are nonetheless restricted in their organizational range of application as avenues of workplace participation and democratic governance structures are attenuated.

For many sectors of workers, skill containment and limited opportunities on the job frustrate their expectations of skill application, development and rewards in the workplace. Moreover, engagement in participatory and democratic forums in workplaces can enable workers, even in low-skill jobs that are ineluctably dull or dirty, to gain and practise wider social and political skills. That practice can provide workers with sources of social and personal development and of dignity and esteem. In a climate of managerially determined strategic learning, these opportunities for learning and knowledge are disfavoured and frequently eliminated in a course of intensified rationalization and technological efficiency. The loss of workers' quality of voice is ignored.

The patterns outlined above in regard to the quality of work occur, as Francis Green (2006) emphasizes, in the high skills, technologically rich sectors, just as readily as in more traditional sectors. The new technologies are biased in the direction of demanding higher skills levels which have typically been positively associated with higher degrees of worker and professional influence and discretion in the workplace. For some workers, those in possession of high-level skills and who are employed in production and organizational activities that utilize such skills, workplace life can be more engaging and satisfying. The ability to apply knowledge and skills and to participate in collaborative work teams, along with receiving higher wages and benefits, brings, for an elite sector of workers, general improvements to working life compared to those reported a generation ago. Nonetheless, recent research presents a picture of diminished worker discretion in workplace decisions, task design, performance targets and conduct of their daily work (Boltanski and Chiapello 2007; Gallie 2007; Kersley *et al.* 2006). Workers and researchers report working life conditions for those on continuing contracts are more demanding and more tightly controlled by employers than higher-skilled workers experienced in former decades (Durand 2007; Gallie *et al.* 1998; Gollac and Volkof 2000; Green 2006).

Seemingly paradoxically, at the same time as we witness the increase in flexibility and contingency, the decline in discretion is correlated with an increasing bureaucratization of work life. Increased bureaucratic control of functionally integrated, flexible organization systems wins, for the firm, increased worker conformity and subordination, and vertical structural integration. In neo-liberal techno-managerial discourse these are assumed as both increased efficiency and increased freedom of action by the firm.

Protection, subordination, regulation

The systematic deregulation of labour markets and the forceful weakening of social and cultural institutions in the regulation of work, most especially trade union and collective workers' associations, which have occurred in varying ways and at varying pace across the European model countries over the past two decades, have had extensive effects. In the place of worker collective bodies and representation, the firm asserts the practice of Human Resource Management (HRM). The remarkable ascendancy and cultural acceptance of the managerial technology of HRM at once obscure the strengthening of the power of the firm and the subordination of the workers. HRM's distinctive demand is of an individualization of workers that enables, through their de-collectivization, weakened power, voice and protection. Through that course, the firm's HRM practice strengthens workers' subordination and promotes their acculturation into the firm's centrally coordinated integration strategy. The integration of workers includes the necessity for workers to accept their subordination and utilization at managerial prerogative and, for many, a contingency of tenure and commitment. The managerial utilization of employees toward managerially defined goals is rendered logical and legitimate by a generalized subordination of workers to an asserted superordinate systems' rationality. The role of trade union representation and bargaining, where retained, is weakened or integrated into corporate firm goals.

HRM assumes unquestioned legitimacy as a morally neutral and rationally efficient in-firm practice in the regulation of employees. It is a technology that translates shareholder demands into micro-objectives for productivity and profit extraction. Worker re-subordination has increased the capacity of the firm to outsource or subsidiarize sectors of its workforce. Outsourcing enables a reduction, through subtle circumvention, of the constraints of forms of labour regulation especially "soft" laws. Work units that are of a small size are not required to have a works council and they are minimally unionized (Whittall *et al.* 2007). Workers employed through commercial contracts with subcontracting service agencies rather than through direct employment contracts are frequently excluded from coverage by collective agreements or on-site agreements. As well, these workers are "off the books" in regard to employer responsibility for sick leave or accident compensation. Multi-employer sites and fragmented work affect the practical adoption of EU labour laws and agreements, including those for gender equality in employment (Grimshaw *et al.* 2006; Marchington *et al.* 2005). The reduction in the role of worker representation and reach of bargaining weakens not only the expression of rights and capacities for workplace regulation. It weakens the role of non-firm sociocultural factors drawn from social life in civil society that can inform and humanize the regulation of work. Moreover, at the core of the knowledge-intensive production sectors themselves, the loss of participatory involvement in the regulation and management or work and production activity generates the loss of trust, collaborative behaviour and social capital necessary for the stimulation of employer-demanded innovation and workplace congeniality. For other sectors of workers, domination by the firm of the terms and contexts in which work life may be negotiated excludes their voice altogether.

The firm-engineered weakened social institutions in the regulation of work render individualized workers vulnerable to extensive powers of the firm. As well as the heightened risk of precariousness through flexible organizational structures and contingent demand for skills, neo-liberalized employment relations have made it possible for firms and labour markets to exclude from stable employment – and the benefits that accompany such stable employment – sectors of workers who are the least qualified, the least adaptable (according to employers' terms) and the least adjustable to pressures for geographic or industry mobility. Boltanski and Chiapello (2007) propose that these forces have been depicted in management literatures as attributable to a process of "natural selection" in which the fittest workers survive in the new labour market conditions in which, it is alleged, there is not a job for every person who wants one. The researchers point out, however, that contrary to this attribution to abstract forces, employers have actively restructured jobs in ways that reduce the quantity of full-time and fully-benefited jobs in order to pay for only directly productive time. The definition of what a job is has changed considerably over the past two decades. That practical, empirical change is not mirrored in policy models and abstract discussions on work which fail to grasp workers' lived experiences of the everyday realities of work. The link between organizational innovations and employment policy is one characterized by employer selectivity that directly affects a polarization in labour markets.

Among serious concerns about the dismantling of protection and construction of vulnerability and the firm's re-regulative power, there is a further concern. The powerful subordination and integration of worker collectivities, especially trade unions, pressure those institutions into a subservient and collaborative role with firms. That occurrence reveals and intensifies the deep embedding of elite corporate firm demands for overarching power and normative legitimacy. It presents a social problem, for democratic societies, of considerable magnitude. The state moves to act for the power of elites, corporate firms and shareholders against provision and respect for negotiated power relations with organized class interests, especially those of workers and the socially marginalized. In so doing, macroeconomic policy-making becomes institutionally insulated from real political life among a wide social public. That development proposes a momentous movement away from a European social model with a heritage of seeking politically negotiated socio-economic regulation.

Disparagement of ordinary work

The manifest limits to the capacities of knowledge-economy firms to absorb the higher numbers of skilled workers who have entered the labour market in recent decades are seldom recognized in policy discourse. In the course of that under-recognition and continued policy pressure for high-level skills acquisition and pursuit of knowledge-rich jobs and their higher social status, a cultural reaction unfolds. The political elevation of the knowledge-based economy and its accompanying pressures on working populations have effected a distinct tendency toward the disparagement of ordinary, moderately skilled and lower-skilled work. The intense policy pressure on individuals to gain higher-level skills for higher productivity jobs has intersected with earlier promoted values in the education expansion that champion the intelligence and learning potential of ordinary people who had historically been excluded from participation in higher education. That promotion of intelligence and demand for betterment has seen educationists similarly extol, on behalf of the excluded ordinary people, the aspirations and opportunities for gaining higher-skilled jobs and their associated rewards. The intersection of these cultural advocacies has generated both demand for entry into higher-skilled jobs and – often unwittingly – a disparagement of those jobs, and workers, deemed lower-skilled and of lower productivity.

The evident discrepancies in the labour market's capacity to utilize and reward skill-upgraded workers pose immediate issues in regard to skill and job matching. The economic retention of relatively low-productivity sectors in which neither high-level skills nor substantial productivity gains are expected is rational and predictable. The aims in the production of these sectors, typically in the services, are to minimize labour costs, maintain production efficiencies and compete on price. These production and labour market practices, as discussed in Chapter 5, show that organizations utilize workers' skills in ways that enable the company to deploy or stockpile skills for strategic utility. Skill sets are retained at low price in order to maximize profitable return for the firm. Retaining routinized, lower-skilled jobs enables lower wage costs and efficient sorting systems for as many types of employees as possible. In the midst of repeated policy and demand by the firm for higher-level skills, despite the erratic utilization of those higher skills, firms gain a further exploitative advantage. In addition to the advantages of stockpiling skills and lowering the premium for skills, firms are able to use the normative demand for higher skills to further strengthen and normalize their superior power over workers. That enables a further reduction of wage costs for the firm and degraded conditions for significant sectors of workers.

Exploiting the normative demand for higher-level skills enables the firm to act toward its workforce to utilize employee sorting on a wider range of desirable employability measures. Large firms, or their agents, now commonly deploy psychometric testing in the selection of new workers, and the sorting of existing ones (Boltanski and Chiapello 2007). That action enables firms to selectively remove employment sectors of workers with lower skill levels or lower capacities to integrate and comply with restructured organizations. Those selected-out workers, who are likely to be older and immigrant (or, as Boltanski and Chiapello, demonstrate, politically active or "old-style" trade unionists), are then at risk of a wider social exclusion or of relegation to lower-skilled jobs. Those lower-skilled jobs are at the same time subject to employers' low commitment and deliberate neglect of quality. Poor quality jobs marketed for desperate workers in turn fuels a disparagement of the work performed in those jobs. The work itself, which is otherwise ordinary work for ordinary workers, could be made decent and respectable if the job structure and relations were not deliberately impoverished. The implementation of policies for labour activation exerts intense pressure on sectors of the working classes to participate in employment even as firms' selection criteria actively exclude them. Workers, urged by governments to take insecure and poorly constructed jobs to maintain their flexicurity, are forced to comply with the firm's prerogative to exploit de-collectivized labour.

Economically low productivity, low-skilled and lower culturally valued sectors include traditional sectors of labouring, agriculture, manufacturing, routine processing, transportation, delivery, retail and warehousing. They also include jobs – typically with traditional origins but often undertaken within the large firm or household – which are regarded as comprising "new" services in expanded custodial, security and maintenance, food and hygiene services, hospitality and personal services, entertainment and sport services. The old and new jobs in these sectors have been systematically subject to declined or stagnated wage rates and increased employer flexibility in their structure and employment relations. The discursive depiction of these diverse jobs as low skilled[3] renders them vulnerable to the disparagement of a wide populace. That cultural disparagement has been encouraged by the knowledge-based economy rhetoric that demands increased higher techno-scientific skills across the population, irrespective of their utilization.

In the midst of a policy-cajoled majority of people striving to compete in the knowledge-based economy sectors, the routine, daily provision of necessary services and products by a majority of moderately and lower-skilled workers is typically ignored. Yet, despite their low economic and cultural value, many of these jobs remain vitally socially necessary. In the prevailing climate of a distorted, hyper-emphasis on knowledge-rich jobs, the lower economic productivity of these ordinary jobs has enabled a discursively forged refusal of cultural recognition of their worth and social value. Socially and culturally undervalued jobs provide vital everyday services and products that are utilized by workers in the higher-skilled, more highly valued sectors and by a wider general public in society. The workers performing ordinary, socially necessary, jobs are subject to implicit or overt cultural disparagement for their failure to gain higher skills and win "better jobs". It is unreasonable and mistaken to advocate the up-skilling of lower productivity jobs beyond a certain general level of efficiency and congeniality. But it is equally and profoundly unfair to blame workers in these lower-skilled jobs for their "skills deficiency" as the reason for their exclusion from knowledge-intensive sectors. The cultural disparagement of ordinary work further permits employers to persist in the degradation of ordinary work through deliberate construction of poor quality, coercively managed and grossly exploitative jobs.

Casualized, poorly paid, highly rationalized and socially impoverished and fragmented "dead-end" jobs are taken by the poor, by migrant workers, and by transient workers, including students, hoping to "escape" them in the future. Disparagement devalues workers and weakens the basis for satisfaction and solidarity. Combined with weakened protection, vulnerability to insecurity and precariousness, pressured to maintain their employability and flexicurity, and disparaged for not winning higher-skilled jobs, workers in many ordinarily skilled jobs face grossly impoverished social conditions. Their weakened status discretely enables employer irresponsibility, poor commitment and further degradation of the quality and dignity of lower-skilled work and workers.

The discursive disparagement of jobs that necessarily require ordinary levels of skills and a mixture of basic training and craft experience serves to discourage people from taking jobs in these sectors, even though they remain relatively labour-intensive and regular features of the labour market. Trade union efforts to affirm and protect workers' rights and dignity in all socially necessary work – even that which contains unavoidable unattractive features such as being dirty, unpleasant to the senses, physically demanding or mentally unstimulating – through demands for decent work are undermined. The causalization of many jobs in these sectors enables them to fall out of range for union organizing, solidarity and protection. That extreme individualization against the collective power of the firm further undermines workers' attempts to find value, dignity and social respect in performing their jobs and in striving for responsibility and participation in their design and management.

Academic and social commentary literature frequently assumes that the cure for "dead-end" jobs is to provide more education and training to persons holding those jobs rather than to contest the assumption that such ordinary, lower productivity jobs may be culturally permitted to be cast-off as dead-end. Literatures on welfare, social exclusion, work and education typically focus on skills development for individuals at risk of social exclusion. The focus is on enabling individuals to seek skills and "better types of work" that would provide "better long-term opportunities" (European Commission 2005b). It is always the individual worker who is pressured to seek training and to find a "better employment situation". The imagined route to betterment is through individual development. The neo-liberal institutional arrangements that allow poor quality jobs and unregulated, grossly exploitative working conditions are exempted from equally moralizing imperatives to improve. Yet, bad jobs being offered to poor and transient workers remain profitable to some employers. Bad jobs persist even if some individual workers are policy-assisted and welfare-assisted to find personal escape from them. Workers who take these employer-created bad jobs are then blamed for their personal deficiency and poor choices. Policy and academic discourse repeatedly emphasize workers' "skills deficiency". In so doing, blame for that deficiency is placed on workers and education and training systems, and employers' negligence in the creation of poor jobs persists without sanction. This easy targeting of blame readily enables employers to escape responsibility and moral opprobrium that is so readily directed to subordinated workers.

The policy promotion of a liberalized knowledge-based economy and extensive prerogatives in the firm's managerial, technical and political control of work and production have brought about a serious paradox: conditions of degradation, insecurity and distortion of cultural value occur in the midst of increasing productivity and consumption. Higher-skilled workers are compensated for these losses and trade-offs by the persuasion of increased consumption. Those holding lower-skilled jobs are differentiated and controlled by fear of precariousness and lack of collective protections – even as they too are encouraged to fuel production through their consumption behaviour often wildly beyond their incomes.

The International Labour Organization's (2001) campaign for "Decent Work", although not primarily aimed at a cultural valuing of ordinary work, takes up some response to the socio-cultural undervaluing and poor treatment of vast sectors of human work and workers. Decent work means that work that meets a social necessity or cultural value, whatever its intrinsic nature in terms of physical effort, sensory unpleasantness or unavoidable risk (sewerage works, mining, soldiering) can be rendered decent and acceptable to those who perform it and to their fellow citizens who benefit from its provision. The ILO has, necessarily, focused extensive effort in improving work and employment in the less developed countries and regions of the world. The conditions which I have elaborated suggest that it must extend demands for decency into the advanced, rich countries of Europe. That demand further exposes the catastrophic consequences of the dissolution of socially controlled capitalism forged in the European model countries in the mid-twentieth century.

CRITICAL CONCERNS AND DILEMMAS FOR EDUCATION

Education is a multifaceted good that accrues both private and public goods. There have always been quasi-market features of education. But it has also been widely assumed that education serves cultural values and ends that cannot be reduced to the economic. That assumption has in recent years been called into question. Renewed debate on the values of education, most especially higher education, animates education and economic discussion. There is little doubt at the present time that economic and market aspects of education have intensified and, many fear, now predominate. The intensive policy focus on education in the course of a general policy imperative in pursuit of the knowledge-based economy and human capital development affects the social and cultural practices of education in unprecedented ways. The intensification of market action and elite demands in education risks a severe marginalization of non-economic, cultural goods of education for wider society. It poses a far-reaching transformation of universities, and a truncation of lifelong learning into a singular rationale of job skills training.

Education in its academic research and practitioner dimensions, as analysts note (Tight 2004), frequently displays an insularity and abstraction from social and economic contexts. The traditional fields and scope of education research, which remains highly important in their own right, have affected a limited reach of social research on education. The relatively small field of social analysis of education has remained marginal to the mainstream of interests in educational research. That delimitation has widened a gap between the academy and the polity. The tendency toward educational institutional insularity, in which education researchers and practitioners predominantly focus on sub-disciplinary problems, has, unwittingly, affected a more general weakness of education as a socio-cultural institution to fully recognize and respond to the techno-science and economic agenda. Among educationists, there has frequently been a predisposition to regard the heightened policy attention to education and education expansion as good for education as traditionally understood in education circles.

The economic incursion reveals a composite set of overarching imperatives. The first of these is the pressure on education institutions to expand and reform practices in accordance with the macroeconomic objectives: mass generation of higher skills, vastly expanded techno-scientific knowledge and innovation capacities, efficiency and rationalization, and heightened market competitiveness. The second is the imperative to increase population participation in formal education, and to increase the length of time individuals spend in formal education and training. Individuals are policy-instructed to take personal responsibility for the alleged "skills deficit" in the economy and among the population. The third is the imperative to shape education institutions into what economists call the scientific episteme and cement education's subordination to economic authoritarianism. A fourth imperative is the shaping of citizens into working, learning, producer–consumers similarly subordinated to economic authoritarianism. In the course of this sweeping agenda, education, as a socio-cultural good with potential to reach beyond modern material knowledge, risks a long eclipse.

The discussion below focuses on a summary of key clusters of concerns and dilemmas. The first set of concerns focuses particularly on internal effects within the education sphere, especially higher education and lifelong learning. Following that are concerns for individual students and families; and third, those for education in society more broadly. All of these concerns and dilemmas overlap to various extents. Drawing out their particular aspects enables a stronger grasp of the considerable social problems arising from the sweep of neo-liberal policies and their economic authoritarianism currently in effect.

CONCERNS FOR THE UNIVERSITY

A burgeoning debate in higher education circles addresses diverse aspects of the new pressures on higher education systems, especially universities. Of course, there are observable national differences. But a more general current of change effected by neo-liberalization displays significant general tendencies. Universities have embarked on processes of reform in accordance with the objectives of mass expansion, marketization and entrepreneurialism. Economic benefits of these reforms undoubtedly accrue to certain sectors and interests in society. But the transformation of the institution of the university in accordance with the demands of a neo-liberal knowledge-based economy policy has far-reaching social and cultural consequences and costs. The epistemological shift of university education, scholarship and research portends a fundamental alteration of the imagined ideal and character of the university and its socio-cultural goods. For many critics, the scale of the expansion and reform programme is seen as nothing less than a social transformation of the university and of the role of higher education in society (Henkel and Little 1999; Scott 2004). That transformation attenuates, or discards outright, the classical values of the university and its forms of education and knowledge.

Critics contend that higher education is in a state of crisis and degradation. University systems are under the sway of a destructive and rampant "new managerialism" (Deem *et al.* 2007) and marketization that alters the cultural character and professional practices of higher education. Many see a globalization of "academic capitalism" (Jessop *et al.* 2008; Slaughter and Leslie 1997) and the marginalization of higher education's inherited ideal of *Bildung* as instrumental rationalities prevail (Jarvis 2001; Peters 2007). Even among those who point out that the classical *Bildung* imaginary was always an elite, conservative and exclusive one, there is much agreement that the new university system with its profound political economy policy influence leaves little trace of the values of that model that had richly informed the modern university. Critics see the "death of the university" (Readings 1996), its "McDonaldization" (Hayes and Wynyard 2002) and its "corruption" (Hussey and Smith 2009).

The elite model, which radical reformers had hoped to democratize in a socially necessary and culturally liberating expansion of universities to historically excluded classes, has instead been powerfully guarded and retained for a powerful few. The educational experience for the majority of people participating in university education is far from that of a democraticized elite model. The economic utility and rationalization agenda and mass expansion have forged the ascendancy of technical and vocational education over liberal and general education and occlusion of cultural knowledge pursuits. The marginalization or exclusion of liberal arts education robs the majority of students of richer cultural values and experiences of university education.

The commodification of knowledge, much criticized in theoretical treatises (Foucault 1972; Lyotard 1984) and earlier taken up in North American critical sociologies of education, extends to the rationalization of degree programmes and structure, of teaching methods and pedagogical relationships. Massified and highly rationalized universities have retreated from providing students and faculty with the relationships once imagined of a community of scholars in shared pursuit of higher knowledge. European universities have begun to adopt a modular degree structure. Echoing the modulation of jobs, modular degree programmes provide students with discrete, short courses of learning and skills sets that can be easily measured and priced. Modular degree programmes also enable institutions to rationalize their teaching which includes increased use of contract teachers who are disengaged from research activity. Modulation of knowledge packages, which may contain little or no cumulative progression of knowledge complexity, enables students to be processed more efficiently.

Students and teachers become positioned in commercial forms of relationship that militate against the formation of pedagogical relationships of teaching and learning. Practices of close pedagogical relationships between teachers and students in which advanced students are apprenticed or mentored into the craft of academic and scientific knowledge have virtually collapsed, or are retained only in the elite universities which are able to maintain a privileged resistance to the reforms of massification and rationalization (Trow 2006). In place of those relationships are efficiency rationalizations in which students are processed through frequently impersonal teaching and learning experiences in a context of market competitiveness between individuals and institutions of higher education. Students are not infrequently depicted as customers, degrees as products, teachers as client managers and employees of a corporate business operation (Hayes and Wynyard 2002; Hussey and Smith 2009).

The modulation of the degree structure and alteration of pedagogical relationships in mass qualifications production also allows universities to intensify research productivity, which they are simultaneously policy-pressured to do. That in turn leads to a separation of research functions from formerly closely related teaching functions in the overarching pursuit of higher knowledge. The heightened role of entrepreneurialism in both research activity and in marketing to new student populations, which includes stimulating a global market of international students for European universities, accelerates the industrial reform of the university. The features that have accompanied mass expansion, entrepreneurialism and business model rationalization alter and transform the design, rationale and quality of university education. Critics argue that these reforms have effected a general lowering of academic standards, a neglect or obsolescence of non-economic knowledge, and a distinct attenuation of the cultural capacities of universities through the course of their capitulation to commercial and instrumental imperatives (Corbett 2005; Mazza *et al.* 2008; Peters 2007).

For many university academics, formed in or influenced by the legacy of the elite cultural ideals of the university and their democratization, the corporate changes to the university qualitatively alter their professional roles and identities. The introduction of new public management and non-participatory hierarchies of decision-making contrasts sharply with the participatory, collegial and inefficient methods of the university imagined as a professional community of variously conflicting and consensual colleagues. The radically intrusive alterations in professional relations of trust, scientific integrity, professional self-regulation and self-identity contradict and undermine forms of academic research practice and scholarship (Deem *et al.* 2007; Dent and Whitehead 2002; Peters 2007). Collegial relations of trust and accountability, that do not readily yield to numerical accountability measures, are transformed into competitive interactions and managerial surveillance. Their incursion brings about a dramatic alteration to the value and esteem of academic work. That alteration and loss of academic capital further occur as the universities pursue business relationships with other actors in its increasingly competitive market environment and reduced state funding provision.

In the course of gaining resources from non-governmental sources, including through increased student fees, and income generation through business partnerships and contracted research programmes, the entrepreneurial university increases its adoption of corporate behaviour and structures and fractures its traditional relationships with society and culture. The university pursues its market actions, corporate organizational agendas and techno-business while putting at risk or openly relegating the quality of educational experience and outcomes for students. In so doing, the university's actions are producing increased inequalities in educational outcomes for students. Historically elite institutions, of which there were and remain very few, in their cultural refusal to massively expand, retain higher qualities and standards enabled through elite pedagogical and apprenticeship relationships and forms of curricula (Brown and Hesketh 2004; Dalton *et al.* 2009).

For the mass of universities competing among themselves, rationalization and commodification appear inescapable. The commodification of teaching disconnects the production of knowledge from its transfer and stifles participatory debate over its constitution. In addition, the heightened emphasis on producing publication outputs and on economically relevant research has led the university to privilege research productivity and its management and to relegate teaching to an inferior role. Intense emphasis on economic capital accumulated through research productivity and performance impact on the university's market generates over-specialization, problem-oriented and short-term research programmes. A publications industry, already led by Anglophone institutions, is spreading across European universities. Its advance takes over university professional life and encourages accumulation of products of little or no relevance to students and teaching. The production of ever-increasing volumes of frequently non-cumulative research, of outputs that do not add value to scientific scholarly debate but rather just add quantity of calculative pieces of information, and pressures on academics to compete for grant funds, further reduce commitments to scholarship and high quality teaching. In this situation, it is not surplus value that is being extracted, it is rather, as Foucault (1980) proposed, surplus discourse production that the knowledge industrialization of the university produces. Even as university critics have been protesting at these occurrences for decades, for knowledge economists, however, surplus discourse production is not only inevitable, it is a constituent of the search for economic capital through competitive innovation and new products.

The university's progressive assimilation into the corporate order and relegation of its historical cultural *raison d'être* places the university at grave risk of losing its unique identity, moral purpose and socio-cultural role. A chief dilemma for the university is one in which it appears forced to ensure its institutional survival through the adoption of corporate firm objectives and behaviour as its political masters have instructed it to do. Or attempt to refuse that political-economic command and risk retracted resources and marginalization in a predominantly marketized world. Yet the price of its survival requires transformation of its once fundamental character. If the university aspires to maintain its traditional ethos of education as principally for cultural and human development and to assert counter-economic rationalities of the irreducibility of that good, it may find its cultural high ground swept away in a much wider tide of commoditization and market competitiveness. The university transformed in this way becomes incapable of recognizing the moral goods of the classically idealized university.

DILEMMAS FOR STUDENTS

Policy pressure for mass expansion of higher education institutions is accompanied by similar pressures on young people to participate in higher education. Mass expansion of provision and participation gains normative public expectation of participation beyond compulsory and state-funded education while at the same time demanding that participants – students and their families – bear the greater burden of its costs. Students' participation in higher education is policy-promoted as the means to maximize their chances of securing jobs and advancing knowledge-based economy dispersion. Students are increasingly pressured to bear the costs of their education and training, while at the same time tolerating erratically unpredictable rates of return from their future labour market participation. They must bear disproportionate costs, in comparison to employers who have successfully offset the costs of skill provisions to the state and to individual workers, of their policy-driven increased participation in higher education. Public funding of universities has considerably declined as a share of higher education revenues as the mass expansion has taken place (Delanty 2001; Hussey and Smith 2009; Mazza *et al.* 2008). Increased student enrolment is achieved at lower national costs to public funds and to industry.

Students must take their chances on the education market in the hope that they will gain skills that employing organizations *may* employ. The uncertainty of the employability and durability of specific skill sets encourages the expansion of the educational provision of various vocational and general skills courses that providers propose will provide marketable skills and indicative qualifications. Yet educational institutions design those programmes with little or severed linkage to industry bodies which had formerly been closely associated with skills formation systems (Crouch 2005b). That institutional knowledge gap incurs, in consequence, increased risk and chance-taking on students' skills investment.

Despite the normative appeal of mass participation in higher education and training, its actual occurrence is not producing a mass distribution of favourable results or a narrowing of social inequalities. Rather than bringing about a true democratization of distribution of higher education and skills, massification proletarianizes the majority of higher education institutions and enables old class-based establishments to reassert their elite differences. The elite institutions have largely resisted expansion – except to international elites – and retain their prestigious positions on the basis of received cultural capital and the continuity of high competition for entry. Mass participation occurs in second tier institutions and especially among students from middle-class backgrounds. Improved participation by students from working-class families remains disproportionately lower than that of students from middle-class and professional families (Ball 2008; Brown and Hesketh 2004; Wolf 2002). Where persons from those traditionally disadvantaged backgrounds do participate, as they are policy-pressured to do, it is in lower rate institutions which preserve their disadvantage. In the UK, ranking systems of higher education institutions inspire keen competitiveness and marketing strategies among institutional providers. In other national systems, such as France and Germany, persistent attachment to unreformed elite demarcations similarly stratifies students and ranks their qualification outcomes (Mazza *et al.* 2008).

In the midst of massification and widened participation, higher education is being re-mobilized to serve and reproduce elite class interests. Students from middle-class and working-class backgrounds are encouraged to purchase higher education participation while persistently excluded from entry into the elite institutions. Their participation, nonetheless, manifestly more so than that of upper middle-class students, constitutes a gamble on their labour market chances for higher-skilled jobs and rewards. The university "knowledge products" being offered to mass entry students are frequently techno-science skills generic, often devoid of cultural "extras", of reflection and discussion of ideas, of permissive intellectual exploration, and of competencies in social criticism and development. Robbed of these educational goods, students are nonetheless disciplined into taking on private debt to fund their participation in universities as qualifications-providing authorities. More recently, students encounter the additional pressure to enhance their job prospects, as their mass degrees lose wage premium, by taking up unpaid internships with employers. Employers, having won the demand for mass increases in skills, persist in claiming a skills deficit even as tertiary-qualified young people cannot find matching jobs (Brown *et al.* 2008). At the same time, the expansion of poor quality, "dead-end" jobs permitted by labour market liberalization and corporate firm skill-sorting utility, intimidates young people into seeking to avoid those disparaged and wilfully impoverished jobs. To escape that fate, young people take on debt burdens to gain university qualifications in the hope that they will personally avoid working in dead-end jobs.

A further concern arises as the neo-liberal state withdraws responsibility for funding the provision of higher education. The state proposes that its retreat will stimulate market action, including students as market actors, to fulfil that function. At the same time, the state has withdrawn regulatory constraints on action by the firm to influence and structure its labour markets and wage levels. The dramatically uneven flexibility, and the widespread lowering or stagnation of wages that has resulted, are assumed to be absorbed by individuals with considerably weakened capacities and protection by the welfare state. That paradox confronts students and their families with a daunting dilemma. The core of that dilemma lies in the risks of purchasing higher education while the uncertain labour market utility and remuneration of those skills, and the variable quality of cultural added-value of the contemporary university experience, may not offset the financial debts incurred. In the course of the mass, business-like provision, students are provided with skills and qualifications while frequently being deprived of the cultural development and personal enrichment insistently retained by the privileged elite universities.

SOCIAL DILEMMAS

Concerns about the future prospects for the cultural quality of universities and the role and value of universities in society are myriad. In addition to the concerns sketched above, are questions in regard to the university's role in serving a public good. The emphasis on entrepreneurial competitiveness, on industry relevance of research and knowledge production, and on international marketing of universities degree products to diverse global populations of consumers alters the relationship of the university in its historical role of service to the public good, or the "good society" (Inglis 2004). The apparent shift in the public good of the university toward an emphasis on private goods and returns occurs as the market and corporate interests play an unprecedented role in the regulation of higher education. The policy-imagined globalization of the knowledge-based economy is accompanied by a movement to globalize the university enterprise disengaged from a public and a conception of public good. Corbett's (2005: 192) study of universities in Europe under the policy imperatives of the knowledge-based economy presents findings that lead to an overarching critical question: "Will universities continue to be seen as a public good or will their prime characteristic be their contribution to Europe's competitiveness?"

There remains a high social and public good attached to a general upgrading of skills across the population. A learning society is made up of learning individuals and the aggregate increase in skilled workers and knowledge-intensive production generates greater opportunity for innovation and competitive advantage. Yet, across the OECD countries, there have been evident trends toward increased privatization of education and training provision and individual responsibility for its access and consumption (Brown *et al.* 2001; Mazza *et al.* 2008). At the same time, employers and firms decline to take up roles in the provision of generalized labour market skill improvements for which they refuse any responsibility. Intensified pressure is placed on individuals, families, and education institutions in business partnerships to provide, through market action, socially desired education and skills training required of the knowledge-based economy. The promotion of education as a social and personal good, that is at once a crucial rudiment of individual life chances and of social cohesion, yet that is available predominantly through market action, poses a serious contradiction for European model social democracies.

Education has long been valued as a multifaceted good of much more than economic utility for persons, firms and society. Its provision and participation contribute vital and irreducible social goods that cannot be provided by market action. Under neo-liberal capitalism and the policy discourse of the knowledge-based economy, these plural goods of education are relinquished to the market and corporate firm action. That gross marketization which undermines socio-cultural purpose and value is, or ought to be, untenable in social democratic societies. In the course of these developments, critics argue that a globalization of higher education adopts an "Americanization" of higher education values and practices (Borghans and Cörvers 2009). That "Americanization" is seen not as the American elite model that leads the world in quality and outcomes for an elite few. It is an Americanization of higher education that is overtly marketized and heavily reliant on private funds and corporate interests. The European model, which has predominantly relied on state funding and a social good agenda has now embarked, through its Bologna Agreement, on the adoption of American models in the course of its pursuit of the liberal knowledge-based economy (Robertson 2008; Robertson and Keeling 2008; Shattock 2009).

As higher education becomes widely marketized and oriented toward competitiveness in a global economy, its connection to societies in which non-economic values and aspirations may be expressed and pursued is fragmented. Notions of the "good society" in cultural and societal models may lose meaning and relevance in what some see as the "postmodern university" of the current age (Scott 2004). In taking this step, the university abrogates its socio-cultural role as conscience and critic of society. Its source of critical ideas and moral perspectives on which societies and cultures may draw and develop is subordinated to techno-science and market innovations. There is no place within the university of the modern scientific episteme for questions to be asked, and recognized, that enquire into non-scientific reason and forms of knowledge. The exclusive humananism of modern knowledge forms (Taylor 1989) forecloses that space. The university's neo-capitulation to the demands of resurgent elite interests poses serious social concerns.

The university's assimilation into the corporate order elides cultural and economic capital into economic capital. In that course, the corporate firm's assertion that its interests be privileged over all other claims on the university in society is triumphant. The corporate order's demand for the university's compliance with its agenda for the generation of competitive techno-scientific knowledge powerfully combines with the demand of old elite universities to refuse a democratization of their cultural goods for the socio-cultural benefit of the many. In the course of this twin action, the university rescinds residual moral claims to serve the public good.

EDUCATION AS ECONOMIC POLICY

Higher education has captured the lion's share of economic policy interest in education's rich goods. In the wake of that interest, lifelong learning has been transposed to refer to work-skills learning and re-training. Its activities in regard to social and cultural development for individuals and communities have been marginalized. As well, attention to early childhood education has relatively declined and its funding and promotion neglected. As Esping-Andersen (2009: 140–1) demonstrates, there is a disproportionate neglect of early childhood education: "human capital investments have, over the past half century, been almost exclusively directed at formal education ... Educational investment in the under-3's is truly marginal." Moreover, parents are emphatically encouraged to participate in labour markets and place young children in the care of childcare workers who frequently lack formal education in child development. The provision of quality childcare is available only to those who can afford its costs. For the majority, that policy neglect leaves too many children in the care of under-educated and under-funded childcare workers. The welfare and learning development of children show class-patterned distortions that indicate a renewed process of class reproduction which, in the post-war decades, had been interrupted.

Education institutions that relinquish their socio-cultural values and distinctive realm deprive all of us of non-economic forms of social and cultural participation. Nonetheless, as education now becomes a strategic arm of macroeconomic policy, education is given a new moral project. That project, which draws heavily on the moral foundations of social democratic lifelong learning ideals developed in the 1970s for human development and character enrichment, differs distinctly from that of progressive education. The new moral project for education, evident since the 1990s, is aimed at shaping a neo-liberal solution to the crisis in the European welfare state. Social policy has shifted emphasis on distribution of welfare and equality of opportunities to an emphasis on individual responsibility for inclusion and participation through employment. Individual participation in education and training systems is policy-theorized as the master key to maintaining a person's "employability" and "flexicurity".

Under "activation" polices of "employability", individuals are expected, and normatively extolled, to invest in themselves as productive agents; to invest in their human capital in order to improve their capacities for successful market participation. The political commitment to employability coincides with pressures on education institutions to adapt to efficiency and market demands. Policies for activation, labour market and education participation are dispersed through economic policy agenda as an effective substitute for social policy.

In concrete terms, employability refers to a person's competency to gain and maintain sufficient skill levels in order that she/he will successfully transition from one job to another in flexible labour markets and avoid unemployment. Persons are expected to personally avoid having to take up jobs in low-skilled and low productivity sectors even as these jobs remain core constituents of contemporary economies. Participation in education and training, especially that undertaken by workers and young school leavers, is intended to ensure access to knowledge-rich jobs that are purportedly expanding at pace. The policy effort to shift responsibility for labour market participation to individuals in the form of "employability" through a person's gaining of appropriate education and skills as capacities for successful labour market participation signifies a significant reorientation of social policy (Streeck 2006). This significant shift marks the new configuration of economic policy, education policy and social policy that is evident in the European Union's Lisbon strategy and its successor *Europe 2020*. Maintaining one's employability is upheld as a duty of citizenship.

Education is now tasked, in that vein, with the political project of citizenship formation (European Commission 2005c, 2007b). The project of citizenship formation is aimed at reducing social exclusion and promoting economic and social participation and cohesion. It therefore has much appeal and much promise. Yet a closer look at the rudiments of the concept of citizenship being imagined reveals the further influence of a macroeconomic perspective. The socially included citizen is one who maintains her or his employability through gaining and maintaining marketable skills and smooth transfer between jobs. Persons failing to accomplish employability risk social exclusion and weak citizen rights. Education, in addition to providing labour market-oriented and lifelong learning workers for the needs of a highly competitive economy, is simultaneously directed to provide citizen-workers newly shaped to be self-reliant, chance-taking, individualized and competitive, who are increasingly independent of a shrinking welfare state.

The neo-liberal policy programme of higher-skilled and re-moralized citizen-workers carries immense and far-reaching political implications. Among them are social and personal dilemmas in regard to societal reproduction. The production of children is, of course, excluded from economic calculus. However, economic and policy-making attention now takes a keen interest in societal reproduction as the problem of low birth rates affecting European welfare states is latterly recognized. The resolution of that problem is implicitly being articulated with yet further demands on the younger generation. Young people, burdened with the demands and debt of skills investments, are simultaneously in the moral scope of policy-makers who hope they will adjust the child-deficit problem of the aging societies of Europe in the coming decades (a matter for which discussion in this book must be deferred).

Education is tasked with a highly ambitious agenda: it is expected to return both financial and social benefits to individuals and to national economies, at the same time as it expected to provide substitution for distributive social policy. Many citizens also wish to see the university maintain its historically unique role in the pursuit of the highest cultural debates and artistic standards as irreducible social goods. Or, at least, they wish to see retention of its role in the dissemination of civilized social attitudes, socially inclusive behaviour and cohesive toleration. Lifelong learning educators continue to cherish the social goals of education for diverse life interests throughout the life-course. The aggressive corporatization and marketization now shaping the character education institutions, especially the university, undermine and may defeat those aspirations. The concurrent weakening of other sources of social participation and civilization as workplaces are rationalized away from valuing such qualities exposes the untenable paradox.

The idealized worker: learning and working in the new economy

Elite demands have won a neo-liberalization of capitalism that manifestly serves elite interests. Government adoption of policies in pursuit of a knowledge-based economy with hoped-for wider social benefits has simultaneously extolled heightened competitiveness and expanded marketization. Those latter forces have, wholly predictably, produced greater social inequalities, skewed distribution of costs and benefits and worsened conditions of poverty and social exclusion. The pursuit of the liberalized knowledge economy, with its low-knowledge service sector accompaniment, places immense burdens on working people. It simultaneously demands more and less of labour: it demands more techno-science skills acquisition and less political power. It demands intensified productivity, greater subordination and compliance to managerial command and less participation and voice in workplace regulation. It demands weakened worker protection, de-collectivization and individualized risk-bearing. Still further, workers are pressured to suppress dimensions of human being that cannot be recognized or understood by economic reason. A worker's conflicts of love and relationality with work and production are presumed to be resolved in the relegation of the non-productive. Children, most saliently, bear that silent cost.

The new ideal of the worker implicit in the European model of the knowledge-based economy is liberalized, activated, and flexible in direct concordance with the demands of the firm, and is simultaneously a devoted consumer of market products. The worker, policy-depicted as entrepreneurial self-manager of her skill acquisitions and risk-taking in the employment opportunities available on labour markets, is required to shoulder a greater burden of market transaction costs. She is simultaneously urged to achieve social inclusiveness and solidarity in these liberalized conditions in which the negative externalities of corporate production costs are displaced from business firms onto de-socialized individuals and a weakened state and civil society.

The ways in which these contradictory developments pose complex challenges to ordinary working people, who have to juggle many responsibilities and interests with the need to earn a living, are typically refused attention in policy discourse. Attention to the practical realities of the world of work into which such activation policies take place is scarce and cursory. In its place is an abstracted projection of an idealized, rationalized workplace in which intensified techno-administrative control and efficiency manage human resources who are otherwise inclined to contrariness and recalcitrant behaviour. The absence of careful attention in dominant policy discourse of the OECD and the European Commission to realistic conceptions of the worker at the receiving end of applications of meta-policy discourses enables an implicit model of the ideal worker to be propagated and dictated. That occurrence reveals of policy elites an ignorance of, if not cynical and dangerous distance from, the lives of ordinary people. It risks an unintended, yet effective, imperialism and tyranny of corporate interests and markets.

The worker, imagined as an abstracted economic unit, a resource for corporate firm production and innovation objectives, is accorded a highly circumscribed status as actor. That worker-actor is policy-imagined as an instrumentally rational agent in regard to her/his choices on education and training markets and in her/his approaches toward work and employment. Matters of work and employment are to be regarded as solely economic activities that must take precedence over all other matters of life. Furthermore, in keeping with the neo-classical model's assumption at the core of this strategy, workers must be extraordinarily knowledgeable. They must be knowledgeable of the requirements of the dynamic knowledge-based, innovative and globalizing economy sufficient to take informed rational decisions that will ensure their participation in education and training, or risk-taking geographic mobility, and achieve their employability – employability that is a shifting quality of market-appropriate skills and competencies, mobility and adaptability.

The current policy expressions place great emphasis on further forms of labour market flexibility: geographic and occupational flexibility. Workers are urged to become willing to relocate across regions and countries in order to find jobs and fill industry needs. They are urged to assume that occupational change and retraining for new jobs will comprise a normal working life for modern, flexible workers. These dimensions of flexibility demonstrate an intensification of worker subordination to both unpredictable employer requirements for worker flexibility and mobility and to the coercive, unmanaged, forces of capitalist economy. The worker is thereby abstracted and idealized as entirely rational and knowledgeable beyond the knowledge expected of firms.

The abstracted worker is also a gender-neutral actor. Economic policy models recognize gender differences solely in regard to labour market participation. There is no recognition of the persistence of normative expectations of gender relations in regard to family life, relationships of care and dependency, and in household maintenance, all of which affect working life. Achievement of gender equalities across a range of measures has stalled (EGGE 2009). Notably, there are gaps between women and men in rates of employment participation, in pay and benefits, in occupational or workplace representation, in opportunities for education and training, and in participation in management and governance of organizations in all sectors of the labour market. (A comprehensive review of gender inequalities in the labour market is found in EGGE 2009; Perrons *et al.* 2005; Walby *et al.* 2007). Policy efforts at EU and national levels endeavour to reduce the gender gaps – especially in regard to harnessing the skilled labour power of women. Gender regimes in society include expectations of women's acceptance of casualized and fragmented jobs to a greater extent than is expected of men. That occurrence renders women workers more susceptible to precarious employment relations and exclusion from opportunities for education and training that, in conventional terms, may enable them (at least as individuals) to escape poor quality jobs. As employers persist in constructing poor quality jobs, they endeavour to exploit an assumed weaker power of women workers which in turn increases a firm's chances of escaping social and trade union pressure to improve those conditions.

There are, moreover, as yet unrecognized factors in the persistence of gender inequalities. These pertain to the broader privileging of techno-scientific and economic reason shaping the worker into rational conformity with its demands. Marketization renders inferior forms of knowledge and social action which do not yield to it calculations of exchange. Women's traditional knowledge in once-valued capacities for prioritizing relations and labours of love and care has been intercepted. It is brought, where possible, into marketized services. Or it is relegated *vis-à-vis* the alleged superior value of any form of marketable knowledge and labour. Women and men are equally urged to conform to traditionally masculinist patterns of prioritization of labour market work, and consume its products. Women, like men, are urged to agree to the rational inferiorization of their humanistic, relational knowledge in exchange for subjugation to firm and market authorities. If they refuse, their equality with men may be withheld. A movement of men seeking equality with women is not encouraged. The momentous socio-cultural project of women's and men's emancipation, which has been championed by feminists since the Enlightenment, risks transposition into androcentric economic rationalization to the exclusion of socio-cultural innovation.

The worker is faced with the concrete demands of the new knowledge-based economy in her or his everyday life. The key question that workers face, and economic policy-makers ignore, is how can one be both a mobile resource for innovative production in capricious capitalist markets and belong to a civil and personal life with its reciprocities of responsibilities and satisfactions? How can one be flexible, adaptable, insecure, and pursue lifelong learning in order to respond to the knowledge-based economy's demands for innovative and dynamic production while raising children, caring for elders, sustaining communities and participating in citizen roles in one's workplaces and polities – all of which require relative stability of geographic space and relational ties? The pervasive neo-liberal economic models dominating macroeconomic and social policy find no place for these questions to be seriously recognized and addressed. As socially central as these questions are, workers are left to themselves to work out personal solutions in the face of demanding economic pressures and instrumental rationalizations.

A surfeit of economic modelling of the idealized worker acting in economic self-interest abstracted from the complexities of real personal and collective life exposes grave weaknesses at the core of this model. Social criticisms of economic modelling and its socially absurd abstractions from historically situated real life have been readily made. They have scarcely reached the attention of mainstream economic and political discourses; indeed, they have been forcefully refused by ideological interests under the guise of economically necessary liberalization. Those critiques of capitalism, now finding their way back in (Streeck 2009), offer renewed potential. They may pose much fruitfulness in the development of and recombination of old and new ideas. Chapter 7 endeavours to draw from these critiques a further exploration of possibilities, renewal and restoration.

CONCLUSION

The neo-liberal knowledge-based economy brings work and education into critical connections as never before. A degradation of cultural quality and supra-market value is a salient shared theme for both education and of work. The loss of dignity, esteem and value for considerable sectors of contemporary work in the midst of the knowledge-based economy's generation of higher-skills, innovative production and increased consumption presents a social paradox.

Higher-level skills, higher productivity and higher consumption are achieved in contradiction to aspirations toward an inclusive, democratic and civilized society. The policy paths of rationalization and liberalization produce momentous social and cultural effects. Discussion in this chapter has pointed to some of them in regard to work and education. Few of them attract full scrutiny in policy discourse. The European Union, in both its Lisbon 2000 agenda and its *Europe 2020* policy successor, asserts the aspiration to create more and better jobs. The latter aspiration of betterment is glaringly unrealized and practically contradicted. At the same time, European model welfare states move to demand greater rates and increasingly longer years of labour market participation and intensified productivity from their citizen workers.

Education rationalizes into the scientific episteme in service of goals its professional institutions no longer set. All of these pose immense concerns. Many critical analysts of work and trade union practitioners find themselves focussed on the extensive demands of immediate conditions for workers that have demonstrably worsened in the 2010s. Critical educationists condemn outright the globally oriented free-market vision for education and the knowledge based economy (Robertson 2008). Yet education critics find themselves in a further dilemma in which, while opposing the market-oriented liberalized reforms of European university systems, they risk rejecting a more socially open Europe, and a more participatory and accessible university system. A more open and widely participatory higher education system allows more educational opportunity for more of Europe's citizens beyond insular nationalistic conventions and expands capacities for post-national solidarity and cultural enrichment.

The left's criticisms are motivated by a cultural defence of earlier, hard-won radical reforms of education in the post-war decades toward more democratic expansion, professional autonomy and democratic governance of universities, more equality of class, gender, and ethnicity in participation, and a retention of cultures of learning and knowledge as intrinsic values. Nonetheless an academic left's elevated attention to globalization and its dangers risks placing its criticism in a newly conservative counter-critique of a return to national interests. Its opposition cannot voice a vision for knowledge and education beyond a modern humanist conception that would be capable of inspiring a substantive cultural critique of the liberal knowledge-based economy and society. Many commentators are drawn to conclusions that the collapse of the university into the capitalist corporation is virtually complete, and student mobility in education a mere reflection of labour market dynamics for an intractably liberalized economy and society. Yet the search for movement beyond neo-liberal capitalism draws on many concerns and newly forging alliances. That search includes possibilities for retrieval and socio-cultural innovation of popular yet neglected social values. Chapter 7 takes up that discussion.

7 Citizens and society, work and education

INTRODUCTION

The neo-liberal political and economic reforms that have been instituted more or less comprehensively in the European model welfare states over the past thirty years continue to prevail. The consequences of socially uncontrolled capitalism portend a worsening crisis of governance. A broadening political recognition of the magnitude of the social crisis may improve the chances of imaginative social innovation after neo-liberalism. The task of renewing social imagination and civic action includes bringing new attention to the civil crises in work and education.

Emancipatory and participatory political action of a socially oriented nature, beyond protestation and unrest, now appears severely constrained or practically ineffective in a world dominated by economic and technological elites and the social forms – including workplaces and universities – they have demanded and instituted. Aspirations of advancing social justice and emancipation within the world of work as well as beyond it, although by no means exhausted, have manifestly diminished scope to support their realization. An apparent resignation to there being no alternative to market liberalism and socially weak institutions may suggest a normative acquiescence. The counter-social irresponsibility of elites, corporate firms and governments complicit in the current crisis of liberal capitalism presents societies and polities with immense challenges of legitimacy and governance. These concerns preoccupy the attention of many seasoned scholars and analysts. Many are inclined to concur that we can see myriad problems and few persuasive arguments for progressive steps forward. In this concluding chapter I explore some efforts of response.

Unleashed capitalism is unlikely to yield to renewed efforts of constraint typical of twentieth century institutions from which it broke free in the past few decades. As much as a renewal and revitalization of trade unions remain a vital agenda, only limited demands can realistically be made of labour institutions. Certainly, a desistance of admonishment of workers for their skills deficits and of unions for their localism, conservatism and capitulation to elites would be an immediate progressive step. As well, a more precise naming of the interests and agents of neo-liberal capitalism and exposition of their deliberate skills deficits: their wilful ignorance and cynical disregard for the disproportionately burdened and marginalized that liberalized, hyper-marketized capitalism predictably generated would be useful. In the interests of society, an engaged, ethical sociological critique enables the search for innovative and just social practices *pro populo*.

The rapacious character of capitalism that has permeated contemporary economic institutions and normalized a public subservience to the logic and power of market action is precisely the reason we cannot expect too much genuine reform-mindedness from those institutions. Popular business claims that "corporate social responsibility" (CSR) can fill the breach must be recognized for their *a priori* interestedness and limits. Corporate social responsibility is a defence of capitalism on the part of elites. It is irrevocably tainted from decades of escalating corporate irresponsibility that is now exposed. The neo-liberal hegemony has set a cultural subordination of organized labour and of the public sphere. It has effected, too, and less explicably, a brazen capitulation of university institutions to the demands of liberalized corporate firms and their implicated policy-makers. Universities, seduced or coerced, by ideologies of economically liberal change, technological and market dynamism, and of the superiority of the techno-scientific episteme have conceded an emancipatory and civilizing cultural vision which, in the mid-twentieth century, was promising a wide social reach.

Policy-makers urge, at best, a pursuit of social cohesion forged through welfare deprivation and frightening people into wilfully degraded jobs or intensified competition for the chance of good jobs. Those better jobs which do utilize and reward higher education and skills are evidently supported by sectors of work which do not. Further pressures are placed on universities to modernize and increase skills generation and astonishingly little pressure is placed on firms to improve the quality of poor jobs and recognize the rights and civil dignity of citizen-workers in the workplace. Sober recognition of the severity of the accumulated degradations incurred in the "creative destruction" of liberal capitalism, which Schumpeter observed, is the most pressing social task. It seems we are, collectively, in much need of reminding of Marx's once-famous recognition of capitalism's "uninterrupted disruption of all social conditions," its "everlasting uncertainty and agitation" and its ensuing social destructiveness. Weber's observation of the "irrational rationality of capitalism" and its evident requirement of social governance are similarly remarkably neglected. Our early twenty-first century "learning society" has forgotten some crucial learnings of our not-so-distant past. The social question returns.

European welfare states strive to revitalize their social models; their leaders speak again of the "big society" and, invoking Durkheim's classical concerns, they speak of social cohesion, citizenship and solidarity. In regard to the social matters of this book, a crucial question arises: can work and education be restored to potentiality beyond their degradation by capitalist appetite? How can social institutions capable of manoeuvre and social construction against monolithic economic reason be newly imagined, and newly effective? Can they be effective in highly market-rationalized work and education?

In response to these questions I propose to draw into discussion explorations of new conceptualizations and forms of citizenship and civil society. Current philosophical attention to citizenship sparks much possibility. Can workers, invoking innovative conceptions and renovated practices of citizenship, mobilize anew for just rights, roles, duties and egalitarian reciprocities in the work spaces of society? What are the roles and responsibilities of education, especially the university, in the practice and dissemination of these and other capacities of citizenship? Despite the university's subordination and adaptation to market imperatives, and the excoriative criticism many are tempted to proffer, its assimilation is not complete. In view of the severe weaknesses of liberalized economic and political institutions and the elevated role of the university in current conditions, much greater social and cultural demands may again be placed on the university. The demand of higher education's revitalized role begins with an interruption of its latter-day role as engine-room for labour market skills production and laboratory of techno-scientific, entrepreneurial knowledge. It is a demand for a reformed and re-civilized role for the university in pursuit of diverse and higher social and cultural knowledge. The university, having embarked on paths of entrepreneurial expansion and adopting business firm models of organization and management and seeking, on a generous view, to serve a wider public at least in the provision of labour market skills, nonetheless retains a cultural heritage of non-economic value and *raison d'être*.

The university, drawing on its rich cultural heritage and social capital, possesses unique capacities to contribute to renewed social institutions and dynamic, self-reflective societies. A new attention to notions of social citizenship, in contemporary transnational and cosmopolitan forms, offers rich potential. The principal aim of the discussions below is to consider the potential of current discourse on citizenship and society and a renewed socio-cultural understanding of education. These non-market interests may offer scope for sources of protecting society and citizens from markets and firms, and advancing social, and planetary, interests. They may inform governments still in the sway of corporate firm interests of the demands and interests of citizens which can never be reduced to markets, trade and consumption. Discussion begins with some remarks on the problem of economic authoritarianism and "corporate social responsibility" (CSR).

ECONOMIC AUTHORITARIANISM

The intensified power of elite interests and the weakening of social institutions in the regulation of economy have encouraged a general public acceptance of the corporate firm's position and action in society. The cultural normalization of the logic of the private interests of the corporate firm enables its market interests to exert an economic authoritarianism over diverse dimensions of social and personal life. In the course of this normalized effect, it has rarely been noticed, as Crouch (2006) points out, that the elite business interests that have persuaded the state of the generality of their interests, have no interest in the maximization of public collective interests. The firm is oriented, and equipped, toward maximizing its own profitability. Indeed, the externalities of public interests, where effective as compliance demands on the firm, are typically regarded as costs which in the firm's interests must be minimized or cleverly circumvented. Worker, and public, collective interests in economic and organizational activity, including in the setting of terms and limits of market action in society, are diminished and de-politicized.

The elevation of the prerogatives of the firm to an uncontested role in the control of work and production relations and the demand of education systems for higher skills and techno-science research exerts more than a practical efficiency. It effects a substantive reduction of work, and education, to economic instrumentalism. The dimensions of work, and increasingly of education, that involve personal, community and social effort, productivity, contribution and meaningfulness beyond the economic are relegated to peripheral, incidental personal matters. Non-economic and cultural domains of life, when they are recognized, are subordinated to a calculus of economic rationalities. Economic discourse speaks of the economic value of art galleries, of green parks, of health, even of children as though a substantive value of these that ignores and refuses the economic is irrational or romantic. In this way, economic pre-eminence dictates values and behaviour over which it ought to have no dominion.

Under a normative climate of neo-liberal economic authoritarianism, policy discourses conceive and promote social inclusion through economic action, especially labour market participation. The quality of that participation and assumed inclusion is measured according to a narrow range of criteria, principally that of the economic value of the job. The values, competencies and social capital factors generated and accumulated in workplace relations in which workers have channels for participation or representation in rule-making and goal-setting, bargaining and negotiation are marginalized under conditions in which the authority of economic principals is paramount. Moreover, as that political-economic authority is constructed and enforced by particular ideological conceptions under the guise of necessity in a competitive globalizing knowledge economy, the avenues for critique and contestation are minimal or foreclosed. The hyper-rationalization of work, the acceleration of market action and the subordination of non-economic values are assumed to be economically necessary. The negative externalities of corporate firm and market action are borne by individuals and liberally compliant governments.

The corporate firm which does recognize the occurrence of negative externalities (the results of market actions that are not themselves involved in such action) proposes in response a promotion of "corporate social responsibility" and of business ethics. Corporate social responsibility (CSR) discourse proposes to voluntarily take into account the externalities of the firm's market behaviour. It proposes to include a range of concerns expressed in public and government arenas such as environmental degradation, community fragmentation and social problems of, for instance, child labour in the manufacturing of mass consumer products or destruction of rainforests. CSR and business ethics have strong normative connotations of being unequivocally good and right endeavours. CSR seeks favourable social, and therefore market, responses to corporate action through displaying the corporate firm's response to high profile social needs. Prominent features include promotion of corporate volunteer programmes for employees, charity fund raising, sponsorship of disadvantaged children, benefactor programmes and educational endowments. In sponsoring these normatively good things, firms promote themselves as "good citizens" in the highly marketized, socially destructive, non-society their demands have wrought. It also includes promotion among corporate employees of notions of good corporate citizenship at work as a moral source of employee behaviour regulation.

Corporate interests promote CSR as an appropriate and sufficient means of constraint on the behaviour of firms. Less visibly than CSR charity sponsorships, CSR methods promote the firm's claim to be sufficiently competent in the regulation of its operational and market actions. It advances the firm's claim for freedom from state regulation and constraint of action by the firm. However, the extensive demands of the corporate firm, as discussed in earlier chapters, incur consequences and implications far beyond the capacities and interests of the firm to recognize. The firm has achieved widely liberalized scope of action. It has forcefully weakened or neutralized sources of regulation from the state, trade unions, civil society actors and educated citizens. The firm's internal hierarchies and boards of governance are frequently the only institutions regulating the firm's behaviour. CSR is defined and regulated entirely within the primacy of the logic of the private firm. Having neutralized former civil society regulatory agents and weakened the state into its service, the firm seeks under its formulation of CSR to be its own self-auditor and governor. That instrument of governance, certainly since 2008, has been vividly displayed as incapable of substantive and necessary regulation of corporate firm action.

A consequence of neo-liberal governance policies subjects the individualized, de-collectivized, worker and citizen to an extreme exposure to corporate firm externalities. The logic of the firm has established organizational forms which are presented to workers and public interests as rational system logics which are reasonably incontestable. Corporate involvement in university governance – which is not invited in reciprocation – increases in European universities. It is a logical progression. That logic has enabled the internal intensification of managerial control and worker re-subordination as rational and legitimate action. It has obscured a serious counter-democratic effect enacted in everyday life. As Crouch (2005a) argues, the prevalence of business authority over other entitlements to participate in collective decision-making narrows the public realm. The social sphere loses a necessary range of effective social institutions in the regulation of social life. These institutions can act to protect society from the market and citizens from corporations. A state distorted in the favour of business interests provides fewer and slower measures of social amelioration. Governments held to ransom by the markets which may "punish" them for market-constraining efforts, lose the faith and confidence of the *demos* which elected them. That loss in turn enables a default technocratic decision-making to be asserted and tolerated.

Yet, once again, as we have known since Weber, market institutions negate non-calculative human bonds, desires and actions. The superordination of market dynamics over increasing areas of human life as a characteristic feature of contemporary society risks a cultural truncation of human life and social imagination that humans persist in wishing to value. Social observers note the rise of communalist and fundamentalist identity and religious movements as a form of counter-action to extreme market logic and failed distribution of socio-cultural goods. Nonetheless, of course, neither markets nor communalisms can succeed in the social tasks of providing public goods and protecting society from public "bads".

Policy aspirations to preserve residual notions of the European social model for citizens alongside accelerated competiveness are shadowed by elements of coercion. A dominant policy discourse represents people reduced to individual market economy actors, as workers, consumers, customers and clients. It has shifted social democratic notions of citizen equality into equality of activation, that is, of employability. Individuals who fail to maintain "economic activation", to gain skills and keep jobs, are threatened with social exclusion. European Union policy visions of free and flexible markets and a modernized social model with more and better jobs come with an escalating price for which it is expected that workers will pay. This grand model risks depriving ordinary people of any mastery over the concrete, immediate conditions of their lives. It risks depriving them, too, of meaningful participation in the shaping of their societies. Workers at once neo-liberalized and powerfully constrained by market authoritarianism are simultaneously expected to deliver for the firm high productivity levels and sustain personal consumption and debt beyond their means to afford. With the new and long-term high levels of government debt, workers are also expected to work longer years and retire later from those same intensified, illiberal conditions of production.

These conditions stir deep-seated objections among European citizens for whom notions of fairness, equality and solidarity are enshrined in their highest political statements. The European Union's Treaty of Lisbon which came into force in December 2009 reiterates its commitment to, and guarantee of, the fundamental rights of "Dignity, Freedom, Equality, Solidarity, Citizenship and Justice". The current crisis intensifies demands for these aspirations. These aspirations require innovative conceptions of citizenship incontemporary conditions. They require, as philosopher, Étienne Balibar (2004) proposes, a movement of popular sovereignty and of "worksites of democracy" and "worksites of citizenship" for their continual effort at realization.

SOCIETY AND SOCIAL CITIZENSHIP

An economic authoritarianism characteristic of the neo-liberalism that permeates economic, political and social spheres contradicts very many social and cultural aspirations which the public and governments continue to express as valued and desired qualities of a good life and good societies. The neo-liberal hegemony undermines and destroys the cohesive social structures on which democratic welfare states depend. But the contradictions of capitalism have long been observed and struggled with. Movements beyond neo-liberalism and toward socially embedded and civilly regulated economies and societies require a considerable re-imagination and vision, as well as willing labour.

An interest in institutional reconfiguration and renewal of social models draws attention to principles of non-market action and institutions which, though frequently ignored, continue to sustain economic activities in society. Among these are qualities of social rights and responsibilities, of trust and obligation, of respect for persons and vague yet effective senses of fairness and limits. They include also notions and practices of citizenship. The weakened social reach of welfare states along with additional challenges of large-scale migration and labour mobility has opened new debates on citizenship roles in social participation. The debates range across traditionally conservative and communitarian to social democratic, republican and cosmopolitan aspirations.[1] Amid a diversity of views, there appears basic agreement on some core aspects of the ideal of citizenship as comprising rights and duties and forums of participation. Citizenship requires a social sphere that reaches beyond the state and the market.

An expansive innovation of the sensibilities of citizenship, in particular of traditional political notions, and a searching development of conceptions of cosmopolitan citizenship propose rich resources for a renewal of society and civil action. The innovative development of the concept of *social* citizenship that may be activated in diverse aspects of social life may enable a regeneration of social cooperation and diminish social exclusion, and forge new ways of living together. It may raise renewed substantive democratic demands on the state and of elite interests for new institutions of market regulation and working life conditions. An irreducible public sphere and a democratic polity are upheld in European Union policy as basic features of European societies. The EU through the European Commission is directing much attention to its proposals of "Europe for Citizens" (European Commission 2005c, 2007b) as its current policy effort toward a regeneration of broad participatory activities and citizen roles in civil society and polity. A potentially useful site to quicken the re-imagination and revitalization of social citizenship lies in the everyday world of work and organizations. Workplaces have extraordinary potential for development into workshops for the practice of social citizenship.

The notion of the citizen starts, crucially, from the recognition that the citizen is not a unit of economy and citizens belong, not to a market, but to societies and communities. Citizenship has traditionally been associated, since its origins in Greek and Roman republican conceptions, with a political status as membership of a political order. In subsequent centuries that political order was imagined as the nation-state. There remains a popular retention of the nation as a normative category of identity and citizenship. But the concept of citizenship as political membership of nation-state is no longer adequate or appropriate for the new conditions in which citizenship must be effective. Certainly, as Wagner and Zimmerman (2004) argue, it is now incapable of sustaining the socially valued European welfare state as transnational European integration proceeds.

A political conceptualization of citizenship does not allow for sufficient socialization of the concept, and practice, of citizenship. Habermas (2006) seeks a model of democratic politics beyond the nation-state, a "post-national constellation", for a cosmopolitan society. Archibugi (2008) and Delanty (2009) argue respectively for a "global commonwealth of citizens", and "a critical cosmopolitan vision". Balibar (2004) argues for a "transnational citizenship" and a transformation of European democracy that deepens and rearticulates the notion of "popular sovereignty" that enables the "direct representation of the population and its social interests". Schnapper (1998) argues for a "community of citizens" that occurs through the contribution of all who share the social space. Benhabib (2004) argues for a "cosmopolitan federalism" and egalitarian reciprocity.

These representatives of the debates seek a renewal of the idea and reach of citizenship. They argue that a re-imagining of *social* citizenship beyond the nation-state is vitally necessary. Citizenship needs to become social to constitute a viable community of solidarity in transnational and globalizing societies. Social citizenship, as Marshall ([1950] 1992) proposed, is the right of persons to the dignity bestowed in their participation and membership of a community. Its practice includes, and requires, recognition of plural forms of participation and value and in diverse sites of action. Crucially, social citizenship refers in practice to concrete situations in which actors have to orientate themselves toward the exercise of solidarity. Wagner and Zimmerman (2004: 39) propose that "the national community of belonging, as defined by nationality laws, is not identical to the community of solidarity which is set up by institutions of the welfare state". The exercise of solidarity that is social citizenship transcends the national framework of citizenship.

A crucial advance of social citizenship, as Étienne Balibar argues, beyond the "national preference" will be capable of "the extension of social rights and of possibilities for intervention in the regulation of the economy" (Balibar 2004: 163). Balibar argues that the European project which includes a "constitution of citizenship" can only emerge on the condition of being *more democratic* than the traditional constitutions of national states. Moreover the wider dimensions and demands of citizenship with a deepened "popular sovereignty" require "worksites of citizenship". "We *are not* 'citizens', but we can 'become' citizens" (ibid.: 198–9, original emphasis). We become citizens through action in plural sites for citizenship creation.

Drawing on these conceptions, and in particular on Balibar's notion of becoming *more democratic* and of a deepening and re-articulation of the notion of popular sovereignty, and of the forging of "worksites of citizenship" and "worksites of democracy", I propose in the following discussion to raise demand and possibilities. I invoke an understanding of the notion of citizen as Touraine (1995: 339) proposes, of the citizen-subject, as a person's quest for subjectivation and self-production and "with the will to live together". It is the subject that "provides the foundation for citizenship". The potential of the acting subject-citizen is the ground for the following explorations. At stake in my effort is the renovation of workplaces as sites, and workshops, of citizen practice and sovereignty. Balibar proposes that "worksites of citizenship" "emphasize a pragmatic dimension: there is matter for trial and error, for apprenticeship on the basis of collective initiatives, some 'global' and others 'local' (ibid.: 198). As Balibar notes, the "labour question" remains a fundamental worksite of democracy. The vast new pressures on Europe as it integrates its member states and diverse migrating persons and the crisis of neo-liberal governance pose a crisis of democracy. I propose that, after a generation of the neglect, or occlusion, of industrial democracy and worker-citizen rights, a new opportunity presents for revitalized discussion and practice of citizenship and democracy at work.

Markets and enterprises increasingly transcend the national sphere of political action and regulation. Yet their actions have relied on the existence of national and cultural institutions to provide disciplined as well as skilled workforces even as their actions simultaneously erode those necessary socio-cultural institutions. Specifically, as flexible labour markets and labour mobility increase discrepancies between peoples' places of residence and identities, national citizenship frequently retains meaningfulness distant from the concrete conditions of a person's life. Furthermore, as the firm de-collectivizes workers, trade unions and workers' institutions of solidarity and political agency are weakened. The bonds and agencies of work, once vital aspects in the practices of industrial citizenship, have been broken. The policy alarm at the visibility of social fragmentation and eroding social solidarity has prompted calls for renewal of social cohesion and citizen activation. The disruption to necessary social solidarities and stabilities brought about by expansive liberal marketization exposes the social limits of the neo-liberal economic model. The economic failure to achieve Europe's social agenda coincides with other calls for a renewal of citizenship and of the neglected realm of civil society.

At the European Union level, much of the policy interest in regard to concern for social fragmentation, inequalities and exclusion is targeted through education and lifelong learning policy programmes (European Commission 2007a, 2007b). A 2007 communication of the European Parliament and Council, *Key Competencies for Lifelong Learning* (European Council 2007) recognizes the breakdown of social cohesion. It proposes new skill development in response:

> Skills for civic competence relate to the ability to engage effectively with others in the public domain, and to display solidarity and interest in solving problems affecting the local and wider community. This involves critical and creative reflection and constructive participation in community or neighbourhood activities as well as decision making at all levels, from local to national and European level, in particular through voting.

These EU communications offer potential for an opening of space for renewed discussion of citizens' rights and roles and their sites of enactment. They stimulate social and cultural contestation of the contradictory economic models that visibly impede these aspirations – including those of EU policy-makers. Current policy depiction of citizens reduces the conception of citizenship to a role of active labour market participation. The rendering of the good citizen as the good worker who maintains her employability reflects a neo-liberal edict. That liberal market reductionism must be exposed in order for a more robust social conceptualization of citizenship and for EU communications calling for citizen competencies and participation to be in the least viable. A social conception of citizenship necessarily includes economic, industrial and occupational actions along with other forms of social participation. A re-imagining of industrial or economic citizenship as a vital dimension of social citizenship adds a further contribution to genuine possibilities for societal renewal, deepened democracy and social protection.

Movements in earlier decades of the twentieth century for expansion of democracy and social participation, especially the campaign for universal adult franchise which won the vote for women, stirred further ideas which promoted embryonic practices of industrial and organizational democracy. Industrial democracy movements, with their range of aspirations and practices, were most notably effective in the European countries in the post-war decades (Blumberg 1973; Casey 2003; Crouch and Heller 1983; Lammers and Széll 1989; Sandberg 1995). Those movements for economic and industrial citizenship and democracy, along with other gains of the organized labour movement, have been severely truncated and frequently trivialized in practice under the neo-liberal firm resurgence. Their ideas, principles and practices have fallen into neglect. A probing reconsideration of the ideals, conceptualizations and practices of those social democratic movements, more richly informed by contemporary innovations in social citizenship conceptualization, can revitalize the practice of worksites of democracy and of citizenship at work. Of course, one recognizes that avenues for re-conceptualization and innovative practice have been seriously destabilized by neo-liberal capitalism. But the conflicts of capitalism and its social degradation have also exposed the limits of individualistic citizen rights and market action.

Industrial democracy movements (the term "industrial" understood as pertaining to all forms of industrious, commercial work including employed professional work) proposed that workers, by virtue of their possession of social and political citizenship in society, have corresponding rights to practise that citizenship in their workplaces. The right to participate, including through representation, in decisions of control and management of production and organizations is a right of citizenship in democratic society. Workers, who are at once social citizens at work, possess capacities to act in communities of solidarity and political representation. The concept of social industrial citizenship differs from a liberal conception of individual rights and freedoms. It is a citizenship as a form of rights and capacities that is based on a sensibility of community of solidarity. That sensibility enables the direct expression of collective citizens' demands toward both market and state institutions.

Industrial democracy, in its earlier conceptualizations, sought extension of expression of citizenship as solidarity through democratic participation and decision-making in the workplace. It generally retained, explicitly or implicitly, an assumed context of, and attachment to, the nation-state ordaining those citizenship rights. The conception now imagined goes beyond the nation. The community of solidarity is not the same as, nor reducible to, the sense of national or communalist community of belonging. Industrial citizenship recognizes the instability and partiality of its community of solidarity, and the necessity to actively construct and reconstruct it. It is, as Balibar (2004) puts it, a "becoming" that recognizes its action for "communities of shared fate". Industrial citizenship claims that the rights accruing to social citizenship are the basis of politics and the legitimate extension of democracy in the workplace. That democracy, as Habermas (1996) theorizes, is a discursive one that allows abstract moral principles such as justice to be invoked and "communicative action" to be practised to solve problems.

A highly social conceptualization of citizenship goes beyond national membership of a polity and of ethnic membership of community. It transcends inherited identities. National political membership is not a requirement of the possession and exercise of industrial social citizenship rights and roles which cross national borders. Indeed, it can be a hindrance that undermines the extension of social rights and capabilities. The increasing migration of peoples, as well as the mobility of capital, requires more appropriate responses. Sensibilities of transnational and post-national solidarity widen the scope of collective life. Balibar (2004) argues that political theories of citizenship must recognize a "citizenship of residency" beyond a "citizenship of belonging". Recognition of that "citizenship of residency" extends toward action in local sites, including workplaces. It mobilizes the idea, as Schnapper (1998) theorized, of a "community of citizens" beyond borders. Balibar argues (2004: 76–7) that the "founding moment of citizenship" that gives it its "democratic power" is constituted in movement beyond inclusion and exclusion, beyond borders, to constitute a "shared act". That shared act, or "common operation" is conducted in such a way as to democratize citizenship and civilize the state and politics.

The propositions I wish to make, following Balibar's general schema, pertain to the constitution and practice of citizenship at work. Citizenship at work cannot be, and is not expected or desired to be, based on membership of the organization. Rather, citizenship at work carries notions of rights and avenues for participation as, following Habermas, an extension of membership of democratic social polities. As Habermas (2001: 107) argues, "The self-referential concept of collective self-determination demarcates a logical space for democratically united citizens who are members of a particular political community." That political and social community claims formation and practice, at once beyond and beneath the national level, in the workplace. A carrying over of the rights and duties of the political and social sphere to the industrial sphere, as was imagined under classical industrial democracy movements, opens space for social citizenship to be practised. Recognition of rights and duties of social citizenship also exposes the obstruction to citizenship practices incurred in corporate firm organizational systems and employment practices.

Firms' practices which have brought about a weakening or incorporation of trade unions, blocked or trivialized worker-citizen participation and intensified domination refuse a social citizenship at work. Yet even from the firm's vantage point, the realities of labour market flexibility and increasing mobility and migration of workers require new forms of social inclusion and expression, unless the firm proposes to rely on intensified coercion and microfascisms in labour management. The social citizenship I propose certainly pertains to identification and solidarity trans-nationally and post-nationally. It includes the sites where those recognitions are made concrete in multi-cultural workplaces. Moreover, it includes recognition of actual social space of workplaces as immediate sites of citizen-formation through contribution and participation. It includes direct, concrete actions at the level of the workplace. Trade union organizations have often sought international infrastructures that express interests in supra-national solidarity and expansion of the rights and interests of workers as citizens (Gold 2003; Whittall *et al.* 2007). There is now immense potential for that transnational movement to spread.

The social citizenship imagined proposes a relationship between citizens, as workers and employers, as equally social citizens engaged in shaping and sharing the same fate. Efforts to claim and practise the rights and duties of social citizenship at work practically shift the normative locus of citizenship beyond political membership of the nation-state, even as that dimension retains necessary levels of effectiveness, and calls on all parties to employment relationships to a solidarity in the "constructive participation" of collective life. A social citizenship also imagined as a "citizenship of residency" extends in principle to the "residency" of being present and engaged and in possession of rights and duties in one's workplace. A highly social concept of citizenship enables and requires a substantive alteration in corporate firm and managerial authoritarianism and normative subordination of workers.

I want to propose, still further than Habermas and Balibar, that citizenship at work and in education invokes a meaning beyond democratic political participation in their regulation, as important as that is. The proposition for an ethic of social citizenship at work that I propose carries the potential for workers' aspirations for quality of being, and doing that transcends the pervasive materiality of their work to be recognized and accommodated. Although those aspirations beyond exclusive materiality have been fearsomely suppressed in hyper-capitalist production, they are far from extinct. Their irrepressibility, which is revealed in simple socialities and good humour, as well as in occasions of luminary effort, excellence and self-transcendence in service and contribution, holds inherent potential for development and expression. The innovation of social citizenship with its demands and expression of popular sovereignty extends, I propose, to an as yet inarticulate appeal for a new order of work. A new order of work includes recognition of human expression in productive labour and creative effort that extends beyond the ordinarily material.

Social citizenship in its political sense as a practice of rights, duties and solidarities at once includes employers, corporate firm agents, shareholders and workers. Amid the current distorted power relations and de-collectivization of liberal institutions, elite firm actors have demanded freedom from the responsibilities of social citizenship. The proposition of an ethic of social citizenship, however, *necessarily* includes those escapees. It places a social duty upon corporate firm actors, as on workers, to participate in communities of solidarity. The reach of social citizenship at work to include employers as citizens recognizes their institutionalized role as corporate firm actors. But it recognizes limits and demands constraint on those roles and their tendency to over-ride citizen and social interests. It recognizes *in situ* the need for and potential capacity to build new institutions of socially responsible citizenship beyond neo-liberal fragmentation and corporate firm vanities. Social citizenship action can build bridges across broken bonds and always fragile complementarities and compensations. As Balibar (2004) argues, European societies had gradually transformed their histories of violence and antagonisms into "collective political capacities". The institutionalization of conflicts enabled the social regulation of antagonistic forces. The decay, or destruction, of those former institutions of representation, participation, distribution and constraint now heightens conflicted interests. But there remain significant resources in these fragile learnings of collective political capacities and their vulnerabilities. Their renewed recognition highlights features of shared interests in shared societal fate.

SOCIAL CITIZENSHIP AND WORK

The current conditions in the world of work, as the learning economy/learning society model founders under the weight of contradictions, hold open new prospects for the intervention of, in Balibar's terms, "worksites of citizenship" and "worksites of democracy". One avenue of potential exploitation opens as a result of worsening problems in organizational workplaces – especially those at the heart of knowledge-rich, innovation and new product pursuers. The firm's highly competitive and individualized workplace is encountering new sets of problems in everyday workplace operations. Firms, which are in pursuit of innovative and high value competitive production and which employ workers with higher education and skills, are encountering skills deficiencies of an unanticipated sort. The education sector's generation of higher skill levels and formal qualifications in the population has certainly occurred. But those higher formal skills and techno-science forms of knowledge are not sufficient to generate continual innovation. That task requires forms of knowledge and qualities of persons which are typically incalculable in economic models but which are assumed as resources upon which everyday production relies.

Organizations show increased need for qualitative and cultural forms of knowledge and competencies. Research in organizations demonstrates that the capacities for the generation and flow of knowledge spillovers – those forms of sharing and interaction that spark learning, new ideas and developments on existing practices, and dispersion – require extensive non-cognitive and non-formal qualities and capabilities. They require qualities of trust, regard, confidence, collaborative cooperation and commitment. The elements of "social capital", which increasingly also include cross-cultural sensitivities and cross-national solidarities, are increasingly recognized as vital dimensions of workplace and productive enterprise.

The problem of a scarcity of social capital and trust now attracts attention among organizational practitioners and business academics. The socio-cultural institutional foundations of organizational trust have been eroding under the neo-liberal conditions of recent years. Heightened individual competitiveness and education's neglect of socio-cultural development are scarcely conducive to social trust formation. That erosion occurs exactly at a time when the goods of social capital are most needed for organizations to become learning organizations of knowledge-generating and knowledge-sharing employees. The necessity for the regeneration of trust and cooperativeness, the development of social competences and personal qualities and their utilization in organizational life presents considerable new challenges for organizations. Social capital is not developed or deployed in the same manner as formal technical or scientific knowledge. These qualities cannot be commanded or codified. Neither is it stimulated or shared by conventional financial incentives. The capacities and sensibilities of inclusion and innovation are not formed or sustained by applications of rational efficiency and managerial command. They need to be learned, motivated and facilitated in concrete social arenas including workplaces, schools, universities and civil society associations.

Heckscher and Adler's (2006) investigation into corporate firms finds evidence for the emergence of what they call new forms of collaborative community. They find that the pressures of complex knowledge-based production and competitive innovation seed the emergence of new forms of collaborative relationships that require "high levels of diffuse cooperation resting on a strong foundation of trust" (ibid.: xi). Neither markets nor hierarchies are sufficient to achieve the organization's learning objectives. They propose, moreover, that these new forms of collaborative community rely on both Weberian value-rationality *and* Durkheimian "organic solidarity". They propose that it has been precisely the explosion of knowledge-intensive industries and the failure of markets and formal contract relations that enables these heretofore ambitious conceptions to gain practical realization.

Heckscher and Adler's proposition of the development of new and sophisticated forms of community among high-tech professionals is certainly redolent with possibility. Its advancement requires a considerable behavioural change on the part of the firm. The firm's recognition of the lack of necessary qualities among personnel, irrespective of their higher formal skills and qualifications, must extend to recognition of other negative consequences of the firm's liberalized successes. The firm's very demand for intensified managerial command, its truncation of workers' voice and genuine participation in the workplace, and its insistence on flexibility, contingency and low commitment to its workforce have produced its counter-actions. The conditions of contemporary economic action stifle the lifeblood of human cooperation, trust and goodwill, and voluntaristic search for innovation and best practice. Authoritarian management in the service of ideological economic imperatives is ultimately limited in its ability to procure creative innovation.

Earlier practices of industrial citizenship demonstrated that participation and negotiation mitigate alienation and generate solidarity in co-worker trust, and enhance social citizenship (Crouch and Heller 1983). The new economies of organization and work now require new forms of citizen participation. These challenges reveal a new need for education of a much broader agenda. They open possibilities for a revitalization of workplace democratic participation and co-determination based on conceptualizations of social citizenship. Heckscher and Adler (2006) propose that the development of collaborative community poses a new form of worker participation and industrial democracy. Collaborative community requires rich social capital of trust, citizen rights, norms and values, and high levels of participation. Learning and developing these qualities require much richer models of worker and organizational learning than those evident in extant managerial models. They require, moreover, new *managerial* learning toward collaborative workplace relationships. These relationships must necessarily include workers in the non-knowledge-intensive sectors of production and service. That inclusion will require a considerable new management learning – one that is currently beyond the capacities and imagination of business schools.

Social competences cannot be achieved under the instrumentalist agenda of higher education for employment skill. Neither can they be achieved under a managerial model of "organizational citizenship" promoted in business literature (Organ *et al.* 2006). That concept is a crude attempt by the firm to appropriate a normative morality of citizen duty and further oblige and discipline employees into dutiful, firm-determined service and forbearance. Employees are expected to practise those virtues even as their employers escape reciprocal commitments and refuse political negotiation of collective conditions. That authoritarian model of "organizational citizenship" is readily exposed as a forgery of social citizenship. It is another attempt to defend capitalist firms, subjugate workers and undermine their becoming citizens and realizing social citizenship's democratizing capacities.

A further avenue for generating sites of democracy and citizenship at work opens in the exposure of a similarly untenable conception of citizenship implicit in European Commission policy discourses. That policy conception has reduced citizenship to a duty of individual responsibility to maintain labour market participation. The implicit model of the citizen as worker; of worker as policy-taker and subject of a complex set of behavioural requirements dictated by the governance practices of the neo-liberal state, is an impoverished and authoritarian one. A more robust conception of social citizenship – which is equally proclaimed in the European Treaty – requires and proposes substantially more. It proposes a renewed recognition of the person of the worker as citizen. The citizen-worker may demand a reactivation of substantive forms of workplace participation as a source of social and political agency and social solidarity. Current conditions, it is well noted, are scarcely conducive to the adoption of these proposals which will necessarily require substantive alteration of shareholder governance over workplace practices, and worker subjugation. Any prospect for development of citizenship practices at work requires a new role for education. Extending the discourse on social citizenship has further potential to contest and alter the dominant conception of CSR. Corporate citizenship under a social citizenship conception renders the firm subject to the rights and duties of individual citizenship. Firms are pressured to behave as responsible citizens, not solely under their own self-styled, self-interested CSR behaviour. Firms, like other citizens, become therefore constitutionally required to accept a share, not a monopoly, of participation in political governance and accept constraint of their actions.

SOCIAL CITIZENSHIP AND EDUCATION

Over the past decade there has been growing policy attention toward the role and tasks of education in the development of learning citizens and workers. That attention has not yet turned to include a new citizenship education of corporate elites. The European Commission declares the objective of increasing social cohesion as a major task of education. A relationship of learning and social cohesion with renovated notions of citizenship open fruitful channels for social development. In the first instance, it is evident that these qualities and competences have not been, and cannot be, generated in the heavily skills biased qualification regimes of education. Their accomplishment requires education and lifelong learning conceived under a different vision and with a new agenda. The vision of humanistic and emancipatory ideals that was especially prominent in the mid-twentieth century has fallen from prominence but is far from extinct. It maintains robust debates especially in fields of lifelong learning. The demand for social citizenship formation enables and requires education institutions to regain a capacity to assert a moral task and to gain necessary latitude from economic demands.

The university may forge an opportunity to revivify its historical role and enliven social imagination for the renewed generation of cultural resources. Again drawing on Balibar's "worksites of citizenship and democracy", we can propose that education institutions must encourage and facilitate a new *Bildung*, the new learning required for post-liberal, post-exclusively market societies and innovated forms of social solidarity. A renewed pursuit of this socially necessary objective would enable education to restore connections with economy that refuse subservience to domination. It proposes a quasi-autonomous domain of knowledge and learning for contribution to the social regulation of economy, and social justice more expansively.

Lifelong learning – its conceptualizations, theories and practical accomplishments in diverse social settings – is strategically placed to enter fully into the heart of debates on new forms of social citizenship. Social citizenship is learned essentially in its practice. Learning across the life course, especially through adulthood, in various social settings can bring the practices of citizenship to bear on diverse decision-making actions. Workplaces are everyday sites of adult learning. Formal and non-formal forms of learning at work have always *de facto* included more than production-oriented learning. Those capacities for active learning at work can be nurtured for the development of sensibilities and practices of social citizenship. Social citizenship necessarily encompasses both individual and collective demands and responsibilities, including those for recognition of non-material dimensions of work. Learning by doing the practice of social citizenship proposes a vital intervention into the problems of institutional and organizational obstructions to better jobs and better workplaces that authoritarian managerialism cannot produce.

Certainly, there is a new and burgeoning interest in citizenship education in schools (Arthur *et al.* 2008; Brookes and Holford 2009; Kotthoff and Moutsios 2007) which opens rich opportunity for social expansion. But as Brookes and Holford (2009) point out, much citizen education of young people takes place within the nation and remains imagined as in service of nation in regard to identities, rights and duties. Citizenship education is rarely pursued beyond levels of multicultural toleration and duties of political membership of nations and communities. Moreover, discussions on citizenship in social, political and philosophical studies seldom reach the attention of educational practitioners. Those practitioners may be more readily influenced by policy directives for types of citizenship education which serve neo-liberal governance purposes. As Field (2006), for instance, points out, much citizen education in recent years has been expressly for the purposes of activating people into work and reducing their expectations and reliance on the welfare state.

There remain considerable obstructions in education fields to participating in broader debates on citizenship and the practicalities of its teaching and learning. Nonetheless, an opportunity arises at the present juncture for education intellectuals to seize. They may assist a re-mobilization of education's progressive cultural capital after the failure of corporate interests to deliver socially valued public goods and as the crisis in neo-liberal governance worsens. That necessarily requires greater cross-disciplinary discussions and knowledge sharing, including in regard to the realities of work and workplaces. It requires, too, a courageous reach among education thinkers to recall and renovate education's vision of learning toward full human development which essentially includes sensibilities beyond the exclusive humanism of modern thought and institutions.

Critical debates in education have been somewhat over-engaged in the residual distractions of postmodernism and focussed on an amorphous "globalization". Education academics, casting attention beyond those often insular concerns and education's contestations with the state, clearly recognize the role of elite private actors. A critical education debate that forges linkages across research disciplines may more powerfully participate in the reform and re-valuing of the economistic university. The university, because of its crucial role in the knowledge-based economy and as repository of an immense reserve of cultural and social capital, is well placed to assert a renewal of its cultural role and ethical quest. Its unique societal position renders the university far more than a business enterprise in the industry of techno-science and skills production. A renewed recognition of the university's unique cultural role in the formation of citizens (including future corporate business leaders and policy-makers) would enable the university to contribute more substantially to the tasks of a comprehensive re-focus of socio-economic agenda. University leaders, if not economists, ought to be eminently capable of dispelling the myths that have arisen through a defiant attachment to *homo economicus* as the sum of the human being that have so liberally disseminated.

Education systems, both schooling and post-compulsory, cannot realistically be imagined as autonomous from economic interests and concerns. But they can recall their cultural institutional aspirations to provide multifaceted skills and competences useful to employment as well as more comprehensive education and human development. The education system has renewed opportunities to adopt a lifelong learning system that starts systematically and comprehensively in early childhood and in the domain of non-cognitive learning. Many educationists are fully aware of the neglect of early childhood education, as they are of the herding of young people through one-way, no-return, conventional schooling systems directed toward the world of work. While educational institutions have been pressured to take up a near-singular emphasis on skills formation and labour market responsiveness, the educational conceptual innovations of lifelong learning and learner-centred curriculum have been shelved.

Education institutions, prominently the university, have adopted corporate firm behaviour and management models. Among the many concerns arising from this action, education institutions are teaching young people entering labour markets how to behave as subordinated labour in accordance with corporate firm imperatives of utility and exploitation. The university's reform of this action requires a revitalization of its irreducible socio-cultural role and active construction of sites of citizenship. As it captures an increasing proportion of the population engaged in higher learning, the university has unprecedented opportunity to teach a mass population of students to be social citizens, capable of reflection, debate and political confidence. Educated citizens gain capacities to recognize and demand social limits of elite interests and behaviour. They may demand an extension and normative legitimation of social rights for intervention in the regulation of economy and workplaces. At the very least, the social limits of corporate firm demands for citizen-worker subjugation may be taught and learned in education programmes and practised in workplaces. An aspiration for egalitarian reciprocity may then become imaginable.

CITIZENS: FOR WORK AND EDUCATION

Cultural interests for social and political action to shape the world of work remain active. Workplace decisions remain some of the most important influences in people's lives and on the quality of civil societal relations. The quality of work and employment relations is a ready indicator of the quality of dignity, freedom and democracy in everyday life. There is little doubt that efforts toward a democratic, participatory and distributive culture in workplace organization have experienced severe political defeat in recent decades. There are, moreover, severe problems for worker action incumbent in the intensification of managerial power under the guise of rational organizational necessity. The expansion of rational control systems, made possible by the codification and mobility of skilled workers' knowledge and the re-proletarianization of salaried labour, is a paradoxical consequence of the knowledge economy and the education expansion. Yet the newly recognized needs of complex production organizations for restored fundaments of social trust and cohesion, and for the education and learning they require, expose a new vulnerability for the corporate organization. They may pose a fruitful intersection with the new debates on contemporary citizenship in social policy, and European Union aspirations toward "Europe for Citizens". An ideal of learning citizen workers may engender an expansion and revitalization of democratic process within organizational life and simultaneously teach citizenship values and identities to new and multi-cultural generation of workers of Europe.

An education sphere that takes up a substantial role in the development of innovative social citizenship fosters social knowledge and behaviour that are capable of revitalizing civil society. The sensibilities of social citizenship include capacities for debate and recognition of diverse knowledge and culture. These sensibilities may extend to citizen behaviour that is capable of altering the degradation of work and the disparagement of extensive sectors of ordinary work. A pivotal dimension of the concretization of that concept and aspiration lies in the vital task of education and social citizenship.

Citizens are, by virtue of their irreducible status as citizens, mutually accorded parity of respect and equality of burden of the rights and duties of that citizenship (with age-specific and impairment modifications allowed for). Education for social citizenship includes its practices among citizens at work. A first virtue of social citizenship must be promotion of a concept, and practice, of *parity of esteem* toward all workers. That entails the recognition of parity of esteem for the productive work of persons irrespective of the job's level of skill and product value. Parity of esteem is a citizen quality that regards the productive work of a bus driver and a kitchen-hand, a software engineer and a surgeon, as myriad other productive occupations, as of intrinsic parity of worth. The persons performing these jobs are of equal social esteem and enjoy parity of rights and treatment, even as the economic value of their jobs is unequal. Labour markets and occupational differentiation unequally remunerate jobs. But taking up the principle of parity of esteem for productive work enables a social and political justification for regulatory interventions to substantively constrain remuneration inequality and dramatically disrupt bifurcation tendencies. On that principle, a narrower differentiation of wage structure and greater egalitarian reciprocity is possible.

In practical terms, citizens' rejection of wide inequalities and status disparities justifies and demands regulatory interventions to raise the minimum wage and narrow the ratio of lowest to highest paid wage and salary earners. It demands delimitation of casual employment and discarding of considerable sectors of workers, it strengthens struggling claims for decency, living wages and equitable citizen dignity for lower productivity workers alongside more fortunate sectors of the labour force. It demands renewed social provision for workers' collective associations to represent and negotiate their interests with employer institutions. Current tendencies of labour market polarization of quality, rewards and benefits extend into a systematic reproduction of privilege and under-privilege that is generating a more socially stratified society not seen for many generations in the European model countries.

Gross inequalities are incompatible with genuine civil societies of respected, participatory citizens. Citizen promotion of parity of esteem demands that the quality of working life be made central to a broader conception of social and economic policy. It also accords due and realistic recognition of the endurance of lower-skilled and lower productivity sectors. Again at a concrete level, such recognition would have a further effect of giving families and individuals more realistic assessment of the costs and benefits of purchasing higher education and training and the chances of winning more highly rewarded and disproportionately esteemed jobs. It would accord to society more everyday solidarity in the parity of regard for diverse persons' work and a narrowing of economic and social inequalities. At the same time it opens scope for demands for education for all persons for their social, cultural and spiritual development free from labour market necessity.

Education for social citizenship and *parity of esteem* is necessarily a grand social and cultural agenda. But its worksites exist in every workplace, school and university. Its effective practice would enable an unburdening of workers from excessive pressures to take chances to reduce their job skills deficits. It would allow education systems, especially lifelong, adult education, the scope to provide and attract participation in learning for diverse life competencies and rich human development. In that course, it would provide learning experiences that nurture the confidence necessary for non-technical-expert workers to participate in social and political forums involved in decision-making and agenda setting over matters that affect a person's life and work, and the societies in which he or she lives. Expanded worker learning for the stimulation of production-required trust, knowledge-sharing and collaboration can be utilized in practice to stimulate and educate for the values of social citizenship. That makes practically viable new prospects for a socio-cultural regulation of economy and work based on social citizenship action. Work-place learning for diverse participatory ends can provide important bases of social solidarity and cohesion beyond the nation-state and basic political roles. And, as Dewey ([1916] 1966) famously argued, learning by doing is typically eminently effective. Learning citizenship, in all its forms, roles and values, may be well practised through participation in its recognitions, conflicts, tensions, compromises and creative energies – by doing it at work.

The recognition and facilitation of a complex learning agenda, rather than its suppression and denial as in managerial models of organization and human resource learning, enable a conception of production organizations which are constructed according to the dynamics of participation, negotiation colla-boration, and collective goal setting. The knowledge-based economy is gen-erating new levels of organizational complexity. These require imaginative governance responses beyond both technological and elite ideological control. Collective productive intelligence depends on coordination, mutual adjustments, respect and personal initiatives in common work. The new economy needs new workers, but these workers must be imagined beyond their instrumentalist and demeaning depiction as human resources. Workers as citizens exercising social citizenship rights provide a basis for their claims not to be treated as objects of corporate firm utility and dispensable human resources. Citizen-based governance practices gain viable foundations. A deepened and re-articulated notion, as Balibar argues, of "popular sovereignty" emerges.

NEW ECONOMIES, NEW CITIZENS, RENEWED SOCIETIES?

Neo-liberal capitalism encourages action by the market and the corporate firm against the interests of society. Market action has encroached into diverse areas of social, cultural, family and personal life that were formerly protected from its logic and demands. A social response to these forces, and their now widely recognized social costs, may be more richly developed through taking up a substantially innovated concept of social citizenship, as ethic and agent, that I have sketched. An inclusive, materialist and post-materialist, conception is an ambitious proposition, yet it must be tabled. Social citizenship, which encompasses parity of esteem for productive workers, advances a civil society premised on equal citizenship of the *cité* – whatever that city may be in concrete situations. Social citizenship diminishes inequalities of esteem for workers in the same way as parity of esteem is accorded to persons across racial, ethnic, religious, regional and other communities of difference within the *cité*. Social citizenship practised at work, in forging new links between different levels of regulation and different issues in the regulatory agenda, nurtures a movement toward greater democratization of the economy and of society.

Social citizenship at once contests the power of market forces, of the technocratic state and of communalist, clan action. Social citizenship, in expressing limits of economic rationality, proposes a means to revitalize education with a semi-autonomous relationship with economy and to release the grip of market forces in its institutions. Moreover, a social citizenship that challenges reduction to instrumental rationality and subservience to elite interests assists a revitalization of the social, and personal, dimensions of work. Citizens recognized as persons with economic and diverse non-economic interests in education and work gain greater avenues for human flourishing. In the workplace, the subject-citizen, in Touraine's term (1995), may organize to forge new demands, including for vital humanization of the workplace, and not least in regard to children and personal relational life which are currently so accustomed to disciplined subordination to economy.

Intensified pressures in workplaces, volatile labour markets, fear of social and personal instability, and pressures to maintain one's consumption habits as worker-consumers are instructed to do, all militate against bearing and raising children. As Esping-Andersen (2009: 104) argues, the much needed humanization of work which includes a "feminization" of work is obstructed and defeated in contemporary conditions. The work environment, "is not conducive to any far-reaching feminisation of either everyday life or of the life course". A more humanized ethic would enable more genuinely family supportive life-styles, would value the care of children and frail elderly, and refuse the invasive encroachment of economic production rationalities into all domains of human life.

Work that is part of what one professes of herself or himself requires development not just of the knowledge, skills and competencies in that professed work – of engineering or teaching, accounting or nursing, of cooking or banking, and so forth – but requires the ethics, habits and responsibilities of craft, of interaction with users or clients of one's work, and of contributions to others. These habits also enable one to deal with the difficulties including boredom with routines and the inevitable irritations of personal and collective human life. It is evidently the case that industrial Fordism and its imagined successor, of flexible, strategically hierarchical and divisional firm and tightly managed flexible workforces, have wrought untenable coercion and debasement of many aspects of work. They have hushed workers' collective voices and heightened competitiveness among them. They have badly damaged, most visibly in many service sectors, workers' sense of responsibility, care and pride.

But it is also the case that postindustrial developments, of which the highly competitive and globalizing knowledge-based economy is the currently favoured path, have brought new emphases on education and skills among wider sectors of workers. The value and dispersion of higher education and skills levels have immense social and cultural potential. Citizen-workers and their revitalized citizen-based unions and, one further hopes, their collaborating university educators, can remobilize demands for more dignified and satisfying work. That more dignified work must include an undoing and surpassing of industrialism's forced separation of mind and heart from so many occupations and jobs in the past two centuries. The restoration of calls for responsible and participatory citizen-workers who are able to problem-solve and thoughtfully, heartedly, participate in the organizing and conduct of their work engenders new potential for both individual human development and in more dignified, democratic and just workplaces and humane societies.

CONCLUSION

The policy discourse of the highly competitive knowledge-based economy is premised on a normalization of the fundamental tenets of modern liberal thought. The core assumption that economic abundance comes before everything else and that markets are the indisputably superior institution for that elevated pursuit and therefore the unavoidable governing principal of production, work and society, has been accepted in policy arenas to our peril. That policy discourse and its assumptions are exposed and found wanting. In that exposure the search and demand for a just economy and society are renewed and reinvigorated.

A just economy requires in the first instance a universal social regulation and constraint of markets and enterprises in the interests of society and persons. It recognizes and honours far more than the imperatives of techno-scientific knowledge and the production and consumption of ever-novel commodities. It recognizes the social retention – at least in the present decades – of non-diminishing sectors of ordinary, moderately skilled work. The ambitious belief in technological advances in production which led very many commentators to conclude that lower-skilled work would be absorbed by technological applications and would, in the advanced economies, inevitably disappear is disproven. Policy projection of a generalized knowledge-based economy and learning society in the midst of liberalized, accelerated competitiveness and empowered firms, is at best an error of economic conceit. At worst, it is an orchestrated deception of the vast majority of working people that portends a wildly unfair burden of cost and frustration. The hypertrophic pursuit of techno-science, the exclusive privileging of its episteme and the distortion of education systems toward its end rob citizens of development of a vast range of human potential for culturally and spiritually rich learning and for contribution beyond the materiality of economy.

The path to a more socially just economy and society cannot be found in the state's and public's compliance to elite demands and imaginaries. A just economy requires a conception of the worker as agentic subject who brings her rich capacities for life – as a desiring, creating, relational person – into her working life and organizational participations. It requires the crucial recognition that workers are, above all, people whose capacities for knowledge, action and life far exceed those required by production. Education, remobilized to contest and refuse economic superordination and authoritarianism may do socially much more than salvage a beleaguered university institution hastily embracing the market and corporate model. Education, led by the culturally unique and privileged place of the university, may nurture the development of a renewed social democracy. It may stimulate and disperse ideas, knowledge, virtues and confidence which must always be shared as widely as possible. And it must play its role in civil society's social regulation of economy and markets.

An innovative and expansive conception of social citizenship, as ethic and agent, offers new possibilities for wider and stronger social, and indeed planetary, solidarities. Social citizenship is a capability which, as philosopher Paul Ricoeur (1996) proposes, must be *awakened* in order to become real and actual in life lived with each other on a finite planet.

Notes

1 Critical reflections on economy and society

1 Sociologies of economy and organization comprised principal areas of classical sociology. Weber's extensive work exemplified and established that central area of pursuit but it later experienced some neglect. The revival of economic sociology, now often termed the "new economic sociology", fuels many current debates on the "new institutional analysis" in economics and in the social sciences more generally. A much revived interest in Karl Polanyi's (1944) work reopens debates with social, political and cultural theory in its critique of mainstream economics. See, for example, Ebner and Beck (2008), Slater and Tonkiss (2001), Smart (2003).

2 A liberal economy of knowledge

1 Keynesian economic policies, which took various forms in European states, were drawn from the theorizations of John Maynard Keynes in the 1930s and 1940s. Keynes (1936) proposed a set of "improvements in the techniques in modern capitalism". Keynes argued, against classical economists, that market economies are intrinsically unstable; that real markets display gaps and imbalances between supply and demand, and between markets. For Keynes, markets on their own cannot ensure a high level of productivity and general distribution and well-being in society. The state must take responsibility for adjusting consumption and investment, including labour supply, and by so doing bring about a more stable demand. That "managed capitalism" enabled social constraints on various sectoral power interests.

2 The United States did not develop Keynesian economic management comparable to that in much of Europe, although some aspects of its Fordist regime readily resembled the Keynesian model (Amin *et al.* 2002; Crouch 1999; Harvey 1989) and the terms Keynesianism and Fordism are often used interchangeably. This was especially evident in those policies favouring full employment of adult males and mass consumption expansion.

3 Economic historian Eichengreen (2007) argues that the role of welfare state policies in the rising levels of unemployment was frequently elaborately over-stated. He points out that the provident welfare state in Europe was well established under conditions of high levels of employment prior to the 1973 oil crisis and downturn. He notes that there were some extensions during the 1970s and 1980s, when times turned bad, of employment protection and unemployment support. But, he argues, "It is a stretch to attribute the entirety of Europe's transformation from a low- to a high-unemployment economy to these limited changes in policy and legislation" (ibid.: 277).

4 The 'seven C's of Brown's (2001) model are: consensus, competitive capacity, capability, coordination, circulation, cooperation, closure. The last factor, closure, addresses social inclusion and exclusion in education, training and the labour market. Brown notes that no existing economy has achieved these targets, but the potential for collaborative participation in regulating relations of economy and education must be emphasized.

5 New institutional approaches in economics share debates with a revived economic sociology and "new institutionalism" in political sciences. The main orientation in the approach is a departure from neo-classical conceptions of abstract economic actions. Institutions are sets of legal rules and social norms that govern economic and political actions. Markets, despite classical claims for their freedom, are always located in sets of socio-cultural institutions. Institutions exert path dependencies (future actions are shaped by their histories) and contextual logics of legitimacy. Attention to the diversity of institutional forms can contribute new knowledge on the development and constraint of innovation (among other things) and further understanding of social and political interests in economic action and governance. Institutions, it is noted, are crucial for the efficiency of markets. See, for instance, Ebner and Beck (2008), North (1990) and Powell (2001).

6 A cluster of economists endeavouring to theorize innovation systems emerged in the 1990s. Prominent in EU debates are the works of Dosi (1988), Foray and Lundvall (1996), Lundvall and Borrás (1999), Archibugi and Lundvall (2001), Nelson (1993), Nelson and Winter (1982). Within variation of emphasis in their models, as the recent collection by Dolfsma and Soete (2006) indicates, a shared orientation in the evolutionary and dynamic nature of knowledge and innovation is evident. Their influence on KBE theorizations is extensive.

3 Work now: The forces of production

1 Many exemplary studies over recent decades address diverse aspects of work and industrial relations in the advanced economies, including, for instance, issues affecting particular occupations or sectors, of work–life balance, health and stress and so forth, which are not explored in this chapter. Many offer particular national or industry studies or focus on particular issues. See, for instance, Ciulla (2000), De Cuyper *et al.* 2005, Gollac and Volkof 2000; Perrons *et al.* (2006), Skorstad and Ramsdal (2009), Williams (2007) for illustrative studies incorporating these issues.

2 Research in industrial and employment relations includes detailed analyses and documentation of legislative changes in particular national contexts or in comparison with sets of national contexts. See, for instance, Gold (2009), Hyman (2001), Leisink *et al.* (2007), Marginson and Sisson (2004), and Széll (2001). For a singularly masterful work of national comparison, see Traxler *et al.* (2001). For a comprehensive comparative study of developments in labour law in the European Union since the mid-twentieth century, see Hepple and Veneziani (2009). That study identifies key convergences among national systems under European Union integration and argues the changes overall make for a "transformation" of labour law and conditions. The authors note especially a convergence in regard to the decline in organized labour and the decentralization of collective bargaining. As they put it, "The most significant change from the 1980s onwards was the decline of collectivism ... Enforcement of employment rights was now typically through individualized judicial procedures. Labour relations had become highly juridified" (ibid.: 2).

3 There is much current discussion in sociological research on organizations and firms that recognizes the firm's institutional context, its roles in a network of relations with other firms and economic actors (Di Maggio 2001; Ebner and Beck 2008; Trigilia 2002). That institutional context was not acknowledged in classical

economic conceptions of the firm and markets. Inter-firm ownership constructs ties across boundaries of enterprises and discrete firms, giving rise to the importance for economic action, and analytical inquiry, of the network form of organization, of vertical business groups and subsidiarization. Castells' (1996) meta-analysis of the "network society" is echoed but not necessarily adopted in this schema. This chapter focuses on the firm's action including through its organizational forms, subsidiary enterprises as business units, profit centres and client networks. Its networks of associations: chambers of commerce, business roundtables, employers' associations, are not discretely studied in this discussion. But it must be noted that large corporate firms have withdrawn from business associations preferring to act individually in relations with governments (Streeck 2006).

4 Economists Lorenz and Lundvall (2006), who are prominent theorists of the learning economy, recall that criticizing wage-cost competitiveness even as late as 1984 was very controversial. Lorenz and Lundvall's promotion of knowledge-based innovation as the key to competitiveness and growth and which required higher wage levels for highly skilled workers was considered by many economists as unorthodox and inefficient.

5 A critical sociological literature addressing social and cultural aspects and effects of marketing includes the illustrative studies of Bauman (1998), du Gay (1996) and Featherstone (1991). The popular criticism of Melanie Klein's (2001) book *No Logo* scrutinizes the rise and power of brand marketing and consumption. A nascent field of critical marketing studies criticizes the development of marketing within the capitalist business world and business schools, and addresses the role of the marketing enterprise in wider society: Brownlie *et al.* (1999), Saren *et al.* (2007), Skålén *et al.* (2008).

6 Some European analysts in the 2000s, looking back over the previous two decades, remark that the emergence of flexibility, especially labour flexibility, had been entirely unexpected (Boltanski and Chiapello 2007; Durand 2007). Even as technological changes were observed and job losses animated much debate in the 1980s, the extent and reach of the move toward flexibility had not been anticipated (Deery and Mitchell 1999; Gallie *et al.* 1998). Standing (2002) identifies seven forms of flexibility: organizational, numerical, functional, job structure, working time, wage system, and labour force flexibility. All of these forms were advocated by economists and politicians with the expectation that their introduction would solve the ills of the advanced economies in the 1990s. Trade unions and labour analysts raised much concern over the rapid and widespread introduction of flexibility.

7 If readers will allow me a biographical note in illustration: As a young factory worker, I operated a heavy metal press in the manufacture of kitchen appliances. My (un-gloved) hands fed sheets of copper and brass into the press for cutting into rounds of various sizes. The components I produced daily were, in the vertically integrated Fordist operation, accumulated in vast quantities beyond the capacities for the manufacture of the final product. Workers observed this internal production inefficiency. But the factory's heavily disciplined liner routinization and lack of horizontal integration made it impossible to share that knowledge and intervene in the production system. Of course, the subsequent ICT-enabled changes to that system are welcome. But the introduction of flexible functional integration co-opted and incorporated workers' new knowledge contributions into further rationalization. It is utilized to effect the re-subordinated integration of workers into managerialist operating systems while enabling flexible firm market action.

8 Reference to "atypical" or "non-standard" jobs, which burgeoned in the Anglophone liberal economies in the 1990s, generally means variation on the mid-twentieth century standard of typically 35–40 hours a week on a continuing (open-ended) contract, and protected by collective agreements on wages and conditions. It can include

forms of seasonal, intermittent, or project work on various fixed term contracts or as self-employed workers.

9 The OECD (2004) reports average decline in union membership as well as average decline in numbers of employees covered by collective agreements, notwithstanding the French exception. The French exception refers to the case in which trade union membership has always been relatively low in comparison with other European countries but its national industrial relations system provides for high coverage of workers by union-negotiated collective conditions and wages. Boltanski and Chiapello (2007) and Jenkins (2000) provide illustrative discussions of the French case.

10 For many analysts, the occurrence of flexibility attracts foremost attention. Studies on the employment effects of flexibility (Felstead and Jewson 1999; Gray 2004, Skorstad and Ramsdal 2009) and on institutional effects (Beck 2000; Gleason 2006; Stråth 2000) have been followed by explorations of responses in the form of policies on "flexicurity", newly introduced in Nordic countries (Muffels 2008), discussed in Chapter 6, to ease the risks for workers.

4 A new economy for education

1 The concept of *cultural capital*, as developed especially by Bourdieu and Passeron (1977), refers to cultural reserves that are possessed by families or individuals and that can be passed on to their children. Cultural capital comprises a stock of valued and advantageous knowledge that include attitudes, behaviours, styles, tastes and elements of socialization and relational networks. This stock of cultural capital, unlike financial capital, can be used without being depleted. Its use, moreover, can further enrich the stock and gain further advantages at later use. Other theorists have added to this concept the notion of *social capital* to refer to similar processes that may not be limited to family sources of acquisition including, for instance, institutions of professions and occupations, civil society organizations, and civil trust.

2 A prominent British educationist, Percy Nunn, expressed these mid-twentieth century aspirations in 1937 in a publication entitled *The Freedom We Seek*:

> the traditional school needs to be radically altered if we desire a new sort of world. There must be less competition and more cooperation … there must be greater informality and complete respect for the individuality of the pupil … There must be free speech and free thought.
>
> (Nunn 1937, cited in Taylor 1963: 94)

3 A vibrant sociology of education of the 1970s–1990s criticized earlier emphases on functionalist approaches and problem-solving for the assumed processes of societal modernization. A critical sociology of education especially prominent in the Anglophone academies with somewhat distinct US and UK traditions drew predominantly on Marxist-informed theoretical traditions and questions of class and ideology in the structures and reproduction of education.

4 The publication in 1968 of the influential comparative study by P.H. Coombs, *The World Crisis in Education*, reported extensive scientific and economic criticism of education. In addition to criticism of the field of study, Coombs criticized the "inherent inertia of education systems" (ibid.: 165) which required widespread and stern reform. The reforms at that time, however, had not yet converged with demands from the business sector which remained profitable based on a prevailing low skill mass production system.

5 The concept of *Bildung* is an ideal of the Humboldtian university founded on the Enlightenment principles of the pursuit of culture, knowledge and truth for their

own sakes. It refers to education that is the development of the whole person, a moral and spiritual education in which personal character and cultural formation are paramount. A similar conceptualization in the Anglo-Saxon context is referred to frequently as the Newman idea of the university based on John Henry Newman's *The Idea of a University* ([1852] 1976).

6 Bourdieu (1988) theorized three types of cultural capital that are fought over in the university. Academic capital refers to socially coded power over academic resources, credentials, status allocation and career influence. Scientific capital is derived from scientific and scholarly knowledge, accomplishments and prestige. The third form (perhaps especially effective in the French cultural context of Bourdieu's study) is that of intellectual capital. That refers to power based on scientific and scholarly capital to influence publics beyond the academy. The role of the public intellectual exemplifies this capital. For Bourdieu, *homo academicus* is a product of these fields of academic power.

7 A succinct illustration of this more generalized orientation is found in Gibb *et al.* (2009) on "leading the entrepreneurial university" prepared for Oxford University's Said Business School for partnership developments with other non-university enterprises in regard to a programme of university entrepreneurial leadership.

5 Labour markets, organizations and the utility of education

1 The technologically enabled obsolescence of labour-intensive jobs was widely assumed. One excerpt from a book published in 1980 boldly entitled *Working in the Twenty-First Century* (Sheppard and Carroll 1980: 213), neatly illustrates the futuristic vision inspired by the developments in advanced technologies:

> Ordinary work, as we now know it, will cease to exist. Computers and other machines will make mail deliveries, bank tellers, store clerks, bus drivers and most similar workers obsolete. Most sales and other business transactions will be done on TV monitors at home ... No printers, no pressmen.

2 Fields of research in organization theory and analysis developed from studies in sociologies of economy, industry, organization and work. In the mid-twentieth century, as the US-style business school developed and expanded, sociological studies of complex organizations were applied to organization science and increasingly associated with administration and management science. Accordingly, there is an extensive applied social science literature that addresses problems of organizational structure, design, behaviour, management and market environments, and so forth. There is, it must also be noted, the globalizing influence of US business school curricula in business and management disciplines in universities in the advanced economies. That curricula normatively adopt the firm's interests in liberal markets in the research questions addressed and subjects taught.

6 Critical dilemmas for work, education and workers

1 For example, many large operators in retail, supermarkets and fast food services in the United Kingdom now frequently employ workers on 4-hour shifts (with Tesco offering workers additional 'slivers of time'). These workers are not required to possess skills beyond secondary school education, nor able to utilize discretion and judgement in the conduct of their work. They are expected to possess skills in self-grooming and toleration of noise, queuing, customer irritations and technological surveillance, and tolerate little negotiation over gaining sufficient continuous hours to ensure adequate pay earnings.

2 For more detailed discussion on models of security and internal functional flexibilities of the firm, and their problems, see Blanpain and Dickens (2008), Furåker and Hakansson (2007) and Muffels and Luijkx (2008).

3 Persistent biases in the measure of skill and what counts as skill affect remuneration and esteem. For example, skill levels required of many so-called women's jobs, especially child-care, have been under-valued on the basis that the personal, relational and social skills required in these forms of work have not been recognized, or formally taught in schooling systems. Similarly, the "soft" skills of interpersonal and congenial relations of customer services workers are required, but not counted, in job design and remuneration.

7 Citizens and society, work and education

1 Discussion on the historical development of citizenship and its conceptual refinements must be deferred for my purposes in this chapter. Suffice to note that T.H. Marshall's ([1950] 1992) seminal thesis continues to engage theoretical discussions today with many writers wishing to add to or revise or compare his categories with more contemporary contexts. Marshall proposed a citizenship characterized by civil, political and social forms. Citizenship is conceived as both a status and a set of rights.

Bibliography

Albert, M. (1993) *Capitalism Against Capitalism*. London: Whurr Publishers.

Amable, B. (2003) *The Diversity of Modern Capitalism*. Oxford: Oxford University Press.

Amaral, A., Jones, G. and Karseth, B. (eds) (2002) *Governing Higher Education: National Perspectives on Institutional Governance*. Dordrecht: Kluwer.

Amin, A., Cameron, A. and Hudson, R. (2002) *Placing the Social Economy*. London: Routledge.

Apple, M. (1979) *Ideology and Curriculum*. London: Routledge and Kegan Paul.

Archibugi, D. (2008) *The Global Commonwealth of Citizens*. Princeton, NJ: Princeton University Press.

Archibugi, D. and Lundvall, B-Å. (eds) (2001) *Europw in the Globalising Learning Economy*. Oxford: Oxford University Press.

Argyris, C. and Schön, D. (1978) *Organizational Learning: A Theory of Action Perspective*. Reading, MA: Addison-Wesley.

——(1996) *Organizational Learning II: Theory, Method and Practice*. Reading, MA: Addison-Wesley.

Aronowitz, S. and Giroux, H. (1986) *Education Under Seige*. South Hadley, MA: Bergin & Garvey.

Arthur, J., Davies, I. and Hahn, C. (eds) (2008) *The Sage Handbook for Education for Citizenship and Democracy*. London: Sage.

Avilés, A. and Vina, J. (2009) "Regulation of the Labour Market", in B. Heppel and B. Veneziani (eds) *The Transformation of Labour Law in Europe: A Comparative Study of 15 Countries, 1945–2004*. Oxford: Hart Publishing.

Bahro, R. (1984) *From Red to Green*. London: Verso.

Balibar, É. (2004) *We, The People of Europe? Reflections on Transnational Citizenship*. Princeton, NJ: Princeton University Press.

Ball, C. (1993) *Towards a Learning Society*. London: Royal Society of Arts.

Ball, S. (2008) *The Education Debate: Policy and Politics in the 21st Century*. Bristol: Policy Press.

Barbier, J-C. (2008) "There is More to Job Quality than 'Precariousness': A Comparative Epistemological Analysis of the 'Flexibility and Security' Debate in Europe", in R. Muffels, (ed.) *Flexibility and Employment Security in Europe: Labour Markets in Transition*. Cheltenham: Edward Elgar.

Barbier, J-C. and Lindley, R. (2002) *La Précarité de l'Emploi*. CCE 4, Noisy-le-Grand: CCE.

Battu, H. and Sloane, P. (2000) "Overeducation and Crowding out in Britain", in L. Borghans and A. de Grip (eds) *The Over-educated Worker: The Economics of Skill Utilization*. Cheltenham: Edward Elgar.
Bauman, Z. (1998) *Work, Consumerism and the New Poor*. Buckingham: Open University Press.
Beardwell, I. (1992) "The New Industrial Relations? A Review of the Debate", *Human Resource Management Journal*, 2(2): 1–7.
——(ed.) (1996) *Contemporary Industrial Relations: A Critical Analysis*. Oxford: Oxford University Press.
Beck, U. (1992) *Risk Society: Toward a New Modernity*. London: Sage.
——(2000) *Brave New World of Work*. Cambridge: Polity Press.
Becker, G. (1964) *Human Capital: A Theoretical and Empirical Analysis with Special Reference to Education*. Chicago: University of Chicago Press.
Bell, D. (1973) *The Coming of Post-industrial Society*. Harmondsworth: Penguin.
Bendix, R. ([1956] 1974) *Work and Authority in Industry*. Berkeley, CA: University of California Press.
Benhabib, S. (2004) *The Rights of Others*. Cambridge: Cambridge University Press.
Bernstein, B. (1975) *Class, Codes and Control*. London: Routledge.
Best, M. (1990) *The New Competition: Institutions of Industrial Restructuring*. Cambridge, MA: Harvard University Press.
Blanpain, R. and Dickens, L. (2008) *Challenges of European Employment Relations: Employment Regulation, Trade Union Organization, Equality, Flexicurity, Training and New Approaches to Pay*. Alphen aan den Rijn, Netherlands: Kluwer.
Blau, P. (1965) *The Dynamics of Bureaucracy*. Chicago: University of Chicago Press.
Block, F. (1990) *Postindustrial Possibilities: A Critique of Economic Discourse*. Berkeley, CA: University of California Press.
Blumberg, P. (1973) *Industrial Democracy*. New York: Schocken Books.
Boisot, M. (1998) *Knowledge Assets: Securing Competitive Advantage in the Information Economy*. Oxford: Oxford University Press.
Bollier, G. and Durand, C. (eds) (1999) *La nouvelle division du travail*. Paris: Editions de L'Atelier.
Boltanski, L. and Chiapello, E. (2007) *The New Spirit of Capitalism*. London: Verso.
Bonham, C. and Cohen, R. (1995) "Testing the Rationality of Price Forecasts: Comment", *The American Economic Review*, 85(1): 284.
Bordogna, L. and Winchester, D. (2001) "Collective Bargaining in Western Europe", in C. Dell'Aringa, G. Della Rocca and B. Keller (eds) *Strategic Choices in Reforming Public Sector Employment*. Houndmills: Palgrave.
Borghans, L. and Cörvers, F. (2009) "The Americanization of European Higher Education and Research", IZA Discussion Paper No. 4445. Bonn: The Institute for the Study of Labor (IZA).
Borghans, L. and de Grip, A. (eds) (2000) *The Overeducated Worker?The Economics of Skill Utilization*. Cheltenham: Edward Elgar.
Bonaccorsi, A. and Daraio, C. (eds) (2007) *Universities and Strategic Knowledge Creation: Specialization and Performance in Europe*. Cheltenham: Edward Elgar.
Bosch, G. and Weinkopf, C. (eds) (2008) *Low Wage Work in Germany*. New York: Russell Sage Foundation.
Boshier, R. (ed.) (1980) *Towards a Learning Society*. Vancouver: Learning Press Ltd.
Bosworth, D. (1992) "The Extent and Intensity of Skill Shortages, 1990", *International Journal of Manpower*, 13(9): 3–12.

Bowles, S. and Gintis, H. (1976) *Schooling in Capitalist America.* New York: Basic Books.
Bourdieu, P.(1988) *Homo Academicus.* Cambridge: Polity Press.
——(1998) *La Précarité est Aujourd'hui Partout. Contre-feux*, Paris: Liber Raisons d'agir.
——(1999) *Acts of Resistance: Against the Tyranny of the Market.* New York: New Press.
Bourdieu, P. and Passeron, J-C. (1977) *Reproduction in Education, Society and Culture.* London: Sage.
Brookes, R. and Holford, J. (2009) "Citizenship, Learning and Education: Themes and Issues", *Citizenship Studies*, 13(2): 85–103.
Brown, P. (2001) "Skill Formation in the Twenty-First Century", in P. Brown, A. Green and H. Lauder (eds) *High Skills: Globalization, Competitiveness and Skill Formation.* Oxford: Oxford University Press.
Brown, P., Ashton, D., Lauder, H. and Tholen, G. (2008) *Towards a High-Skilled, Low-Waged Workforce? A Review of Global Trends in Education, Employment and the Labour Market.* Centre on Skills, Knowledge and Organisational Performance, Cardiff and Oxford Universities, Monograph No. 10, October.
Brown, P., Green, A. and Lauder, H. (2001) *High Skills: Globalization, Competitiveness and Skill Formation*, Oxford: Oxford University Press.
Brown, P. and Hesketh, P. (2004) *The Mismanagement of Talent: Employability and Jobs in the Knowledge Economy.* New York: Oxford University Press.
Brown, P. and Lauder, H. (2006) "Globalisation, Knowledge, and the Myth of the Magnet Economy". *Globalisation, Societies, and Education*, 4(1): 25–57.
Brownlie, D., Saren, M., Wensley, R. and Whittington, R. (eds) (1999) *Rethinking Marketing: Towards Critical Marketing Accountings.* London: Sage.
Brynin, M, (2002a) "Over-qualification in Employment". *Work, Employment and Society*, 16(4): 637–54.
——, (2002b) "Graduate Density, Gender and Employment". *British Journal of Sociology*, 55(3): 363–81.
Buchel, F., de Grip, A. and Mertens, A. (eds) (2003) *Overeducation in Europe: Current Issues in Theory and Policy.* Cheltenham: Edward Elgar.
Burawoy, M. (1979) *Manufacturing Consent.* Chicago: University of Chicago Press.
Burchell, B., Lapido, D. and Wilkinson, R. (eds) (2002) *Job Insecurity and Work Intensification.* London: Routledge.
Burke, R. and Cooper, C. (2008) *The Long Work Hours Culture: Causes, Consequences, and Choices.* Bingley: Emerald.
Cantor, L. (1986) "A Coherent Approach to the Education and Training of the 16–19 Age Group", in G. D. Worswick (ed.) *Education and Economic Performance.* Aldershot: Ashgate.
Casey, C. (1995) *Work, Self and Society: After Industrialism.* London and New York: Routledge.
——(2002) *Critical Analysis of Organizations: Theory, Practice, Revitalization.* London: Sage.
——(2003) "The Learning Worker, Organizations and Democracy", *International Journal of Lifelong Education*, 22(6): 620–34.
——(2004) "Knowledge-Based Economies, Organizations, and the Socio-Cultural Regulation of Work", *Economic and Industrial Democracy*, 25(4): 613–33.
——(2009) "Organizations, Workers, and Learning: New Prospects for Citizenship at Work?" *Citizenship Studies*, 13(2): 169–84.

Casey, C. and Alach, P. (2004) "Just a Temp? Women, Temporary Employment and Lifestyle". *Work, Employment and Society*, 18(3): 459–80.

Castells, M. (1998) *End of Millennium*. Oxford: Blackwell.

——(1996) *The Rise of the Network Society*. Oxford: Blackwell.

Ciulla, J. (2000) *The Working Life: The Promises and Betrayal of Modern Work*. New York: Three Rivers Press.

Clark, B. (1998) *Creating Entrepreneurial Universities: Organizational Pathways to Transformation*. Oxford: Pergamon.

Clarke, J. and Newman, J. (1997) *The Managerial State: Power, Politics and Ideology in the Remaking of Social Welfare*. London: Sage.

Cohen, D. and Prusak, L. (2001) *In Good Company: How Social Capital Makes Organizations Work*. Boston: Harvard Business School Press.

Conceicao, P., Heitor, M.V. and Lundvall, B-Å. (2003) *Innovation, Competence Building and Social Cohesion in Europe:Towards a Learning Society*. Cheltenham: Edward Elgar.

Cooke, P. (2002) *Knowledge Economies*. London: Routledge.

Coombs, P. (1968) *The World Crisis in Education*. London: Oxford.

Corbett, A. (2005) *Universities and the Europe of Knowledge: Ideas, Institutions and Policy Entrepreneurship in European Union Higher Education Policy, 1955–2005*. Basingstoke: Palgrave Macmillan.

Coriat, B. and Weinstein, O. (2002) "Organizations, Firms and Institutions in the Generation of Innovation", *Research Policy*, 31: 273–90.

Coutrot, T. (1998) *L'Entreprise néo-liberale, nouvelle utopie capitaliste?*. Paris: La Découverte.

Crafts, N. (1988) "The Assessment: British Growth over the Long Run", *Oxford Review of Economic Policy*, 4(21): i–xxi.

Crouch, C. (1986) "Conservative Industrial Relations Policy: Towards Labour Exclusion?", in O. Jacobi, B. Jesson, H. Kastendiek, and M. Regini (eds) *Economic Crisis, Trade Unions and the State*. London: Croom Helm.

——(1999) *Social Change in Western Europe*. Oxford: Oxford University Press.

——(2000) *Coping with Post Democracy*. London: Fabian Society.

——(2005a) *Capitalist Diversity and Change: Recombinant Governance and Institutional Entrepreneurs*. Oxford: Oxford University Press.

——(2005b) "Skill Formation Systems", in S. Ackroyd, R. Batt, P. Thompson and P. Tolbert (eds) *The Oxford Handbook of Work and Organization*. Oxford: Oxford University Press.

——(2006) "Modelling the Firm in its Market and Organizational Environment: Methodologies for Studying Corporate Social Responsibility", *Organization Studies*, 27: 1533–51.

Crouch, C., Eder, E and Tambini, D. (eds) (2001) *Citizenship, Markets, and the State*. Oxford: Oxford University Press.

Crouch, C., Finegold, D. and Sako, M. (1999) *Are Skills the Answer?* Oxford: Oxford University Press.

Crouch, C. and Heller, F.A. (eds) (1983) *Organizational Democracy and Political Processes*. Chichester: John Wiley & Sons, Ltd.

Cycert, R. and March, J. (1963) *A Behavioral Theory of the Firm*. Englewood Cliffs, NJ: Prentice-Hall.

Dale, R. and Robertson, S. (eds) (2009) *Globalisation and Europeanisation in Education*. Didcott: Symposium Books.

Dalton, P., Asplund, R. and Barth, E. (eds) (2009) *Education and Inequality across Europe*. Cheltenham: Edward Elgar.

Daly, H. (1996) *Beyond Growth: The Economics of Sustainable Development*. Boston: Beacon Press.

Davenport, T., and Prusak, L. (1998) *Working Knowledge: How Organizations Manage What They Know*. Boston: Harvard Business School.

Davis, S. and Botkin, J. (1998) "The Coming of Knowledge-Based Business", in D. Neef (ed.) *The Knowledge Economy*. Boston: Butterworth-Heinemann.

Dearing, R. (1997) *Higher Education in the Learning Society*, The Report of the National Committee of Inquiry into Higher Education. Norwich: HMSO.

Debels, A. (2008) "Transitions Out of Temporary Jobs: Consequences for Employment and Poverty across Europe", in R. Muffels (ed.) *Flexibility and Employment Security in Europe: Labour Markets in Transition*. Cheltenham: Edward Elgar.

De Cuyper, N., Isaksson, K. and De Witte, H. (eds) (2005) *Employment Contracts and Wellbeing among European Workers*. Farnham: Ashgate.

Deem, R., Hilyard, S. and Reed, M. (2007) *Knowledge, Higher Education, and the New Managerialism*. New York: Oxford University Press.

Deery, S. and Mitchell, R. (eds) (1999) *Employment Relations: Individualism and Union Exclusion*. NSW, Australia: Federation Press.

De Fraja, G. (2004) "Hierarchies in Organisations and Labour Market Competition", *Labour Economics*, 11: 669–96.

Delanty, G. (2001) *Challenging Knowledge: The University in the Knowledge Society*. Buckingham: SRHE and Open University Press.

——(2009) *The Cosmopolitan Imagination: The Renewal of Critical Social Theory*. Cambridge: Cambridge University Press.

Dennison, E. (1962) *The Sources of Economic Growth in the United States and the Alternatives Before Us*. New York: Committee for Economic Development.

Dent, M. and Whitehead, S. (eds) (2002) *Knowledge, Identity and the New Professional*. London: Routledge.

Desjardins, R., Garrousted-Norelius, C. and Mendes, S. (2004) *Benchmarking Education and Training Systems in Europe*. Brussels: CEC D-G Education and Culture.

Dewey, J. ([1916] 1966) *Education and Democracy*. New York: Free Press.

Di Maggio, P. (2001) *The Twenty-First Century Firm*. Princeton, NJ: Princeton University Press.

Doeringer, P. and Piore, M. (1971) *Internal Labor Markets and Manpower Analysis*. Lexington, MA: D.C. Heath.

Dolfsma, W. and Soete, L. (eds) (2006) *Understanding the Dynamics of a Knowledge Economy*. Cheltenham: Edward Elgar.

Doogan, K. (2009) *New Capitalism? The Transformation of Work*. Cambridge: Polity.

Dosi, G. (1988) "Sources, Procedures, and Microeconomic Effects of Innovation". *Journal of Economic Literature*, 26(3): 1120–71.

Dosi, G., Teece, D. and Chytry, J. (eds) (1998) Technology, Organization, and Competitiveness: Perspectives on Industrial and Corporate Change. Oxford: Oxford University Press.

Dribbusch, H. and Schulten, T. (2007) "The End of an Era: Structural Changes in German Collective Bargaining", in P. Leisink, B. Steijn and U. Veersma (eds) *Industrial Relations in the New Europe*. Cheltenham: Edward Elgar.

Dronkers, J. (2008) "Education as the Backbone of Inequality: European Education Policy: Constraints and Possibilities", in F. Becker, K. Duffek and T. Mörschel (eds)

Social Democracy and Education: The European Experience. Amsterdam: Friederich Ebert Stiftung.

Drucker, P. (1993) *Post-Capitalist Society*. New York: HarperCollins.

Dubois, P., Heidenreich, M., La Rosa, M. and Schmidt, G. (1995) "New Technologies and Post-Taylorist Regulation Models", in W. Littek and T. Charles, *The New Division of Labour: Emerging Forms of Work Organisation in International Perspective*. Berlin: Walter de Gruyter.

du Gay, P. (1996) *Consumption and Identity at Work*. London: Sage.

Duke, C. (1992) *The Learning University*. Buckingham: Open University Press.

Durand, J-P. (ed.) (1994) *La Fin du modèle suédois*. Paris: Syros.

——(2007) *The Invisible Chain: Constraints and Opportunities in the New World of Employment*. Basingstoke: Palgrave Macmillan.

Easterby-Smith, M. and Lyles, M. (eds) (2003) *The Blackwell Handbook of Organizational Learning and Knowledge Management*. Oxford: Wiley-Blackwell.

Ebner, A. and Beck, N. (eds) (2008) *The Institutions of the Market: Organizations, Social Systems and Governance*. Oxford: Oxford University Press.

Edwards, P. and Wajcman, J. (2005) *The Politics of Working Life*. Oxford: Oxford University Press.

EGGE (European Network of Experts on Employment and Gender Equality) (2009) *The National Reform Programmes 2008 and the Gender Aspects of the European Employment Strategy*. Brussels: CEC.

Eichengreen, B. (2007) *The European Economy since 1945: Coordinated Capitalism and Beyond*. Princeton, NJ: Princeton University Press.

Elias, P. and Purcell, K. (2004) "Is Mass Higher Education Working? Evidence from the Labour Market Experiences of Recent Graduates", *National Institute Economic Review*, 90: 60 – 74.

Eliasson, G., Fölster, S., Lindberg, T., Pousette, T. and Taymaz, E. (1990) *The Knowledge-Based Information Economy*. Stockholm: Almquist & Wiksell International.

Esping-Andersen, G. (1990) *The Three Worlds of Welfare Capitalism*. Princeton, NJ: Princeton University Press.

——(2002) *Why We Need a New Welfare State*. Oxford: Oxford University Press.

——(2009) *The Incomplete Revolution: Adapting to Women's New Roles*. Cambridge: Polity.

Esping-Andersen, G. and Regini, M. (2000) *Why De-Regulate Labour Markets?* Oxford: Oxford University Press.

European Commission (1993) *Growth, Competitiveness and Employment* (Delors White Paper). Luxembourg: Office for Official Publications of the European Communities.

——(1995) *Teaching and Learning: Towards the Learning Society*. Brussels: CEC.

——(1997) *Partnership for a New Organisation of Work*. COM (1997) 128. Brussels: CEC.

——(1998) *Modernising the Organisation of Work*. COM (1998)512. Brussels: CEC.

——(1999) *The European Employment Strategy*. Luxembourg: Office for Official Publications of the European Communities.

——(2000) *A Memorandum on Lifelong Learning*. SEC (2000)1832. Brussels: CEC.

——(2001) *Making a European Area of Lifelong Learning: Communication from the Commission*. COM (2001)678. Brussels: CEC.

——(2005a) *Working Together for Growth and Jobs: A New Start for the Lisbon Strategy*. COM(2005)24. Brussels: CEC.

——(2005b) *Delivery on Jobs and Growth: A New and Integrated Economic and Employment Coordination*. COM (2005)24. Brussels: CEC.

——(2005c) *Citizens for Europe*. SEC(2005)442. COM 2005 116. Brussels: CEC.

——(2005d) *Mobilising the Brainpower of Europe: Enabling Universities to Make their Full Contribution to the Lisbon Strategy*. COM(2005). Brussels: CEC.

——(2006) *Delivering on the Modernisation Agenda for Universities: Education, Research and Innovation*. COM(2006)208. Brussels: CEC.

——(2007a) *Employment in Europe 2007*. Luxembourg: Office for Official Publications of the European Communities.

——(2007b) *Europe for Citizens*. D-G COM, EACEA. Available at: http://ec.europa.eu/citizenship. Brussels: CEC.

——(2008a) *Renewed Social Agenda: Opportunities, Access and Solidarity in 21st Century Europe*. COM (2008)412. Brussels: CEC.

——(2008b) *An Updated Strategic Framework for European Cooperation in Education and Training*. COM(2008)865. Brussels: CEC.

——(2008c) *New Skills for New Jobs: Anticipating and Matching Labour Market and Skills Needs*, COM (2008)868. Brussels: CEC.

——(2010) *EUROPE 2020: A Strategy for Smart, Sustainable and Inclusive Growth*. COM(2010)2020. Brussels: CEC.

European Council (2007) *Council Resolution on Modernising Universities for Europe's Competitiveness in a Global Knowledge Economy*. 16096/1/07REV 1. Brussels: CEU.

——(2008) *Presidency Conclusions of Spring Council, Brussels*, CONCL1 7652/1/08. Brussels: CEU.

European Round Table of Industrialists (1989) *Education and Competence in Europe*. Brussels: European Round Table of Industrialists.

——(1997) *Education for Europeans: Towards the Learning Society*. Brussels: ERTI.

Fagerland, I. and Stromquist, G. (eds) (2004) *Reforming Higher Education in the Nordic Countries: Studies of Changes in Denmark, Finland, Iceland, Norway and Sweden*. Paris: International Institute for Educational Planning.

Fairclough, N. and Wodak, R. (2008) "The Bologna Process and the Knowledge-Based Economy", in B. Jessop, N. Fairclough and R. Wodak, *Education and the Knowledge-Based Economy in Europe*. Rotterdam: Sense Publications.

Faure, E. (1972) *Learning to Be: The World of Education Today and Tomorrow*. Paris: UNESCO.

Featherstone, M. (1991) *Consumer Culture and Postmodernism*. London: Sage.

Felstead, A., Gallie, D. and Green, F. (2002) *Work Skills in Britain 2001*. London: DfES.

Felstead, A. and Jewson, N. (eds) (1999) *Global Trends in Flexible Labour*. Basingstoke: Macmillan.

Field, J. (2006) *Lifelong Learning and the New Educational Order*. London: Trentham.

Finegold, D. and Soskice, D. (1988) "The Failure of Training in Britain: Analysis and Prescription", *Oxford Review of Economic Policy*, 4(3): 21–53.

Floud, J., Halsey A. and Martin, F. (1956) *Social Class and Educational Opportunity*. London: Heinemann.

Foray, D. (2004) *The Economics of Knowledge*. Cambridge, MA: MIT Press.

Foray, D. and Gault, F. (2003) *Measuring Knowledge Management*. Paris: OECD.

Foray, D. and Lundvall, B-Å. (eds) (1996) *Employment and Growth in the Knowledge-based Economy*. Paris: OECD.

Fourastié, J. (1979) *Les Trente Glorieuses*. Paris: Fayard.

Fourcade-Gourinchas, M. and Babb, S. (2002) "The Rebirth of the Liberal Creed: Paths to Neo-Liberalism in Four Countries", *American Journal of Sociology*, 108: 544–9.

Foucault, M. (1972) *The Archeology of Knowledge*. London: Tavistock.
——(1980) *Power/Knowledge: Selected Interviews and Other Writings*, ed. C. Gordon. New York: Pantheon Books.
Freeman, C. and Lundvall, B-Å., (eds) (1988) *Small Countries Facing the Technological Revolution*. London: Pinter.
Freeman, C. and Soete, L. (1997) *The Economics of Industrial Innovation*. London: Pinter.
Frege, C. and Kelly, J. (eds) (2004) *Varieties of Unionism: Strategies for Union Revitalization in a Globalizing Economy*. Oxford: Oxford University Press.
Friedman, M. (1953) *Essays in Positive Economics*. Chicago: University of Chicago Press.
——(1962) *Capitalism and Freedom*. Chicago: University of Chicago Press.
Furåker, B. and Hakansson, K. (eds) (2007) *Flexibility and Stability in Working Life*. Basingstoke: Palgrave Macmillan.
Gadrey, J. (2000) *Nouvelle Economie, nouveau mythe?*. Paris: Flammarion.
Galbraith, J. (1967) *The New Industrial State*. Harmondsworth: Penguin.
Gallie, D. (ed.) (2004) *Resisting Marginalization: Unemployment Experience and Social Policy in the European Union*. Oxford: Oxford University Press.
——(2007) *Employment Regimes and the Quality of Work*. Oxford: Oxford University Press.
Gallie, D., White, M., Cheng, Y. and Tomlinson, M. (1998) *Restructuring the Employment Relationship*. Oxford: Oxford University Press.
Garibaldo, F. and Telljohann, V. (eds) (2006) *Nuove Forme di Organizzazione del Lavoro e Relazioni Industriali: Dov'è Italia?* Bologna: Maggioli Editore.
Garicano, L. and Rossi-Hansberg, E. (2006) "Organization and Inequality in a Knowledge Economy", *The Quarterly Journal of Economics*, Nov.: 1383–435.
Gibb, A., Haskins, A. and Robertson, I. (2009) *Leading the Entrepreneurial University*. Oxford: Oxford University Said Business School.
Giddens, A. (1998) *The Third Way: The Renewal of Social Democracy*. Cambridge: Polity.
——(ed.) (2003) *The Progressive Manifesto: New Ideas for the Centre-Left*. Cambridge: Polity.
Gleason, S. (ed.) (2006) *The Shadow Workforce: Perspectives on Contingent Work in US, Japan and Europe*. Kalamazoo MI: Upjohn Institute for Employment Research.
Glyn, A. (2006) *Capitalism Unleashed: Finance, Globalization and Welfare*. Oxford: Oxford University Press.
Gold, M. (2003) *New Frontiers of Democratic Participation at Work*. Aldershot: Ashgate.
——(ed.) (2009) *Employment Policy in the European Union: Origins, Themes, Prospects*. Basingstoke: Palgrave Macmillan.
Goldin, C. and Katz, L. (2008) *The Race Between Education and Technology*. Cambridge, MA: Harvard University Press.
Gollac, M., and Volkof, S. (2000) *Les Conditions de Travail*. Paris: La Découverte.
Goos, M., and Manning, A. (2007) "Lousy and Lovely Jobs: The Rising Polarization of Work in Britain", *Review of Economics and Statistics*, 89(1): 118–33.
Gorz, A. (1982) *Farewell to the Working Class*. London: Pluto.
——(1989) *Critique of Economic Reason*. London: Verso.
Gottdiener, M. and Komminos, N. (eds) (1989) *Capitalist Regulation and Crisis Theory*. Basingstoke: Macmillan.

Gray, A. (2004) *Unsocial Europe: Social Protection or Flexploitation?* London: Pluto Press.

Green, A. (2001) "Models of High Skills in National Competition Strategies", in P. Brown, A. Green and H. Lauder (eds) *High Skills: Globalization, Competitiveness and Skill Formation*. Oxford: Oxford University Press.

——(2002) "The Many Faces of Lifelong Learning: Recent Educational Policy Trends in Europe", *Journal of Education Policy*, 17: 611–26.

Green, A., Preston, J. and Germen, J. (2006) *Education, Equality and Social Cohesion: A Comparative Analysis*. New York: Palgrave Macmillan.

Green, F. (2006) *Demanding Work: The Paradox of Job Quality in the Affluent Economy*. Princeton, NJ: Princeton University Press.

Griffin, C. (2006) "Research and Policy in Lifelong Learning", *International Journal of Lifelong Education*, 25(6): 561–74.

Grimshaw, D., Marchington, M. and Rubery, J. (2006) "The Blurring Organizational Boundaries and the Fragmentation of Work", in G. Wood and P. James (eds) *Institutions, Production and Working Life*. Oxford: Oxford University Press.

Grubb, N. and Lazerson, M. (2004) *The Education Gospel: The Economic Power of Schooling*. Cambridge, MA: Harvard University Press.

Habermas, J. (1989) *The Theory of Communicative Action*, Vol. 2. trans. T. McCarthy. Boston: Beacon Press.

——(1996) *Between Facts and Norms: Contributions to a Discourse Theory of Law and Democracy*. Cambridge: Polity.

——(2001) *The Postnational Constellation: Political Essays*, trans. M. Pensky. Cambridge, MA: MIT Press.

——(2006) *The Divided West*. Cambridge: Polity.

Hall, P. and Soskice, D. (2001) *Varieties of Capitalism*. Oxford: Oxford University Press.

Halsey, A. (1992) *Decline of Donnish Dominion: The British Academic Professions in the Twentieth Century*. Oxford: Oxford University Press.

Halsey, A., Floud, J. and Anderson, A. (1965) *Education, Economy, and Society: A Reader in the Sociology of Education*. New York: Free Press.

Hartley, D. (2003) "New Economy, New Pedagogy?", *Oxford Review of Education*, 29(1): 81–94.

Hartog, J. and Van der Brink, M. (eds) (2007) *Human Capital: Advances in Theory and Evidence*. Cambridge: Cambridge University Press.

Harvey, D. (1989) *The Condition of Postmodernity*. Oxford: Blackwell.

——(2005) *A Brief History of Neoliberalism*. Chicago: University of Chicago Press.

Hayek, F. von (1945) "The Use of Knowledge in Society", *American Economic Review*, 35(4): 519–30.

Hayes, C., Fonda, N. and Hillman, J. (1998) "Learning in the New Millennium", in S. Ranson (ed.) *Inside the Learning Society*. London: Cassell.

Hayes, D. and Wynyard, R. (eds) (2002) *The McDonaldization of Higher Education*. Westport, CT: Bergin & Garvey.

Heckscher, C. (1988) *The New Unionism*. New York: Basic Books.

Heckscher, C. and Adler, P. (2006) *The Firm as a Collaborative Community: Reconstructing Trust in the Knowledge Economy*. New York: Oxford University Press.

Heery, E. (2001) "Learning from Each Other: A European Perspective on American Labor", *Journal of Labour Research*, 22(2): 307–19.

Heery, E. and Salmon, J. (eds) (2000) *The Insecure Workforce*. London: Routledge.

Henkel, M. and Little, B. (eds) (1999) *Changing Relationships between Higher Education and the State*. London: Jessica Kingsley Publications.
Hepple, B. and Veneziani, B. (eds) (2009) *The Transformation of Labour Law in Europe: A Comparative Study of 15 Countries, 1945–2004*. Oxford: Hart Publishing.
Holt, J. (1976) *Instead of Education*. Harmondsworth: Penguin.
Hursén, T. (1974) *The Learning Society*. London: Methuen.
Hussey, T. and Smith, P. (2009) *The Trouble with Higher Education*. London: Routledge.
Hutchins, R. (1968) *The Learning Society*. Harmondsworth: Penguin.
Hyman, R. (2001) *Understanding European Trade Unionism*. London: Sage.
Inglehart, R. (1977) *The Silent Revolution: Changing Values and Political Styles among Western Publics*. Princeton, NJ: Princeton University Press.
——(1997) *Culture Shift in Advanced Industrial Society*. Princeton, NJ: Princeton University Press.
Inglis, F. (ed.) (2004) *Education and the Good Society*. Basingstoke: Palgrave Macmillan.
International Labour Organization (2001) *Reducing Decent Work Deficit: A Global Challenge*. Geneva: International Labour Organization.
Jacobi, O., Jesson, B., Kastendiek, H. and Regini, M. (eds) (1986) *Economic Crisis, Trade Unions and the State*. London: Croom Helm.
Jarvis, P. (ed.) (2001) *The Age of Learning: Education and the Knowledge Society*. London: Kogan Page.
——(2007) *Globalisation, Lifelong Learning and the Learning Society*. London: Routledge.
Jenkins, A. (2000) *Employment Relations in France: Evolution and Innovation*. New York: Kluwer.
Jessop, B., Fairclough, N. and Wodak, R. (eds) (2008) *Education and the Knowledge-Based Economy in Europe*. Rotterdam: Sense Publications.
Kahin, B. and Foray, D. (eds) (2006) *Advancing Knowledge and the Knowledge-Based Economy*. Cambridge, MA: MIT Press.
Kalleberg, A. (2009) "Precarious Work, Insecure Workers: Employment Relations in Transition", *American Sociological Review*, 74(1): 1–22.
Kanter, R. (1989) *When Giants Learn to Dance*. New York: Simon and Schuster.
Karabel, J. and Halsey, A. (1977) *Power and Ideology in Education*. New York: Oxford University Press.
Keating, M., Loughlin, J. and Deschouwer, K. (2003) *Culture, Institutions and Economic Development: A Study of Eight European Regions*. Cheltenham: Edward Elgar.
Kersley, B., Alpin, C. and Forth, J. (eds) (2006) *Inside the Workplace: Findings from the 2004 Workplace Employment Relations Survey*. London: Routledge.
Keynes, J. (1936) *General Theory of Employment, Interest and Money*. New York: Harcourt Brace & World.
Klein, M. (2001) *No Logo*. London: Flamingo.
Kochan, T., Locke, R. and Piore, M. (eds) (1995) *Employment Relations in a Changing World Economy*. Cambridge, MA: MIT Press.
Kotthoff, H-G. and Moutsios, S. (eds) (2007) *Education Policies in Europe: Economy, Citizenship, Diversity*. Münster: Waxman.
Kuhn, M. and Sultana, R. (eds) (2006) *Homo Sapiens Europæus: Creating the European Learning Citizen*. New York: Peter Lang.
Kuhndt, M., Geibler, J. and Villar, A. (2003) "Challenges for SMEs in a Globalized World Economy", *Industry and Environment*, 26(4): 7–9.

Lammers, C. and Széll, G. (eds) (1989) *International Handbook of Participation in Organizations*. Oxford: Oxford University Press.

Lane, J-E. (2000) *New Public Management: An Introduction*. London: Routledge.

Lasch, C. (1995) *The Revolt of the Elites and the Betrayal of Democracy*. New York: W.W. Norton.

Lash, S. and Urry, J. (1987) *The End of Organized Capitalism*. Cambridge: Polity Press.

Lauder, H. (2001) "Innovation, Skill Diffusion and Social Exclusion", in P. Brown, A. Green, and H. Lauder (eds) *High Skills: Globalization, Competitiveness and Skill Formation*. Oxford: Oxford University Press.

Laursen, K. (2004) "New and Old Economy: The Role of ICT in Structural Change and Economic Dynamics", *Structural Change and Economic Dynamics*, 15(3): 241–3.

Leadbeater, C. (2000) *Living on Thin Air: The New Economy*. London: Viking.

Leisink, P., Leemput, J. and Vilrokx, J. (eds) (1996) *The Challenges to Trade Unions in Europe: Innovation or Adaptation*. Cheltenham: Edward Elgar.

Leisink, P., Steijn, B. and Veersma, U. (eds) (2007) *Industrial Relations in the New Europe: Enlargement, Integration and Reform*. Cheltenham: Edward Elgar.

Levy, F. and Murnane, R. (2004) *The New Division of Labor*. New York: Russell Sage.

Littek, W. and Charles, T. (eds) (1995) *The New Division of Labour: Emerging Forms of Work Organisation in International Perspective*. Berlin: Walter de Gruyter.

Littlewood, P. (2004) "Putting the Garden on the Market: Vocationalism, Commodification and Privatisation in Education and Training in Great Britain", in P. Littlewood, I. Glorieux, and I. Jonsson (eds) *The Future of Work in Europe*. Aldershot: Ashgate.

Lloyd, C., Mason, G. and Mayhew, K. (eds) (2008) *Low Wage Work in the United Kingdom*. New York: Russell Sage.

Lomba, C. (2005) "Beyond the Debate over 'Post'-vs 'Neo'-Taylorism", *International Sociology*, 20(1): 71–91.

Lorenz, E. and Lundvall, B-Å. (eds) (2006) *How Europe's Economies Learn*. Oxford: Oxford University Press.

Lucas, R. (1988) "On the Mechanics of Economic Development", *Journal of Monetary Economics*, 22: 3–42.

Lundvall, B-Å. (2002) *Innovation, Growth and Social Cohesion*. Northampton, MA: Edward Elgar.

Lundvall, B-Å. and Archibugi, D. (2001) *The Globalizing Learning Economy*. New York: Oxford University Press.

Lundvall, B-Å. and Borrás, S. (1999) *The Globalising Learning Economy: Implications for Innovation Policy*. Brussels: CEC.

Lyotard, J-F. (1984) *The Postmodern Condition: A Report on Knowledge*. Minneapolis: University of Minnesota Press.

Magnusson, L. and Stråth, B. (2004) *A European Social Citizenship?* Brussels: Peter Lang.

Marchington, M., Grimshaw, D., Rubery, J. and Willmott, H. (2005) *Fragmenting Work: Blurring Organizational Boundaries and Disordering Hierarchies*. Oxford: Oxford University Press.

Marginson, P. and Sisson, K. (2004) *European Integration and Industrial Relations: Multi-level Governance in the Making*. Basingstoke: Palgrave Macmillan.

Marshall, T. ([1950] 1992) *Citizenship and Social Class*. London: Pluto.

Matthews, J. (1998) "Organizational Foundations of the Knowledge-based Economy", in D. Neef (ed.) *The Knowledge Economy*. Boston: Butterworth-Heinemann.

Mayhew, K., Deer, C. and Dua, M. (2004) "The Move to Mass Higher Education in the UK", *Oxford Review of Education*, 30(1): 65–82.

Mazza, C., Quattrone, P. and Riccabone, A. (eds) (2008) *European Universities in Transition*. Cheltenham: Edward Elgar.

Méda, D. (1995) *Le Travail: Une valeur en voie de disparition*. Paris: Flammarion.

Méhault, P. (2006) "The Learning Society: The French Debate", in M. Kuhn and R. Sultana (eds) *The Learning Society in an International Discourse*. New York: Peter Lang.

Metcalf, D. (1989) "Trade Unions and Economic Performance: The British Evidence", *London School of Economics Quarterly*, 3: 21–42.

Mishel, L., Burnstein, J. and Allegratto, S. (2005) *The State of Working America, 2004–05*. Ithaca, NY: ILR Press.

Muffels, R. (ed.) (2008) *Flexibility and Employment Security in Europe: Labour Markets in Transition*. Cheltenham: Edward Elgar.

Muffels, R. and Luijkx, R. (2008) "Labour Market Mobility and Employment Security of Male Employees in Europe: 'Trade-Off' or 'Flexicurity'", *Work, Employment and Society*, 22(2): 221–42.

Musgrove, F. and Taylor, P. (1969) *Society and the Teacher's Role*. London: Routledge and Kegan Paul.

Nelson, R. (1993) *National Innovation Systems: A Comparative Analysis*. Oxford: Oxford University Press.

Nelson, R. and Romer, P. (1996) "Science, Economic Growth, and Public Policy", in B. Smith and C. Barfield (eds) *Technology, R&D, and the Economy*. Washington, DC: Brookings Institution.

Nelson, R. and Winter, S.G. (1982) *An Evolutionary Theory of Economic Change*. Cambridge: Cambridge University Press.

Newfield, C. (2008) *Unmaking the Public University*. Cambridge, MA: Harvard University Press.

Newman, J. ([1852] 1976) *The Idea of a University*. Oxford: Oxford University Press.

Nolan, P. (1996) "Industrial Relations since 1945", in I. Beardwell (ed.) *Contemporary Industrial Relations*. Oxford: Oxford University Press.

North, D. (1981) *Structure and Change in Economic History*. New York: Norton.

——(1990) *Institutions, Institutional Change and Economic Performance*. Cambridge: Cambridge University Press.

Odin, J. and Manicas, P. (eds) (2004) *Globalization and Higher Education*. Honolulu: University of Hawaii Press.

OECD (1974) *Towards Mass Higher Education: Issues and Dilemmas*. Paris: OECD.

——(1996a) *Measuring What People Know*. Paris: OECD.

——(1996b) *Lifelong Learning for All*. Paris: OECD.

——(1996c) *The Knowledge-Based Economy*. Paris: OECD.

——(1999) *The Knowledge-Based Economy: Facts and Figures*. Paris: OECD.

——(2001) *OECD Science, Technology and Industry Scoreboard: Toward a Knowledge-Based Economy*. Paris: OECD.

——(2004) *Innovation in the Knowledge Society: Implications for Education and Learning*. Paris: OECD.

——(2008a) *Higher Education to 2030*. Vol. 1: *Demography*. Paris: OECD.

——(2008b) *Growing Unequal? Income Distribution and Poverty in OECD Countries*. Paris: OECD.

——(2009) *Society at a Glance 2009: OECD Social Indicators*. Paris: OECD. Available at: www.oecd.org/els/social/indicators.

Offe, C. (1985) *Disorganised Capitalism*. Cambridge: Polity Press.

Offe, C. and Preuss, U. (2006) "The Problem of Legitimacy in the European Polity: Is Democratization the Answer?", in C. Crouch and W. Streeck (eds) *The Diversity of Democracy: Corporatism, Social Order and Political Conflict*. Cheltenham: Edward Elgar.

Olssen, M. and Peters, M. (2005) "Neoliberalism, Higher Education and the Knowledge Economy: From the Free Market to Knowledge Capitalism", *Journal of Education Policy*, 20(3): 313–45.

Organ, D., Podsakoff, P. and MacKenzie, S. (2006) *Organizational Citizenship Behaviour*. Thousand Oaks, CA: Sage.

Perrons, D., Fagan, C., McDowell, L., Ray, K. and Ward, K. (eds) (2006) *Gender Divisions in Working Time: Changing Patterns of Work, Care and Public Policy in Europe and North America*. Cheltenham: Edward Elgar.

Peters, M. (2007) *Knowledge Economy, Development and the Future of Higher Education*. Rotterdam: Sense Publishers.

Peters, T. (1989) *Thriving on Chaos*. London: Macmillan.

Peters, T. and Waterman, R. (1982) *In Search of Excellence*. New York: Harper and Row.

Pfau-Effinger, B. (2009) "Varieties of Undeclared Work in European Societies", *British Journal of Industrial Relations*, 47(1): 79–99.

Phillips, R. and Furlong, J. (eds) (2001) *Education, Reform and the State: Twenty-Five Years of Politics, Policy and Practice*. London: Routledge.

Piore, M. and Sabel, C. (1984) *The Second Industrial Divide*. New York: Basic Books.

Plasman, R., Rusinek, M. and Rycx, F. (2007) "Wages and the Bargaining Regime under Multi-Level Bargaining", *European Journal of Industrial Relations*, 13(2): 161–80.

Polanyi, K. ([1944] 1957) *The Great Transformation: The Political and Economic Origins of Our Time*. Boston: Beacon Press.

Popkewitz, T. (ed.) (1987) *The Formation of the School Subjects*. New York: Falmer Press.

——(2000) *Educational Knowledge: Changing Relationships Between the State, Civil Society, and the Educational Community*, New York: SUNY Press.

Porter, M. (1990) *The Competitive Advantage of Nations*. London: Macmillan.

Powell, W. (2001) "The Capitalist Firm in the Twenty-First Century: Emerging Patterns in Western Europe", in P. Di Maggio (ed.) *The Twenty-First Century Firm*. Princeton, NJ: Princeton University Press.

Rajan, R. and Wulf, J. (2006) "The Flattening Firm: Evidence from Panel Data on the Changing Nature of Corporate Hierarchies", *The Review of Economics and Statistics*, 88(4): 759–73.

Ranson, S. (ed.) (1998) *Inside the Learning Society*. London: Cassell.

Readings, B. (1996) *The University in Ruins*. Cambridge, MA: Harvard University Press.

Reed, M. (2002) "New Managerialism, Professional Power and Organisational Governance in UK Universities", in A. Amaral, G. Jones, and B. Karseth (eds) *Governing Higher Education: National Perspectives on Institutional Governance*. Dordrecht: Kluwer.

Reich, R. (1991) *The Work of Nations: Preparing Ourselves for 21st Century Capitalism*. New York: Alfred Knopf.

Reinalda, B. and Kulesza, E. (2006) *The Bologna Process: Harmonizing Europe's Higher Education*. Opladen: Barbara Budrich Publications.

Ricoeur, P. (1996) "Fragility and Responsibility", in R. Kearney (ed.) *Paul Ricoeur: The Hermeneutics of Action*. London: Sage.

Rifkin, J. (2000) *The Age of Access*. New York: Putnam.

Rinne, R. and Koivula, J. (2009) "The Dilemmas of the Changing University", in M. Shattock (ed.) *Entrepreneurialism in Universities and the Knowledge Economy: Diversification and Organizational Change in European Higher Education*. Maidenhead: Open University Press.

Robertson, S. (2008) "Embracing the Global: Crisis and the Creation of a New Semiotic Order to Secure Europe's Knowledge-Based Economy", in N. Fairclough, R. Wodak and B. Jessop (eds) *Education and the Knowledge-Based Economy in Europe*. Rotterdam: Sense Publishers.

Robertson, S. and Keeling, R (2008) 'Stirring the Lions: Strategy and Tactics in Global Higher Education', *Globalisation, Societies and Education*, 6(3): 221–40.

Robison, R. (ed.) (2006) *The Neo-Liberal Revolution: Forging the Market State*, Basingstoke: Palgrave Macmillan.

Rodrigues, M. (2002) *The New Knowledge Economy in Europe*. Cheltenham: Edward Elgar.

Rogers, J. and Streeck, W. (eds) (1995) *Work Councils: Consultation, Representation, Cooperation*. Chicago: University of Chicago Press.

Romer, P. (1986) "Increasing Returns and Long-run Growth", *Journal of Political Economy*, 94: 102–37.

——(1990) "Endogenous Technological Change", *Journal of Political Economy*, 98(5): S71–102.

Rooney, D., Hearn, G. and Ninan, A. (2005) *Handbook on the Knowledge Economy*. Cheltenham: Edward Elgar.

Rouban, L. (ed.) (1999) *Citizens and the New Governance: Beyond New Public Management*. Amsterdam: IOS Press.

Rubery, J., Earnshaw, J., Marchington, M., Cook, F. and Vincent, S. (2002) "Changing Organizational Forms and the Employment Relationship", *Journal of Management Studies*, 39(5): 645–71.

Rubery, J., Smith, M. and Fagan, C. (1999) *Women's Employment in Europe*. London: Routledge

Salais, R. (2003) "Work and Welfare: Towards a Capability Approach", in J. Zeitlin and D. Trubek (eds) *Governing Work and Welfare in a New Economy*. Oxford: Oxford University Press.

Salverda, W., Van Klavernen, M. and Van Meer, M. (eds) (2008) *Low Wage Work in the Netherlands*. New York: Russell Sage.

Sandberg, A. (ed.) (1995) *Enriching Production: Perspectives on Volvo's Uddevalla Plant as an Alternative to Lean Production*. Aldershot: Avesbury.

Saren, M., Maclaran, P., Goulding, C., Elliott, R., Shankar, A. and Catterall, M. (eds) (2007) *Critical Marketing: Defining the Field*. Oxford: Elsevier.

Schnapper, D. (1998) *Community of Citizens: On the Modern Idea of Nationality*. New Brunswick, NJ: Transaction Publishers.

Schomman, K. and O'Connell, P. (eds) (2002) *Education, Training and Employment Dynamics*. Cheltenham: Edward Elgar.

Schön, D. (1971) *Beyond the Stable State: Public and Private Learning in a Changing Society*. New York: Norton.

Schonberger, R. (1986) *World Class Manufacturing*. New York: Free Press.

Schuetze, H. and Casey, C. (2006) "Models and Meanings of Lifelong Learning: Progress and Barriers on the Road to the Learning Society", *Compare: Journal of Comparative Education*, 36(3): 279–87.

Schultz, T. (1960) "Capital Formation by Education", *The Journal of Political Economy*, 68(6): 571–83.

Scott, P. (1995) *The Meanings of Mass Higher Education*. Buckingham: Open University Press.

——(2004) "The Transformation of the Idea of a University", in F. Inglis (ed.) *Education and the Good Society*. Basingstoke: Palgrave Macmillan.

Senge, P.(1990) *The Fifth Discipline: The Art and Practice of the Learning Organization*. New York: Random House.

——(1999) *Challenges of Sustaining Momentum in Learning Organizations*. New York: Doubleday.

Sennett, R. (2006) *The Culture of the New Capitalism*. New Haven, CT: Yale University Press.

Shattock, M. (ed.) (2009) *Entrepreneurialism in Universities and the Knowledge Economy: Diversification and Organizational Change in European Higher Education*. Maidenhead: Open University Press.

Sheppard, S. and Carroll, D. (eds) (1980) *Working in the Twenty-first Century*. New York: Wiley.

Skålén, P., Fougère, M. and Fellesson, M. (2008) *Marketing Discourse: A Critical Perspective*. New York: Routledge.

Skorstad, E. and Ramsdal, H. (2009) *Flexible Organizations and the Working Life*. Farnham: Ashgate.

Slater, R. and Tonkiss, D. (2001) *Market Society*. Cambridge: Polity Press

Slaughter, S. and Leslie, L. (1997) *Academic Capitalism*. Baltimore, MD: Johns Hopkins University Press.

Smart, B. (2003) *Economy, Culture and Society*. Buckingham: Open University Press.

Smeets, V. and Warzynski, F. (2008) "Too Many Theories, Too Few Facts? What the Data Tell Us about the Link between Span of Control, Compensation and Career Dynamics", *Labour Economics*, 15: 688–704.

Soete, L. (2006) "A Knowledge Economy Paradigm and its Consequences", in A. Giddens, P. Diamond and R. Liddle (eds) *Global Europe, Social Europe*. Cambridge: Polity Press.

Soguel, N. and Jaccard, P. (eds) (2008) *Governance and Performance of Education Systems*. Dordrecht: Springer.

Standing, G. (2002) *Beyond the New Paternalism: Basic Security as Equality*. London: Verso.

Steinmueller, W. E. (2002) "Knowledge-Based Economies and Information and Communication Technologies", *International Social Science Journal*, 54(171): 141–53.

Stewart, T. (1997) *Intellectual Capital: The New Wealth of Organizations*. New York: Doubleday.

Stiglitz, J. (1999) *Public Policy for a Knowledge Economy*. London: Centre for Economic Policy Research.

——(2002) *Globalization and its Discontents*. New York: W.W. Norton.

Stråth, B. (ed.) (2000) *After Full Employment: European Discourses on Work and Flexibility*. Brussels: Peter Lang.

Streeck, W. (1992) *Social Institutions and Economic Performance*. London: Sage.

——(1997) "Industrial Citizenship under Regime Competition: The Case of European Work Councils", *Journal of European Public Policy*, 4: 643–64.

——(ed.) (2006) *Governing Interests: Business Associations Facing Internationalization*. London: Routledge.

——(2009) *Re-forming Capitalism: Institutional Change in the German Political Economy*. New York: Oxford University Press.

Supiot, A. (2001) *Beyond Employment: Changes in Work and the Future of Labour Law in Europe*. Oxford: Oxford University Press.

Svensson, G. (2000) "A Conceptual Framework for the Analysis of Vulnerability in Supply Chains", *International Journal of Physical and Logistics Management*, 30: 731–47.

Széll, G. (ed.) (2001) *European Labour Relations*. Aldershot: Ashgate.

Taylor, C. (1989) *Sources of the Self: The Making of the Modern Identity*. Cambridge, MA: Harvard University Press.

Taylor, W. (1963) *The Secondary Modern School*. London: Faber.

Teece, D. (ed.) (1987) The Competitive Challenge: Strategies for Industrial Innovation and Renewal. New York: Harper & Row.

Tight, M. (ed.) (2004) *The Routledge Falmer Reader in Higher Education*, London: Routledge.

Tilly, C. and Tilly, C. (1998) *Work Under Capitalism*. Boulder, CO: Westview Press.

Tolsby, J. and Kirkebak, P. (2006) "The Neo-Tayloristic Role of Information and Communication Technologies in Knowledge-Based Economies", *International Journal of Knowledge, Culture and Change Management*, 6(3): 121–8.

Touraine, A. (1971) *The Post-industrial Society*. New York: Random House.

——(1995) *Critique of Modernity*. Oxford: Blackwell.

——(2001) *Beyond Neoliberalism*. Cambridge: Polity Press.

Traxler, F., Blaschke, S. and Kittel, B. (2001) *National Labour Relations in International Markets*. Oxford: Oxford University Press.

Trigilia, C. (2002) *Economic Sociology: State, Market, and Society in Modern Capitalism*. Oxford: Blackwell.

Trow, M. (1973) *Problems in the Transition from Elite to Mass Higher Education*. Berkeley, CA: Carnegie Commission on Higher Education.

——(2006) "Reflections on the Transitions from Elite to Mass to Universal Access: Forms and Phases of Higher Education in Modern Societies since WWI", in J. Forest and P. Altbach (eds) *International Handbook of Higher Education*. Dordrecht: Springer.

UNICE (Union of Industrial and Employers' Confederations of Europe) (2003) *Lisbon Strategy 2003, Time is Running Out*, Brussels: UNICE.

Upchurch, M., Taylor, G. and Mathers, A. (2009) *The Crisis of Social Democratic Trade Unionism in Western Europe*. Farnham: Ashgate.

van Vught, F. (2009a) *Mapping the Higher Education Landscape: Towards a European Classification in Higher Education*. Dordrecht: Springer Press.

——(2009b) "Closing the European Knowledge Gap?", in L. Weber and J. Duderstadt (eds) *Reinventing the Research University*. London: Economica.

Wagner, P. and Zimmerman, B. (2004) "Citizenship and Collective Responsibility: On the Political Philosophy of the Nation-Based Welfare State and Beyond", in L. Magnusson and B. Stråth (eds) *A European Social Citizenship?* Brussels: Peter Lang.

Walby, S., Gottfried, H., Gottschall, K. and Osawa, M. (eds) (2007) *Gendering the Knowledge Economy*. Basingstoke: Palgrave Macmillan.

Warhurst, C., Grugulis, I. and Keep. E. (eds) (2004) *The Skills that Matter*. Basingstoke: Palgrave Macmillan.

Weber, M. [1922] 1978) *Economy and Society: An Outline of Interpretive Sociology*. Berkeley, CA: University of California Press.

Webster, J. (2007) *Changing European Gender Relations: Gender Equality Policy Concerning Employment and the Labour Market*. EUR23163. Brussels: European Commission.

Webster, J., Wickham, J. and Collins, G. (2003) *Innovations in Information Society Sectors: Implications for Women's Work, Expertise and Opportunities in European Workplaces*. Final Report SOE-CT 98–1119. TSER, CEC DG Research. Available at: http://ec.europa.eu/research/social-sciences/pdf/finalreport/soe1ct981119-final-report.pdf.

Weishaupt, J. (2010) "A Silent Revolution? New Management Ideas and the Reinvention of European Public Employment Services", *Socio-Economic Review*, 8: 461–86.

Wenger, E. (1998) *Communities of Practice: Learning, Meaning, and Identity*. Cambridge: Cambridge University Press.

Westergaard-Nielson, N. (2008) *Low Wage Work in Denmark*. New York: Russell Sage.

Wexler, P. (1987) *The Social Analysis of Education*. New York: Routledge.

Whitley, R. (1999) *Divergent Capitalisms: The Social Structuring and Change of Business Systems*. Oxford: Oxford University Press.

Whittall, M., Knudsen, H. and Huijgen, F. (eds) (2007) *Towards a European Labour Identity: The Case of the European Work Council*. London: Routledge.

Williams, C. (2007) *Rethinking the Future of Work: Directions and Visions*. Basingstoke: Palgrave Macmillan.

Williams, G. (2004) *The Enterprising University: Reform, Excellence and Equity*. Maidenhead: Society for Research into Higher Education and Open University Press.

Wilthagen, T. and Tros, F. (2004) "The Concept of 'Flexicurity': A New Approach to Regulating Employment and Labour Markets", *Transfer: European Review of Labour and Research*, 10(2): 166–86.

Wolf, A. (2002) *Does Education Matter?: Myths about Education and Economic Growth*. London: Penguin.

World Bank (2003) *Lifelong Learning in the Global Knowledge Economy: Challenges for Developing Countries*. Washington, DC: The World Bank.

Wright Mills, C. (1959) *The Sociological Imagination*. New York: Oxford University Press.

Index